# THE LIFE OF EDWARD
# THE BLACK PRINCE

# THE LIFE OF

# Edward the Black Prince

## 1330—1376

## THE FLOWER OF KNIGHTHOOD
## OUT OF ALL THE WORLD

### BY

## HENRY DWIGHT SEDGWICK

*"It is blasphemy to say that we
can be beaten while I am alive"*
—The Black Prince, at Poitiers

BARNES
&NOBLE
BOOKS
NEW YORK

This edition published by Barnes & Noble, Inc.

1993 Barnes & Noble Books

ISBN 1-56619-156-4
Printed and bound in the United States of America

M 9 8 7 6 5 4 3

*To*
# H. D. S. II

*Home dit et si est de ce voir*
*Qu'il n'est chose que ne delzeche,*
*Ne qil n'est arbres que ne seche*
*Q'un soul c'est luy arbres de vie,*
*Mais sil arbres en cest vie*
*Fflorist et botonne en toutz champs.*

—THE HERALD CHANDOS.


There is a common saying rife
That nothing is that doth not rot,
There is no tree that withers not
Excepting one, the Tree of Life,
And if on earth that blooming be
'Twill bourgeon everlastingly.

# CONTENTS

# CONTENTS—*Concluded*

# INTRODUCTION

FROM the royal house of England, three martial heroes have come forth. Of these Richard Cœur de Lion has received his meed, for out of the dim recesses of Matthew Paris's chronicle he stepped into the sunlight of *Ivanhoe* and *The Talisman*, and for three generations became one of the idols of all English-speaking boys who were lucky enough to be bred in civilized homes. The second, Henry the Fifth, Shakespeare took as the exemplar of English manhood, and extolled "the mirror of all Christian kings," making his name a household word, with the same deep tenderness with which he described:

This blessed plot, this earth, this realm, this England.

To Edward the Black Prince, no such fortune has befallen. This could hardly have been from lack of appreciation. In England his has always been a famous name. "We can scarcely recall a period of our early studies when the exalted character of the Black Prince, his brilliant achievements, his noble frankness, and his chivalric courtesy in peace and in war, had not already excited our attention and interest" (*Memorials of the Order of the Garter*). Nevertheless, his chief monument is his tomb in Canterbury Cathedral, and the best that literature has offered in his honor is a poem in French, written by a Walloon gentleman who served in one of the Prince's campaigns. I can not tell why the Elizabethan dramatists, Greene, Marlowe, Peele, Cyril Tourneur, passed him by, unless it was because they could not find in his simple straightforwardness such traits of passion, revenge or treachery as would befit their tempestuous verse. He is a better subject for drama or romance than for biography. A playwright or novelist may take one trait, the essential trait, in his hero, magnify it, glorify it and encompass it with suitable exploits; but all a poor biographer can do is to accept what the chroniclers say the hero did, repeat what they say the hero said, and reconcile conflicting statements as best he may, and, when he comes to ambiguities or impossibilities, guess and guess.

The speeches that I have attributed to the Black Prince are all taken from contemporary chroniclers, Froissart, Chandos, Geoffrey Baker, Cuvelier and so on. That they are verbally correct is most unlikely, but the substance may well be true, for in those days what great men said on great occasions was often handed from mouth to mouth with an accuracy that no hearsay would have in these days of print. I have invented nothing.

To show the opinion of the Prince entertained by his first modern biographer, let me quote from Alexander Bicknell's *The History of Edward Prince of Wales* (1776): "The Prince, whose history is the principal subject of the annexed sheets, appears to have been graced with every quality natural or acquired which constitute the real Hero: to those were superadded the more important ones that form the virtuous man. *Take him for all in all,* estimate his worth from this union of characters, and we may safely pronounce, that England, or indeed any other country, never gave birth to a person whose actions more justly claimed the notice, or deserved the encomiums of Historians."

H. D. S.

# The Life of Edward the Black Prince

## CHAPTER I

### GENEALOGICAL

EDWARD the Black Prince, eldest son of King Edward III, is often considered to be a Frenchman, but, in spite of his descent, which was in great part foreign, in spite of his daily speech, for he spoke French to his familiars, and in spite of his family claim to the French crown, he was a typical Englishman, simple, fearless, keen for his interests—which always appeared to him under the names Duty, Honor or Patriotism, and, had they not done so, he would have been far less keen—unintellectual, incurious of things of beauty, tenacious, resourceful, cruel where cruelty seemed to him justice, loyal, true to his word, a good friend, disdainful of foreigners and their ways, strong of body, active and vigorous, and with somewhat of the bulldog's temperament. To realize his English character, you have but to compare him with his contemporaries, Charles V of France, clever, politic, *rusé, très fin;* the Duc de Berry, Charles's brother, cultivated, sensitive, very Latin; Charles le Mauvais of Navarre, a man of Oriental sinuousness, or Don Pedro the Cruel, a morose, savage, suspicious man, who were all allied to the Black Prince by blood.

The Black Prince talked French because that was the practice of the upper class in England, he heard it all about, it was his natural tongue, but he spoke English to his grooms, his valets, his yeomen, and sometimes to his knights when he did not wish the Frenchmen present to understand what he said. As to the French crown, if no distinction of sex had been made, he was as close in blood as the French King. As to his foreign ancestry, his mother was Philippa of Hainaut, his grandmother, Isabella of France, his great-grandmother, Eleanor of Castile, his great-great-grandmother, Eleanor of Toulouse, his great-great-great-grandmother, Isabella of Angoulême, his great-great-great-great-grandmother, Aliénor of Aquitaine. The French King's grandams were not more barren of Englishry than his. Nevertheless, the Black Prince was English; he was born and bred in England. Oxford, Northampton, Lincoln, Hants, at first, other shires later, with their green fields, their forests, their rivers and brooks, their fresh verdure, their birds and beasts, their plowed lands and fallow, made him an Englishman. England's knights, who loved "chivalry, truth and honour, freedom and courtesy," England's squires, "wonderly deliver and great of strength," England's yeomen clad in green, with mighty bows and sheaves of peacock arrows, England's monks often "manly men," her wanton merry friars, her solemn merchants in their Flandrish beaver hats, her clerks educated at Oxford, her sergeants of law, wary and wise, her franklins, who loved a sop of wine in the morning, her haberdashers, carpenters, weavers, dyers, seamen, untroubled on the high seas by too nice a conscience, her physicians, parsons, plowmen, millers, manciples, reeves, had themselves all been molded and fashioned by English life into what they were; and they made England England. And England made its Prince, born of French stock, speaking French, claiming the land of France as his own, a typical Eng-

lishman. Indeed, at this very time England was converting all
its French aristocracy, all the descendants of the conquerors,
who had come with Duke William from Normandy, into Englishmen, and the English language was beginning to elbow out
French in castle and palace. The court spoke French, scholars
at Queen's College, Oxford, and monks in their monasteries
spoke French, when the rules did not oblige them to speak Latin.
The statutes of the realm were in French, the pleadings in court
were in French, writers of memoirs, like Thomas de la More,
for instance, wrote in French, the educated class, when not
writing Latin, wrote letters in French; nevertheless, the English
language was swelling like a rising tide, and the Black Prince
was but ten years old when Dan Chaucer was born, and Chaucer
enacted that the literature of England should be English.

And the human stuff, the character, temperament, disposition,
which this environing England was to mold, train and educate
in order to produce the Black Prince, was of the choicest. You
might seek the whole world round and not find another such
ancestry. The Prince's father, Edward III, was a man of
goodly frame and "godlike face," valiant to rashness, a lover
of danger, dominion and power. If Edward II was of a different quality, according to some obscure Mendelian law, the
Prince's grandmother, Isabella, "she wolf of France," had the
spirit to depose him and urge on her paramour to murder him.
Edward I, "Martellus Scottorum," a tall, big-limbed, handsome
man, devoted to tournaments and the chase, hot of temper but
of disciplined character, of "domestic life unstained," a lover of
justice, and loyal to his friends, was a very royal personage.
Henry III, "unbridled in temper and tongue," was an indifferent
warrior but he built Westminster Abbey. King John, according
to John R. Green, together "with the supreme wickedness of his

race, inherited its profound ability"; and John's brother Richard
Cœur de Lion, he, too, as Sir Walter Scott has depicted, a
"Black Knight," would have ennobled any lineage. Even the
old chronicler, Ralph of Coggeshale, succumbs to enthusiasm
when he speaks of him. The scene is a seacoast in Palestine,
the Turks line the seashore, Richard, with all his armor on, leaps
upon the beach and lays about him right and left, *velut leo
furibundus*, like lion wode, till the Turks, thinking he must have
a mighty host following close, run in rout. Or, when he has
heard that the Duke of Austria, a fellow crusader mind you, had
dared, as Walter Scott says, had dared "to plant the paltry rag of
Austria beside the banner of England," how he strode to the
spot, pulled down the Austrian flag and flung it into the *cloaca.*
Or, again, when he fought at Joppa, where "the story of how the
King's valor flashed in the battle . . . would seem incredible,
unless divine assistance is acknowledged." And Richard's
father, Henry II, a fiery Angevin, with his ebullient energy and
big heavy hands, was "one of the foremost on the roll of those
who have been the makers of England's greatness." And there
is Richard's mother, Aliénor of Aquitaine, about whose
memory a wreath of legend has twined itself. Wife of Louis
VII of France, she took the cross with him at Vézelay under the
oratory of the great Saint Bernard; but out there, in the Holy
Land, she with her Uncle Raymond, or with a Saracen, one of
Satan's brood, gave use to uncharitable ears, *thori conjugalis
fidem oblita, elle n'estoit mie lors sage fame:* after that, di-
vorced, but not till four years later, while hastening from Paris
to Aquitaine, she escaped first one lover in ambush, Thibaut de
Champagne, then a second, Geoffrey Plantagenet, and married
Henry II. Then she poisoned Fair Rosamond (I follow the
legend), listened to words of love from Bertrand de Ventadour,

gave judgment in a *Cour d'Amour* that there could never be true love between people legally united, conspired with her rebel sons against their father, was imprisoned for seventeen years, and finally laid her bones at Fontevrault, beside those of her husband and of her son Richard, and received an epitaph that gives the lie to legend: "By integrity of life, purity of conduct, sweet blossoming virtues, she exalted the greatness of her birth and by her *vie sans reproche* surpassed almost all queens in the world."

And back of Henry II comes the great House of Anjou that was descended, as their neighbors believed, from a demon. "From the devil they came and to the devil they will go." Geffroi le Bel, *"batailleur et autoritaire, vir magnae probitatis et industriae* [a fighting, autocratic man, very brave and very clever]," who at fifteen married the Empress Maud, heiress of England, a widow of twenty-six, but more famous because of his custom of seeding the *planta genesta* in unwooded lands, *miricem plantans,* in order not to let cultivated fields encroach upon his hunting grounds (so it is surmised), a custom that gave his race the name Plantagenet. His grandfather Foulques *le Réchin* and grandmother, *mulier versipellis,* who had so much charm and art that she induced her husband Foulques to show the greatest respect and honor to her acknowledged lover, Philip I of France. And Foulques Nerra, a figure of fantastic energy, fighting, love-making, breaking all the Ten Commandments, building churches, abbeys, and a long line of castles that we go to see, the châteaux de Langeais, de Montrichard, de Montbazon, de Montboyan, de Montrésor, de Montrevault, de Montfaucon; and when his crimes overflowed all measure, off he went a pious pilgrim to the Holy Land, to scourge himself naked in the streets of Jerusalem and give rise to strange stories, altogether the very embodiment of mad Angevin energy. And finally, through the Empress Maud, to William the Conqueror and that Norman breed that left its cicatrice red and raw on Saxon, Italian, Greek and Saracen. Such was the inheritance that, molded, shaped and polished by English nurture, produced the Black Prince, to stand out conspicuous in that long line of martial heroes from Richard Cœur de Lion to the Duke of Wellington.

# CHAPTER II

THE Black Prince was born in the year 1330. At that time western Europe was entering into a new political phase. The old medieval theory that European Christendom was a single political body, under two great guiding powers, the Empire, dominant in things secular, and the Papacy, dominant in things spiritual, had vanished into the limbo of outworn ideas, although Dante, its greatest exponent, was but nine years dead; and the new order, in which nationality was to play so great a part, for evil and for good, had not as yet become a political theory. Nations were darkly groping, following their primitive appetites of swallowing and incorporating lesser political neighbors. Unconsciously they were seeking what they have since called their natural boundaries. The feudal system was crumbling away, and no one knew what would take its place. Here and there streaks of light indicated the coming day, but still too vague to be of general acceptance. In England a Parliament sat from time to time at Westminster. At Avignon, Venice or Milan, Petrarch was living a life that has earned him the soubriquet of the first modern man, but, so confused was the mingling of the departing old ideas and of the oncoming new ideas, that even he, in the year when the Black Prince attained his eleventh birthday, did homage to the old order by receiving the poet's laureate wreath on the Capitol in Rome.

Nations were acting, as I have said, like rudimentary organisms. England, in her instinctive effort to incorporate the

21

whole island, had conquered Wales and was struggling to conquer Scotland. France, hemmed in between the Empire to the
east, and the English province of Guienne and independent
Brittany to the west, was eagerly contemplating expansion
wherever she might. In the Iberian Peninsula, there was too
much equality for any one of the five kingdoms there to swallow
up the others; Castile, Aragon, Navarre, Portugal and the
Moorish Kingdom of Granada quarreled and fought, but none
attained to mastery. The Empire had fallen into a mere aggre-
gate of heterogeneous states, mostly German, and including on
the western front, nominally at least, Provence, Burgundy,
Lorraine, Alsace, Brabant, Hainaut, Namur and Luxembourg.
The Emperor was elective, and the Houses of Austria, Bavaria
and Luxembourg struggled over candidates. The Papacy, which
still played a great political part, for no ruler knew how far
an interdict or ban of excommunication might affect his subjects, had recently committed a great blunder. It had emigrated
from Rome, the source of its strength, city of the Claudii, the
Scipios, the Cæsars, of St. Paul's preaching, of St. Peter's
martyrdom, of Hildebrand and Innocent III, and had, at the
good pleasure of the Kings of France, settled in Avignon. A
migration of which a turbulent young Roman, Cola di Rienzo,
spoke rudely: *"De suo proprio loco sancto ad lupanar, tamquam
ad burdellum, ut nomen consonaret effectu, meretricanda de-
fluxit* [forsaking its own holy place, it migrated to a bawdy
house]"; an opinion that, more moderately formulated, was held
in England, and was one of the causes why papal attempts to
smooth the differences, and make peace, between France and
England, were nearly or quite futile.

Of all these countries, France enjoyed the most renown for
riches, for chivalry, for power. Philippe Auguste had wrested

from King John of England almost all the Angevin possessions; Philippe le Bel had taken the Pope by the beard in his
stronghold at Anagni; and their successors had rendered the
Papacy, a subservient ally. And now, with all the glamour of
being cock of the walk, France entered the fatal valley of the
shadow of the Hundred Years' War. A fatal valley for England, also, for it was as true then, as it is now, or nearly so,
that both victors and vanquished come out from such maimed
and mutilated. The English historian, John Richard Green,
says: "No age of our history is more sad and sombre than the
age which we traverse from the third Edward to Joan of Arc."
That age has four periods: In the first the English were the
victors of Crécy and Poitiers, of which the Black Prince is
the hero; in the second the French under du Guesclin drove the
English out; in the third, Henry V won the battle of Agincourt; in the fourth, Joan of Arc performed her miracles. As
this first period is the drama in which the Black Prince plays
his heroic part, it needs some introduction.

The causes of the Hundred Years' War make none too good
an excuse for it. In the first place, it was impossible for a
King of England to forget that, a few generations earlier,
his ancestors had held Brittany, Normandy, Maine, Anjou, Poitou, Guienne, Gascony, a territory larger than that ruled by the
French Kings. Now scarce an eighth was left. It was hard to
believe that the English crown had lost so much rightfully.
That diminution was a thorn in the foot of a proud, young, ambitious king, and all the harder to bear because many persons
of importance assured him that his title, not merely to the lost
provinces, but to the crown of France itself, was better than that
of Philip of Valois, the king de facto. Edward's title, according to these English counselors, would have been good, had not

the French craftily pretended that only males could inherit and transmit title to the crown of France. I will not bore you by recounting the steps by which this decision was reached. Suffice it to say that an assembly of Notables did decide that in France no woman could inherit the crown, or transmit a right to the crown. The decision was probably affected by considerations of the undesirability of having a woman for queen or a foreigner for king. But every law should depend on large considerations, and this law simply extended the Salic law, governing feudal estates, to the crown, and undoubtedly was in accord with the wishes of the people. King Edward, who was then sixteen years old, or his counselors, at first entertained thoughts of asserting his claim by force, but affairs at home made that impossible, and when King Philip summoned him as his liegeman to do homage for the Duchy of Guienne, he went and did so. He raised, indeed, a technical point of feudal law as to the nature of the homage he should profess, and at the time only agreed to a curtailed ritual; but, on going back to England, he formally acknowledged the full ceremonial homage of liegeman. This was as complete a renunciation of title to the crown of France as well could be.

Another serious cause of antagonism between France and England was this: England had set out to conquer Scotland, and Edward Longshanks, after several victories, had annexed that kingdom; but the Scots refused to acquiesce in the annexation, and long wars gave now one side, now the other, the advantage. France, out of self-interest, allied herself with Scotland, and helped with money, munitions and ships, whether or not she happened to be at peace with England at the time. And, very much after the fashion that France intrigued in Scotland against England, England intrigued against France in Flanders.

This western part of modern Belgium had been assigned to Charles the Bald on the famous division of Charlemagne's empire into three parts (A. D. 843), and had been, ever since, under the suzerainty of France, and, at the time of which we are speaking, its Count was strongly French in his sympathies, whereas the mercantile classes were strongly pro-English. Bruges, Ghent and Ypres, prosperous cities, had grown great by weaving English wool into cloth, and it was of the utmost economic importance for both English and Flemish merchants to maintain peace and friendship between their countries. When the Count of Flanders, pursuing his pro-French policy, interfered with the English trade, the burghers rebelled against him, and made a treaty on their own account with England. Their leader, Jacques van Artevelde, whom Froissart describes as *un sage homme et imaginatif durement, hautain, subtil et bien enlangagé*, came to an understanding with King Edward and they agreed between them that Edward should assume the title, King of France, for then the Flemings might lawfully recognize him as their suzerain. Edward did so, and quartered his arms with the arms of France, the Leopards alternating with the Fleurs-delys, and also put on his seal the motto *Dieu et mon Droit.*

Again, to the northwest of France there was more trouble between the two countries. The Duchy of Brittany, where more than half the people spoke a language unintelligible to the French, was virtually a separate principality, though under the nominal suzerainty of France. It was claimed by two rival claimants, Jean de Montfort, who was upheld by the English, and the Comte de Blois, who was upheld by the French.

Add to these various causes of jealousy and dissension, the circumstance that it was even easier and more natural for contiguous states to quarrel in feudal times than it is now. A lord in one country might have vassals in the other, and under feudal law a vassal's duty was to his immediate superior; it would be difficult to make a more ingenious political device to provoke continual contention. A French lord might have vassals in Guienne, an English lord vassals in France; or it might even be more elaborate than that. The King of England as Duke of Guienne, was vassal to the King of France; he might have a French count in Poitou for vassal, and that Count might have lesser vassals in Guienne. Also the border multiplied trouble. Cattle lifters could cross the border, and if a sheriff pursued them into their own country, there would be a cry of invasion. Altogether the boundary between Guienne and the neighboring confines of France, like that between England and Scotland, was inevitably the scene of frequent border warfare.

Add to all this the idleness of the feudal nobility. Gentlemen disdained to be farmers or merchants, they had nothing to do but hunt and joust, and both the chase and the tourney were tame pleasures compared with fighting. A foray in France was a delightful adventure. Marauding, too, might be very profitable. In short, the nobility of a country was a martial yeast swelling it to aggression and war. It is not strange that there was a Hundred Years' War, but rather that there ever was peace at all.

# CHAPTER III

NOBODY knows for certain how our hero came by his name the Black Prince. Joshua Barnes, writing in the time of Charles II, says: "For courage and conduct, policy and courtesy, the most renowned captain in the world, being for his dreadful deeds in war (as most agree) surnamed by the French *le Noir*, or Black Prince." A more popular theory, nowadays, is that he acquired the epithet because it was his habit to wear black armor. But, as the name does not appear in recorded history until two hundred years after his death, it is not likely that there will ever be a certain explanation. A similar obscurity hangs over the Prince's boyhood. He was born on June 15, 1330, at Woodstock, near Oxford, "a very fair, lusty and well formed infant." (Barnes.) The King, on hearing the good news, rewarded the messenger, Thomas Prior, with a grant of fifty marks per annum. And, of the Prince's household, his nurse, Joan of Oxford, received ten pounds per annum, a handsome salary, and his bersatrix, Matilda Plympton, ten marks. Great hopes, Barnes says, were immediately conceived of the royal babe, from the beauty of his shape, the largeness of his size and the form and contexture of his body. Every one agrees that his mother, Queen Philippa, was a very good and charming person. Barnes says that she exceeded most ladies in the world for sweetness of nature and virtuous disposition; Froissart: "The moost gentyll quene, moost liberal, and moost courtesse that ever was quene in her dayes." She nursed her baby.

27

The Prince, at the age of three, became Earl of Chester, at six, Duke of Cornwall, and at thirteen, with coronet, gold ring and silver rod, he was created Prince of Wales. As soon as he was of an age to concern himself with books, Dr. Walter Burley, of Merton College, Oxford, the Queen's almoner, a distinguished philosopher, scholar and diplomat, became his tutor. From that time until the campaign that led to Crécy, there is but scanty information concerning him. He had two little sisters, Isabel and Joan, near his age, and his mother also took charge of a little orphaned cousin, another Joan, destined to grow up to be *"la plus belle de tout le royaume d'Engleterre et la plus amoureuse,"* the prettiest girl and greatest coquette in England, the Fair Maid of Kent. We also know one member of the Queen's household, a young gentleman from Hainaut, who had come over in her train, as her carver, *ecuyer tranchant,* an important functionary in the days before forks, and was destined to immortality in the pages of his fellow countryman, Jean Froissart, Sir Walter Manny, or Gaultier de Maunay, if you prefer the Hainaut spelling to that of England. It is said that the Prince and his brothers, who came along at intervals, Lionel, John of Gaunt (Ghent), Edmund, Thomas, were all stout, well-made young men, and also that the Prince, in the honorary positions imposed upon him even in early boyhood by his rank as heir apparent, made a very favorable impression.

The Prince probably sat in the Parliament of 1344 as a peer of the realm, when it voted "to end the French war either by battle or an honorable peace," with the added injunction (you remember that the Popes were at Avignon, *cette ville pécheresse,* and were regarded in England as subservient to France) that "if the King shall attempt the war eftsoons, he do not stay the same on the letters or requests of the Pope, or of any whomsoever, but end the same by dint of sword." That same year King Edward, wishing to follow in the footsteps of King Arthur, founded a Round Table, from which a few years later the Order of the Garter proceeded; and celebrated the occasion very handsomely with entertainments and junketing. A great festival was held at Windsor on the Sunday next after the feast of the Purification of the Virgin, at which were present the Prince of Wales, aged fourteen, earls, barons, knights, Queen Philippa and her younger children, the dowager Queen Isabella, countesses, baronesses, ladies and damsels and a great concourse of people. There was eating and drinking, viands and wines most delicate and in greatest plenty, enough and more than enough to satisfy every one. The ladies and gentlemen danced, kisses and hugs were given and returned; which means that the King and Queen did not exact Victorian behavior. After the ball, followed three days of tournaments, mountebanks, minstrels; and many presents were given. But the next day, Thursday, attained the zenith of royal splendor. The King, in velvet robes, with his crown on his head, and attended by his Queen, his mother, the Prince of Wales and all the great lords and ladies, made a solemn vow on the Bible to revive King Arthur's Round Table, and then trumpets and clarions burst forth and everybody hurried to the banquet, always among Western peoples, the seal of solemnity. The banquet was complete, with all the resources of culinary art and of the cellar, the merriment was indescribable, the enjoyment inestimable, mirth without backbiting, gaiety free of care. In other words, they had a jolly good time. But with these vague exceptions, there is little knowledge of the Prince of Wales and his doings until he was sixteen years old and went on the famous campaign that led up to the battle of Crécy and provided his *Lehrjahre* and *Wanderjahre*.

The Hundred Years' War had already been going for a 'decade. There had been fighting by land and sea. The Earl of Derby had made one of the forays, such as I must describe more particularly hereafter, he had raided from Bayonne into Languedoc, *en ravissant hommes et femmes sans nombre,* so successfully, that he was able to report: *"Nous avons fait une belle chevauchée, Dieu merci,* [We have made a splendid raid, thanks be to God]"; and King Edward had ordered such thanks to be given with due ecclesiastical ceremony. But now, in 1346, the King himself was to lead an invading army. There was lively enthusiasm in the country over the King's purpose. Laurence Minot, a poet of the north country, who spoke for the common people, wrote:

> Now God that is of mightes maste,
> Grant him grace of the Holy Gaste,
> His heritage to win,
> And Mari Moder, of mercy fre,
> Save oure King and his menye
> Fro sorrow, and schame, and syn.

Great preparations were made. The chief feudatories, the sheriffs of the shires, all local commissioners, were called on for their tales, of men-at-arms, archers, spearmen, light-armed irregular horse, called hobilars, and so on. As the chroniclers are extremely loose in the matter of figures, when it comes to reckoning the size of an army, I will say, roughly, that we may estimate one earl to eight bannerets, one banneret to a dozen knights, one knight to four men-at-arms, one man-at-arms to four archers, and that of the archers, one-fifth might be mounted, and that there would be about as many spearmen as mounted archers, and besides these a small number of hobilars. That is, using round numbers, an estimate for a unit of all arms led by an earl, would give ten bannerets, five hundred men-at-arms (including knights), two thousand archers, five hundred spearmen and fifty hobilars, about three thousand men all told. The heavily armed men-at-arms would constitute one-sixth of the force, and the archers two-thirds. I base this estimate on the figures of the English army before Calais in 1347. On a border foray, where the purpose was mere destruction, every man had a mount. The pay was as follows: Prince of Wales, £1 per diem, an earl, 6s8d; a banneret, 4s; a knight, 2s; men-at-arms, 1s; mounted archers, 6d; hobilars, 6d; foot archers, 3d; Welsh spearmen, 2d.

It was given out in the fleet that Bordeaux was to be their destination, but instead of that, whether owing to contrary winds or to the persuasion of Harcourt, a Norman nobleman, or whether the King wished to mislead the French, he landed in Normandy at Saint-Vaast-la-Hougue, which is not far from Cherbourg, on July 12, 1346. The English army may have numbered about twenty thousand men. The French were not prepared for a serious resistance, and such troops as they had collected were easily driven away. The King, that same day, conferred the order of knighthood on the Prince of Wales, the young Earl of Salisbury, Roger Mortimer and others, and then set about his business of destruction. Geoffrey Baker, the chronicler, tells the tale, simply, as such a tale should be told: *"Per residuum diei et totam noctem rex in villa de Hogges ospitabatur, et, in crastino, die Jovis, per exercitum villa combusta, deinde per patriam Constantin profectus.* [For the rest of that day and all the night the King lodged in the town of La Hougue, and on the next day, Thursday, after the town had been burned by the army, he marched through the Cotentin country.]" But my English does not do justice to the chronicler; unless it be pure fancy that his subconscious pity shows itself. Something in the Latin word *ospitabatur* (lodged as a guest) suggests the eager readiness of the poor Norman peasants and their wives to hide their fear under the bravery of hospitality, for they may well have heard that all the English nobility were of Norman descent. And a recognition of this kinship crops up in the word *patria,* which Baker applies to the Cotentin; he was a Christian, and in orders, and may not have seen what this destruction of the houses and towns of Norman peasants had to do with King Edward's claim to King Philip's crown.

If you have motored through that pleasant land, with the *planta genesta* in golden bloom, with magpies in twos and threes flashing their black and white across the road, or when the apple trees are in blossom, or their young fruits beginning to swell, you can picture the march of twenty thousand marauders in this inexpectant land. The main body marched southward a few miles to Morsalines, and there tarried several days while detachments rode roundabout to do what the expedition had come to do. *"Tota patria cum villa de Barbeflete combusta fuerat, vastata cum tota illa costa marina.* [Barfleur was burned down, and all the land and seacoast was laid waste.]" Then on to Valognes; next, southeast along the route the visitor now drives his car, to Saint-Côme-du-Mont, and on across the marsh lands of the Douve, rich in cattle, to Carenton. The route, then marked by burned villages, harried crops, dead bodies of any foolish enough to resist, and weeping women, is known by the records with complete accuracy from town to town. The expedition had been carefully prepared, and the English officers knew then, as now, that the primary factor in a successful campaign is food; and the halting places of the King's kitchen were regularly noted and the record kept.

Twenty thousand men, under orders to destroy, can cover a wide sweep of land. Froissart, who must have talked to men that had been in the expedition, says: "They went burning and ravaging the land. The barns were full of grain of all sorts, the houses full of riches; the inhabitants had lived at ease, possessing wagons, carts, horses, pigs, sheep and everything, in abundance. The soldiers took what they chose, and turned them over to the King's officers, except gold and silver, of which they rendered no account. The people of the country had never seen any men-at-arms, and knew nothing of war or battles, and fled as soon as they heard that the English were coming, leaving all their belongings, for they had no means to save them." You can picture the handsome young Prince, still a boy, galloping about, shouting out where to set fire, what booty to load on the carts, what cattle to lift, enjoying the game with all the zest of first experience. On they went, to Pont-Hébert, Saint Lô, a charming town, whose cathedral was rebuilt after the passage of the English, Cormolain, Torteval, Fontenay-le-Pesnel. "*Omnia combusserunt.* [They burned everything.]" There is universal agreement as to their thoroughness: "*Destruant et gastaunt, tute le pais envyroun et myst en fieu et en flamme villes grosses et hameletz par queles il passa.* [Destroying and laying waste all the country round, and setting fire to all cities and hamlets through which they passed.]" Customs have not greatly changed in six hundred years. You may read General Sherman's campaign from Atlanta to the sea; or that of the Malakand Field Force on the borders of Afghanistan. Winston Churchill says: "We proceeded systematically, village by village, and we destroyed the houses, filled up the wells, blew down the towers, cut down the great shady trees, burned the crops and broke the reservoirs in punitive devastation." So far, except at the landing, there had been no defense; all had been riding, robbing, lifting cattle, fire and rapine. Then they came to Caen, the city of William the Conqueror, and here they met the old Norman spirit. I quote a contemporary chronicle: "This city, with its strong citadel, was fair to see. Its churches and houses were wonderfully handsome. On one side was a ditch and a new stockade, on the other a stone wall, a marsh and the rough waters of the sea [the river Orne], for a creek crossed by a stout bridge came up by the town. To human eyes it looked impregnable, but the King's most righteous quarrel quickened every heart, and the Prince, displaying his prowess in his father's quarrel to his soldiers, marched up with his column, without stopping, right up to the city. Contrary to his expectation there was no opposition. He and his men took possession of the Abbey of Nuns, where Matilda, once Queen of England, lies buried. The King stopped in the suburbs, and the rearguard pitched its tents in the fields, for the enemy had withdrawn into the city." You remember that Caen had been the residence of William the Conqueror, that he built there the *Abbaye aux Hommes,* where his ashes lie, and that Queen Matilda built the *Abbaye aux Dames.* These two tourist-haunted monuments of Norman Romanesque architecture, and the citadel, as well, lie to the west of the river, while the main city, except some suburbs, lay on the east bank. The citadel was too strong to take, but it could give no help to the town, which was not walled but was protected by the river and could only be reached by crossing the bridge. Within was the Constable of Normandy, with some soldiers hastily collected to defend it, for it was full of a great wealth of cloth and all sorts of merchandise, of rich burghers, and of noble ladies, and of very beautiful churches. The invaders summoned the city to surrender but the townspeople refused "to obey the English King." The English, therefore, marched to the assault; but I will content myself with quoting a letter written by one of the marauders, Michael de Northburgh, one of the King's clerks:

"You may remember that our lord the King landed at Saint-Vaaste-la-Hougue on the 12th of July [I skip the description of the earlier part of the campaign]. On Wednesday, about noon, they arrived before the town of Caen, and learned that a great number of men-at-arms were in the town. The King set a good part of his army in battle array, and dispatched scouts to reconnoiter. They reported that the castle was strong and well built, and manned by knights and men-at-arms under the Bishop of Bayeux. On the side toward the river the town is well fortified. In one quarter there is an abbey, as noble as can be, where William the Conqueror lies buried. It is enclosed by walls, with large well battlemented towers. Nobody had remained there. In another quarter of the town there was another noble abbey, for ladies, but nobody remained there, no one at all in that part of the town on the same side of the river as the castle. The inhabitants had gone to the half of the town across the river. The Constable of France was there, the Chamberlain of Tankerville, who is a very great lord, and many gentlemen, to the number of five or six hundred, as well as the common people. Our soldiers, without orders and without military formation, attacked the bridge, which had been fortified with battlements and barricades. There was much to do, for the French defended it very stoutly, and endured a great deal before they gave way. Then the Constable and Chamberlain were made prisoners, together with about a hundred knights and six or seven score squires. A great multitude of knights, squires, and people of the town, were killed in the streets, and in the houses and gardens; no one can tell how many of note were killed, for the bodies were stripped stark naked and could not be recognized. On our side not a gentleman was slain, except one squire, who was badly wounded and died two days later. Wines, provisions, and other goods, things that could be carried away, were found without number, for the town is larger than any in England except London. . . . On the Thursday after the King had left Caen, the citizens of Bayeux asked leave to surrender themselves and their city and do him homage, he would accept of no conditions, other than they should not be harmed."

In the south at this time, the cultivated Tuscans, Petrarch, Boccaccio, Coluccio Salutati and their friends, or the revolutionary idealist, Cola di Rienzo, were highly rhetorical letter-writers, but in the north, among the English warriors, the art was held in mean esteem, and their letters, written in French, were singularly jejune, as you see. Sir Bartholomew Burghersh's letters to the Archbishop of Canterbury are in the same style. He says: "At Caen between six and seven score knights were taken or slain, and about five thousand squires, citizens and common people, so that, Praised be Our Lord! our business hath gone hitherto as favorably as it could. . . . May the Holy Ghost keep you in your honors, in good life and long." The chroniclers are equally concise. Thomas Walsingham rivals Cæsar: "*Cepit, spoliavit, combussit.* [He captured, looted, burned.]" It is certain that Caen was a very rich city when the English came, full of rare merchandise, of gold and silver plate, jewelry, all sorts of articles of comfort and luxury, and that they left it stripped to the bare walls. The booty was conveyed down the River Orne to its mouth, and there loaded on the

English ships.  One chronicler says: "The slaughter and pillage were too horrible to record."  So it seems to us, but the feeling in England, rapidly becoming national, was that the Normans merely got what they deserved.  Laurence Minot expressed their views on the burning of Caen:

> That fire ful many folk gan fere
>    When thai se brandes o-ferrum [afar] flye,
> This have thai wonen of the were [war],
>    The fals folk of Normandy.

Such were the occupations and practices that constituted the curriculum for a hero, such the arena where he learned the art of war.  It is not necessary to follow the rest of the campaign with particularity.  We know how the young Prince fleshed his sword, how he rounded out by a field course the education, whatever it was, that he had received from Dr. Walter Burley.  And, if one pauses to think, the Muse of History has done well to turn our eyes away from the multitudinous horrors of it all, deaths, mutilations, rapes, robberies, arson, and lift them up to one high heroic figure of courage, resolution and will.

King Edward does not appear to have had any very definite plan.  He went up the left bank of the Seine, hoping to cross, but found the bridges broken, until he came close to Paris; he crossed the river at Poissy and marched northward past Beauvais, on through the towns of Summereux and Poix to Airaines.  By this time the whole situation had changed; instead of advancing triumphantly onward with the enemy scattering to cover before him, he was now pursued by the vastly larger army that King Philip had at last got together.  His object now was to cross the Somme and join his Flemish allies, who had been besieging a town in northern France, sixty thousand strong. At Airaines it will be necessary to take up the narrative again more fully. Here I will merely record an anecdote of the other side of war, for these gentlemen, who seem to trample so ruthlessly upon the humane and tender values of life, had a rigorous code of chivalry. At Poix the English captured the castle of the Comte de Poix and with it his two handsome daughters. The young ladies would have fallen a prize to the brutality of the soldiers, if Sir John Chandos and Lord Basset had not been there to interfere. These gentlemen, to make sure that the ladies were not subjected to insult, conducted them to the King, who entertained them graciously, asked where they wished to go, and sent them there under a trusty escort. The great French soldier, Bertrand du Guesclin, whose bones lie buried beside the bones of the Kings of France in the sacred precincts of Saint Denis, called Sir John Chandos *"le plus illustre chevalier du monde."*

# CHAPTER IV

## THE VIGIL

KING EDWARD was beginning to regard his situation as awkward. The contrast between a victorious advance, with an enemy shutting itself up in walled towns, and a retreat, with that enemy at your heels, rapidly becoming three or four times as numerous, is dispiriting. The English had not diminished much in numbers since landing, there had been no great fighting, no bad illness, probably few desertions, and not many had gone home; nevertheless, a long march in the months of July and August dulls the edge of adventure. The prospect of joining their Flemish allies, in Picardie or Artois, wore a pleasant look. Edward pushed rapidly northward; Philip followed hard. By the time the English were at Airaines, the French were at or near Amiens, some twenty miles to the southeast.

In order to join the Flemings, King Edward had to cross the River Somme, which runs northwesterly from Amiens to the English Channel. He sent the Earl of Warwick with a strong detachment to look for a crossing. Warwick made a reconnaissance all along the river for miles, even to Abbeville, and in some places tried to capture a bridge-head, but he was obliged to return and report no success. King Edward was perplexed; *il commença fort à muser et fort à merancolyer,* but his words were brave: "Gentlemen, be ye not dismayed, for we have passed through many perils with God's help, and I am persuaded that God, Our Lady and Saint-George, will find us a passage." He left Airaines at daybreak, going north. That same day at noon, the French vanguard entered the town and found tables ready spread, bread and pastry in the oven, meat on the spit, not to mention barrels of wine. From Airaines the English marched to Acheux, thirteen miles northwest. Their situation was now ticklish. They were being pushed farther and farther into the angle formed by the Somme and the sea; and the farther they went wider and wider grew the river. The King offered a rich reward to any man who would show them where and how to cross it. Luckily for him, a native of the region was brought in as prisoner, a man of low degree, Gobin Agache. Tempted by the reward, this fellow said that he could guide the army to a place called Blanchetaque, between Abbeville and Saint-Valery-sur-Somme, where the water at ebb-tide was no deeper than the knee, and twelve men could walk abreast. You can find the place now, even after many changes, for Blanchetaque got its name from the marl, or chalky clay, of the river bed.

The English broke camp at midnight and proceeded to the ford. The moon was near the full, and the tide was consequently high, and would not be at complete ebb at the ford until after eight o'clock in the morning. Their road, it seems, led from the village of Saigneville, a mile and a half or two miles, across swampy land, to the ford. Froissart's account is difficult to accept; he was not there, and he is always delightfully un-methodical, and careless of what he regards as unimportant details. In the first place, it is a little singular that the English should have had any difficulty in discovering the ford; which seems to have been the only one between Abbeville and Saint-Valery, and was so well known that King Philip had sent Sir Godemar du Fay with thousands of men to guard it. Another difficulty is that Froissart's story implies that only twelve men could cross abreast, but it would seem impossible for an army to cross at so narrow a ford in the face of a thousand men-at-arms, and masses of foot soldiers, as well as Genoese crossbowmen. The answer is that "twelve men abreast" is a rhetorical phrase and sounded well to Froissart; King Edward wrote afterward to Sir Thomas Lucy, "The army crossed on a front of a full thousand men at a place where before that scarce three or four men were accustomed to cross," and Richard Wynkeley, in a letter home, says, "Our men crossed indifferently in almost every place." Nevertheless, Froissart was historically right. "Twelve men abreast" gives the truer picture. He paints, with verisimilitude (just as Van Eyck painted his angels to represent spiritual Flemish qualities), the gay, gallant, devil-may-care, chivalric gentlemen adventurers of the fourteenth century,— kings offering to draw up their army at such a time and place as the opposing monarch might find convenient, knights riding up to the enemy's battle array begging for a preliminary encounter before the battle began, or, bachelors, for the love of a lady, binding up one eye until they should perform some deed of note. As the weavers of Bruges and Ghent wove into their tapestries blues, yellows, greens and reds, so Froissart fills his pages with trumpets, pennons, swords, spears and resplendent glory, with honor and renown, and pays little or no heed to slovenly, unhandsome corpses, that lie thick in order to make a solid foundation for fame, and not much to improbabilities, inconsistencies or even irreconcilable facts. At all events, this is Froissart's account: "So, when the tide had wholly ebbed, on the other side Godemar du Fay came to the pass of Blanchetaque, with a great multitude of men-at-arms sent by the King of France. Sir Godemar, also, on his way to Blanchetaque, had gathered together a great multitude of the country people, so that, reckoning these with the others, there were twelve thousand, who were drawn up by the side of the river, to defend the passage. But King Edward, notwithstanding, did not forbear crossing. He bade his marshals plunge in the water, and his archers to shoot hard at the French, who were in the water and on the bank. Then the two marshals of England bade their banner-bearers advance in the name of God and Saint George, and followed themselves. The boldest and best mounted knights plunged into the water with a dash. And there was many an encounter in the river itself, and many a man unhorsed on both sides. A great combat began, for Sir Godemar and his men defended the crossing valiantly. There were some French knights and squires, from Artois and Picardie in Sir Godemar's retinue, who for their honor's sake plunged into the water, and did not wish to be found on the field, but held it more worthy to perish in the water than on land. There were, I tell you, many a joust and many pretty feats of arms. And the English had a very hard fight there at the beginning; for all those who had been sent there with Sir Godemar were picked men, *gens d'eslitte,* and stood in good array on the narrow approach to the ford. So that when the English came out of the water, and stood on land, they had a hard fight. There were Genoese who did much mischief with their crossbolts. But the English archers shot so hard, and in such volleys, that it was a wonder, and, in the meantime, while the archers were keeping the French well occupied, the men-at-arms crossed."

The gist of the matter is that under cover of the English archery, the men-at-arms crossed and speedily put the French to rout. The shooting of the English archers won the victory. The French had never experienced such deadly artillery before. One thinks of Montezuma's Aztecs facing the Spanish harquebuses, or of the Dervishes at Omdurman mowed down by

Kitchener's Maxim guns. Only well trained and disciplined troops could have held their ground. And the great mass of Sir Godemar's motley army was composed of city train-bands, yeomen in wagoners' frocks, plowboys and carters with chance weapons, who had come up *cum exclamacione valde superba,* to drive the English back into the river, but very quickly made up their minds to get out of the way. Nevertheless Sir Godemar had a good number of men-at-arms, and if he had had any military capacity or knowledge, he might well have defended the ford; all the fords and bridges above had been easily defended. One infers from some of Froissart's sentences that Sir Godemar was a conservative officer, of old-fashioned military notions, and had drawn up the bulk of his men-at-arms in the fields in order to give them space to charge. Whatever it was that he did, it was badly done. After the men-at-arms had crossed, the French soon gave way; the mounted men escaped, but great numbers on foot were killed or captured. The pursuit lasted more than a league. And now after Froissart's brilliant Flemish narrative, I will quote what Magister Michael Northburgh, "an excellent clerk," wrote home about it on September fourth. "And then the King of England, whom God save, drew towards Ponthieu on the day of Saint Bartholomew, and came to the River Somme, which cometh to the sea from Abbeville in Ponthieu. And the King of France had appointed five hundred men of arms and three thousand of the commons armed, to hold the passage; and thanks be to God, the King of England and his host took that water of the Somme, where never man passed before, without loss, and fought their enemies and slew more than two thousand armed men and chased the rest right up to the gate of Abbeville, and took of knights and squires in great number." In the meantime Philip's light horse had reached the west bank of the river before the English rear-guard had wholly crossed, and captured some baggage.

A chivalric episode, not told by Froissart, adds a high light to the scene. The tide had come in and the river was no longer fordable and scarce passable, when a French knight in Philip's army rode up along the bank and shouted across to know if there was not some English knight who would come over and joust three courses for the love of his lady. An Englishman from the north country, Sir Thomas Colville by name, heard the challenge, mounted his horse, and plunged into the river at peril to his life. But, *loez en soit Dieu,* he reached the farther bank safely. The gallants ran two courses. At the second the Frenchman's shield was broken. Colville cried, "Take my shield, or let us run a third course without any." But, apparently by those present, objections were made to this very dangerous offer, and, instead, the two young men pledged themselves to be friends for ever.

From the Somme the main corps of the English army marched northeast, toward the forest of Crécy. And as for twelve hours at least there would be no danger of pursuit from Philip, raiding parties rode off to devastate and plunder, and brought in large supplies. The King, his larder stocked, was now free to proceed upon his retreat, but he suddenly decided to face the enemy. It was a volte-face in every sense. Up to now he had been running away from a battle, and now he accepted it. Froissart offers one explanation. Crécy is in the Comté de Ponthieu, of which Edward's grandmother, Eleanor of Castile, had been countess in her own right; his mother, too, had a claim upon it. When the English reached the field of Crécy, the King said: "Let us post ourselves here. We will not budge till we have met the enemy. I have a right to face them here. This land is my mother's lawful inheritance, and I mean to defend it against Philip of Valois." The old belief in wager of battle, that God would defend the right, had not wholly passed away. At Poitiers and at Navarette, the Prince of Wales harangued his men on the righteousness of their cause. The orthodox believed in God's justice; and very likely the King himself, and certainly many in his host, felt that God would be far more inclined to favor a man when defending his own feudal territory—*Dieu et mon Droit!*—than when aggressor in a foreign land; as to his claim to the throne of France, the King, in the bottom of his soul, did not set much store by it. But, to my thinking, the King was influenced by a very different consideration. At Blanchetaque, for the first time, he and his officers had taken the measure of the enemy's strength. The battle there had shown that the French infantry, so formidable in numbers, consisting in the main of city train-bands and country yeomen, was badly armed and wholly undisciplined, and had little value as a fighting force, and that their men-at-arms were not able to withstand the fire of the English archers, and further that the French officers, if one was to judge by Sir Godemar du Fay, were not comparable to the English captains, Warwick, Salisbury, Chandos and a score of others.

Ponthieu, in this neighborhood, is an undulating country, nearly flat; the downs roll like gentle waves of the sea, rising to a crest, and then flowing down into an almost imperceptible valley, and then rising again. One of these crests lies to the east of the forest of Crécy, and rolls gently down to the southeast, a slope of sixty feet, with the fall of one foot in ten, to the Vallée des Clercs, a stretch of perhaps six hundred yards, and then rises, still more gradually toward another but lower crest, in the direction of Estrées, a village about two miles to the east.

The village of Crécy was situated on the southwest end of this ridge or crest, or rather, set a few hundred yards back, and was separated from the forest only by the little brook Maye, that flows northerly through marshy banks. It is the sort of place where some old Ponthevin Caspar, when his work was done, might sit beside his cottage door and watch his little grand-daughter at play; while at the other end of the ridge lies the hamlet of Wadicourt. The English army drawn up on this ridge, facing the Vallée des Clercs, with its right flank protected by the brook and the forest, and its left by the hamlet or forest of Wadicourt, held a very strong position. This distance is a mile and a quarter, or a little over two thousand yards. The King arrived there on Friday, August twenty-fifth, approved the spot and encamped. That night the soldiers looked to their arms and armor; and the King gave a supper to his nobles, at which they made good cheer, drinking the wines they had captured in French ships at the mouth of the Somme. On their taking leave he retired to his oratory and prayed that, if he was to do battle the next day, he might come off with honor. Though he did not go to bed till midnight, he was up betimes on Saturday morning, and he and the Prince of Wales heard mass and took communion; the army also heard mass, confessed and received absolution. Then each man repaired to the place assigned him by his orders.

The battle array was this. The army was divided into three divisions, corps, or "battles," as they were called. The first division, under the command of the Prince of Wales, assisted by the Earls of Warwick and Oxford, Lords Cobham and Stafford, and many other able officers, was stationed on the right wing, and Sir John Chandos and Sir James Audeley, were especially assigned to the Prince's person. Theirs was the better protected position, on account of the brook and the forest, and because the land fell away more steeply, but it also squarely faced the direction from which the enemy would come, and therefore was most likely to bear the brunt of the attack, as it did. The numbers, as always, are uncertain; Froissart's later figures are more likely to be correct than the earlier, they put the Prince's division at twelve hundred men-at-arms, four thousand archers, and one thousand Welshmen. The second division, under the Earls of Northampton and Arundel, was stationed behind and a little to the Prince's left, with its left flank protected by the hamlet or forest of Wadicourt, and, apparently, in part, by an improvised rampart of some interlocked carts and wagons. This division was smaller and subsidiary to the first; it consisted of twelve hundred men-at-arms and four thousand archers. The third division, commanded by the King, and held as a reserve, was stationed behind the other two; it consisted of fifteen hundred men-at-arms, and six thousand footmen including archers. At some distance in the rear a corral was made, stockaded by the rest of the carts and wagons; and within were placed the horses, the baggage and non-combatants. The whole army may be estimated at thirty-nine hundred men-at-arms, ten thousand archers and five thousand Welsh. These Welshmen were a species of infantry armed with spears and knives. The men-at-arms and archers were all dismounted.

The Prince's division was distinctly in front. Its men-at-arms, all on foot, fell into line, let us say, two hundred lengthwise, and six deep, and small pits, a foot wide, a foot deep, were dug in front of the line. The archers were, at the commencement of the battle, ranged in lines, not more than two or three deep, I should suppose, across the whole front, in such a way that those behind could shoot between those in front. It was of the first importance to bring the whole force of the archery to bear upon the advancing front ranks of the enemy. When the French men-at-arms charged, the archers fell back to right and left of the English front, and from there could enfilade the attackers.

On Saturday morning, August twenty-sixth, the English army, drawn up at the top of the slope, every man in his place, quietly awaited the enemy.

# CHAPTER V

KING PHILIP, *tyrannus Francorum* as Geoffrey Baker patrioti-
cally calls him, had been prevented by the incoming tide from
pursuing the English across the Somme; so he returned from
Blanchetaque to Abbeville, and crossed the river there. Early
the next morning, after religious exercises, he set forth in pursuit. He supposed that the English had retreated by a road
running to the west of the forest of Crécy, and started in that
direction, but learning his mistake, turned eastward and followed what is now route nationale No. 28. His army streamed
out of Abbeville in most disorderly fashion, and it was past noon
before the hindmost had left the city. After a few miles, he
attempted to arrange the battalions in marching sequence according to his proposed battle array, but it is evident that this attempt
was imperfectly executed. Everything was helter-skelter for
they did not expect to overtake the English that day. The
Genoese, who were ordered to the van, left their shields and a
great part of their crossbolts on the baggage wagons. It occurred to somebody that it would be well to reconnoiter; and
four knights were sent forward to obtain what information they
could. It was then about three o'clock and the army, having
already marched eight or nine miles, was straggling on in its
disorderly fashion, the Genoese bowmen at the head, then bodies
of mounted men-at-arms and footmen, each troop, sometimes
each man, marching as was easiest, and so on, all the great
multitude strung out half-way back to Abbeville. Nobody

49

knows how many there were, probably six thousand Genoese crossbowmen, and all told, feudal nobles with their followers, mercenaries from Germany and Savoy, city train-bands and rustic militia anywhere from thirty thousand to sixty thousand men.

When the four knights came back from scouting, the etiquette of chivalry—one finds the conservative spirit that animated Sir Godemar du Fay everywhere in the higher command of the French army—prevailed over military exigency, and no one of the four was willing to take precedence of his colleagues and speak first. So they stood looking at one another, while the sweating troops marched wearily on. The King addressed himself to Sieur Le Moine de Bazeilles, a knight from Luxembourg, in the retinue of John of Bohemia, and bade him speak out. The knight answered: "Sire, I will speak since you are pleased to bid me, but under correction from my companions. We advanced far enough to reconnoiter the enemy. They are drawn up in three divisions and are waiting for you. For my part, I should advise (subject to wiser counsel) that you halt your army here, and encamp them for the night. It will be very late before the rear comes up; and the army then will have had time to take a good position. Your men are tired and in disorder, whereas the enemy is fresh and in advantageous battle array. To-morrow you will be able to deploy, and post your army at your convenience, also to reconnoiter at greater leisure and determine where it will be best to launch the attack. You may rest assured that the enemy will wait for you." The King approved the advice, issued the order, and officers rode forward and back, crying out: "Halt, in the name of God and Saint Denis!"

Meanwhile on the crest of the downs at Crécy, the English had been quietly waiting. There was confidence in their camp.

Since the battle of Blanchetaque, it had been obvious to the officers that the French army was a mere jumble, no coordination among its units, no foresight in the high command. Besides, rest and abundance of food and wine had made their bodies comfortable. King Edward, cheerful and light-hearted, mounted on a small palfrey, with a white rod in his hand, rode slowly along the ranks. He bade the soldiers remember his honor and defend the right. His look, his manner and his words, were so full of assurance and cheer that even those who had been apprehensive were comforted. By ten o'clock he had ridden down all the lines. He then returned to his division, the reserves, drawn up in the rear, and gave orders that rations should be served, that the men should eat well and each have a glass of wine; and he commended all things to God and the Blessed Virgin. His orders were obeyed, dinner was eaten in leisurely fashion, and the pots and pans were packed up and loaded on the carts in the corral. That done, each man returned to his place, and sat down on the ground with helmet and arms beside him, to await what might happen.

Across the Vallée des Clercs and miles beyond, there was none of this calm and quiet. The afternoon had already begun to cast long shadows by the time the French officers were trying to halt their troops. The long, slouching, perspiring line extended for miles, and the van was approaching the plateau on the southeasterly side of the Vallée des Clercs. From the higher uplands they could already see the English in battle array. When the order to halt reached the generals of the Genoese mercenaries, Grimaldi and Doria, it found the men quite ready to obey; though their shields and the supply of crossbolts had been left in the baggage wagon, their crossbows were heavy and they had marched some fifteen miles or more, they were tired and said that they were in no condition to attack. The Duc d'Alençon, the King's brother, on being told of this, said: "This is what comes from employing these rascally fellows, they are only good at eating, and hinder us more than they help." But no one, except the Genoese, paid any attention to the King's orders. All the French noblemen wished to begin the fight, each impatient to be the first; they had already quarreled as to who should have what prisoners. The Duc d'Alençon, who commanded the foremost division of men-at-arms, pressed upon the bowmen, and those behind him came crowding on. All jostled, pushed, shoved, as if they were escaping from a theater on fire, all in a mad passion of rivalry to be the first. The propulsive force was too great to be checked, and, when the young officers saw the English army, the last chance of order was done, their fighting blood kicked over all discipline, and the crossbowmen, willy-nilly, were shoved down the slope into the Vallée des Clercs. The experienced eyes of the old soldiers foresaw the outcome. On the English side, Sir John Chandos or some other, cried "They are ours." A flock of crows flew over the field, an augury. Then, as often happens in that region during the month of August, black clouds gathered, thunder roared, lightning flashed, and rain fell heavily. The storm soon passed, and the setting sun, coming out brilliant in the freshened air, shone full in the faces of the advancing columns. The Genoese crossbowmen advanced. They had no choice; not only were they pushed by the disorderly ranks of the impatient horsemen behind, but King Philip, on coming within sight of the English, lost his self-control; his blood too began to boil. "Unfurl the Oriflamme!" he cried, and shouted to his generals to order the Genoese forward. The grumbling reluctant Genoese tramped wearily across the wet ground, wet themselves, and the strings of their bows moist and slack; when they entered the little valley, they shouted their battle cry. Froissart describes the scene (Lord Berners' translation) : "Whan the Genowayes were assembled toguyder and beganne to aproche, they made a great leap and crye to abasche the Englysshmen, but they stode styll and stridde not for all that. Than the Genowayes againe the seconde tyme made another leape and fell crye and stepped forwarde a lytell, and the Englysshmen remeued not one fote; thirdly agayne they leapt and cryed, and went forth tyll they came within shotte; then they shott feersly with their crossbowes. Than the Englysshe archers step forthe one pase and lette fly their arowes so hotly and so thycke that it semed snowe, whan the Genowayes felte the arowes persynge through heedes, armes and brests, many of them cast downe their crossbowes and dyde cutte their strynges and retourned dysconfited. Whan the Frenche Kynge saw them flye away, he said, 'Slee there rascals, for they shall lette and trouble us without reason.' Than you shoulde have sene the men-of-armes dasshe in among them and kylled a great numbre of them. And even styll the Englysshmen shot where as they saw the thyckest preace, the sharpe arowes ranne into the men-of-armes and into their horses, and many fell horse and men amonge the Genowayes, and when they were downe they coude not relyne agayne; the preace was so thycke that one overthrewe another, and also amonge the Englysshemen there were certayne rascalles [the Welshmen] that went a fote with great knyves, and they went in among the men-at-armes and slew and murdredd many as they lay on the grounde, both erles, barownes, knyghts, and squyers, whereof the King of Englande was after dyspleased, for he had rather they had been taken prisoners."

It seems, in less picturesque language, that the Genoese bowmen, first ordered to halt, then to advance, and wet to the skin,

had pushed forward, while behind them the men-at-arms, on
horseback, came tramping on their heels, amid an immense din
of drums, trumpets, clarions, and had begun shooting too soon.
Their bolts fell short. They had to stop to draw their bows
again; and, in disorder to begin with, they became more and
more disorganized. When they arrived within range, the English bowmen, drawn up over the whole front, poured their
volleys of arrows with a speed, accuracy and power that the
Italians had never experienced before. From the survivors, reports got back to Italy that the flight of arrows was like a cloud,
and that the English had cannon which made such a noise and
concussion that it seemed as if God were hurling thunderbolts,
*che facieno si grande tremoto e romore, che parea, che Iddio
tonasse,* but whether the cannon were really there, or the Genoese
merely heard the thunder, nobody is very sure.

Behind the crossbowmen, the Duc d'Alençon and the Count of
Flanders had done their best to deploy their divisions into battle
formation, but with such little success that the chroniclers do
not agree how many battalions were marshaled; one says four,
another seven, another eight, another nine. In fact there was
little, or no, order. The front rank of men-at-arms, mounted
and clad in heavy armor, had after a fashion deployed behind
the Genoese bowmen; but when there rose from the Genoese
ranks shrill screams and cries as the arrows, of a long cloth
yard, struck them in every unguarded spot, the hind ranks of
men-at-arms took the noise to be English shrieks, and pressed
eagerly on, especially the young noblemen, of whom there were
many, all eager not to lose their share of glory. Alençon's
men, some, no doubt, surmising treachery among the Italian
mercenaries, rode through them, hurling them to right and left,
trampling them down; and when the horses in their turn were hit

by the arrows—the English archers aimed at the horses—the confusion was indescribable; the maddened beasts reared and kicked, unhorsed their riders and careered riderless hither and there. The French showed courage; a troop of Alençon's knights forced their way to the Prince of Wales' division. The English men-at-arms, on foot, awaited attack; the bowmen fell back to the right and left of the battalion, or slipped through its ranks to the rear. The French gained the top of the ridge, and for a time the Prince was in the thick of it. The second battalion moved up. Sir Thomas Norwich, seeing the Prince's danger, went in great haste to the King, who had taken his station by a windmill that stood on a hillock a little back of the Prince's division, between it and the reserves. "Sire," said Sir Thomas, "the Earl of Warwick, Lord Stafford, Lord Reginald Cobham, and other suche as be about the Prince your Sonne, are feersly fought withal, and are sore handled; wherefore they desire you that you and your batayle wolle come and ayde them for if the Frenchmen increase, as they dout they woll, your sonne and they shall have much ado." The King asked: "Is my son dead, or hurt or on the earth felled?" "No, Sire," the Knight replied, "but he is hardely matched, wherefore he hath need of your ayde." The King said: "Sir Thomas, go back to them that sent you, and tell them from me that they sende no more to me for any adventure that falleth, as long as my son is alive. And also say to them, that they suffre him this day to win his spurs, for if God be pleased, I woll this journey to be his, and the honor thereof and to them that be about him." Sir Thomas Norwich returned to his battalion and reported the King's answer. It mightily encouraged them, and made them repent that they ever had sent such a message. The need had been great. One of the stories, told after the battle, said that the Prince had been struck down twice upon his knees, and that his standard-bearer, Richard Fitz Symon, dropped the flag, put his foot on it and, swinging his sword with two hands and shouting "Rescue the King's son," advanced and stood over him. The King, who could judge from the vantage of his hillock better than those in the mêlée how the battle was going, in spite of his words, sent a band of twenty knights to the rescue. This small number shows how few of the French knights had been able to reach the English line. Other post-bellum stories had it that this band of rescuing knights, sent by King Edward, found the Prince and his men leaning on their swords and spears, beside a heap of corpses, getting their breath, and awaiting another attack. The Prince won great commendation. When the English soldiers were at home again, they described him (at least so Geoffrey Baker heard the story) as standing in the front rank, "where he proved to the Frenchmen his admirable valor, *equos perforando, equites prosternado, cassides conquatiendo, lanceas truncando, ictus objectos prudenter frustrando, suos juvando, se ipsum defendendo, amicos prostratos errigendo, et suis omnibus exemplum benefaciendi exhibendo* [piercing horses, prostrating knights, shattering helmets, lopping spears, warding blows, etc., etc., and setting an example of good deeds to all his men]," nor did he rest from such labors till the foemen, barred by the rampart of their own dead, drew off.

The victory was won by the English archers; but the primal cause was the disorder in the French army, for French bravery was as conspicuous as ever. The men-at-arms essayed, fifteen times it is said, to ride over the dead and dying and attack the English lines. All in vain, they were *navrés, blechiés, tués, pestelés, affolés et esquellés,* or in literal English, cut to pieces. The Duc d'Alençon, the King's brother, was killed, so was the Count of Flanders, the Count of Blois (the King's nephew) and the Duke of Lorraine (his brother-in-law) and many another great noble. The blind King of Bohemia, son to that Emperor, Henry of Luxembourg, whom Dante hoped would restore the distracted Empire to peace and order, was killed, and in death won great renown. A legend concerning him soon arose, with what truth one can not say. He asked how the English army was arrayed. Somebody answered: "Excellent well for fighting, they have stacked their carts and wagons in the rear." The King said: "They mean to die where they stand to-day or else to be the victors." Somebody remarked that there were many crows and carrion birds flying over the French. "A bad sign," he said, "the army goes to slaughter." (Winston Churchill says that when the British army marched across the desert to Omdurman, "a hundred vultures joined it, flying or lazily waddling from bush to bush . . . it was freely asserted that these birds of prey knew that two armies were approaching each other, and that this meant a battle, and hence a feast.") The King of Bohemia then asked those about him if his son, Charles, afterward Emperor, was in the fight. They could not answer for sure, but thought that he was. "Gentlemen," the King said, "you are my people, you are my friends and brothers in arms this day; as I am blind, I ask you to lead me into the fight so far that I may strike one blow with my sword." His horse was led, it would seem, by a tie-strap. King and his bridle-leaders rode to their deaths. On the morrow they were found side by side, and the tie-strap not cut. Laurence Minot says triumphantly,

> Ye King of Beme was cant and kene,
> But there he left both play and pride.

King Philip, at the opening of the battle, had been well behind the first column of men-at-arms, and did not bring his battalion into the fight till Alençon's battalion had been discomfited. Then he behaved well. His horse was shot under him, and he himself was wounded by an arrow in the jaw. It was now late, darkness was coming on, not sixty knights of all his battalion were left. The confusion was hideous. It was obvious that all was lost. Sir John of Hainaut found the King a horse, and said he must go: "Sire, retreat while opportunity serves, and do not expose yourself like a common soldier. This battle is lost, but another time you will be the victor." And taking the King's bridle he led him away. A handful of them rode off together to the south. They reached the castle of la Broyes late at night. The gates were shut. Their shouts brought the commandant to the walls: "Who is it that calls at such an hour?" The King called: "Open, open, Warder, it is the unfortunate King of France." The Warder opened the gate and let down the drawbridge. But the fugitives only halted for rest and food. At midnight they rode forth again and at daybreak reached Amiens.

The silence on the battle-field made the English sure that the victory was theirs; but the King's orders were strict that no man should quit the ranks, so they stayed on the ridge. Torches were lighted and bonfires made. The King led his battalion down to the Prince's position. He put his arms round his son and kissed him: "Fair Son, God give you good perseverance. You are my good son, and nobly have you acquitted yourself this day. You are worthy to be a King." The Prince bowed very low and did obeisance and gave all the honor to his father. There were no wild rejoicings, for the King had commanded quiet, but they rendered thanks to God.

The next day a detachment in force, making a reconnaissance, came upon French reenforcements, who had no news of the battle, and mistook the English for French.  The French were routed; and then again, the English encountered another body of ignorant French levies, and defeated them.  And they came upon many stragglers, in ones and twos or little troops, wandering lost, seeking some way to safety.  The English put every man they met to the sword, and it is said that the slaughter then was four times as great as in the battle.  The rest of the Sunday was spent in reckoning up the dead and sorting the bodies of knights and noblemen.  Froissart says that they found eighty banners, the bodies of eleven princes, twelve hundred knights and about thirty thousand common men.  This must be far too large, but it shows the impression left of multitudinous slaughter.

# CHAPTER VI

## CALAIS

THIS glorious victory, the first great English victory on the continent, stirred all England and swelled the national sentiment with pride. Laurence Minot dipped his goose quill deeper into his inkhorn to celebrate the deeds of King Edward, and likened him to a wild boar (bare) at bay:

> Then come Philip, ful redy dight,
>     Toward the town, with all his rowt,
> With him come mani a kumly knight,
>     And all umset the bare about.
> The bare made tham ful law to lout,
>     And delt tham knokkes to thaire mede;
> He gert them stumbill that war stout,
>     Thare helpid nowther staf ne stede.

An inevitable corollary to this national praise of King Edward was disparagement of King Philip, who is rather badly treated by the English chroniclers. One calls him, as I have said, *tyrannus Francorum*, another *intrusor Franciae*, a third *coronatus*. John of Reading, speaking of Philip's flight from Crécy, says: *"Retraxit se cum residuo suorum praedictus Philippus* inglorious, or as the French say, *Noster beal retreit* [our excellent retreat," a favorite English joke]. And Geoffrey Baker says that the Oriflamme was a signal to give no quarter, and got its name from *oleum inflammatum*, blazing oil, which spared nothing. Nevertheless, under the stress of war, nationality showed its beneficent aspect as well. Out of the carnage, dev-

60

astation and horrors of it all, a hero stepped forth, clothed in *probitas admiranda* and *honor militaris,* marvelous prowess and martial honor. From that time on the Black Prince swam in a sea of glory. As Thomas Walsingham said (after that flashing career had ended), "He never met the enemy without a victory, never attacked a town that he did not take; under his lead the English were afraid of nothing, for he was feared, like another Hector, by both Christians and Pagans alike." One must travel far in the pages of military story, to find another lad of sixteen with such a laurel crown. The author of *Wynnere and Wastour* (1352) describes him as "one of the ferlyeste frekes [most wonderful champions]." He says that the Prince never failed his father, that, when the King commanded, the Prince answered, "Lord, I serve while my life endures," and that he "was youngest of years and yarest of wit, that any wight of this world wist at his age."

And the Prince was fortunate in this, that his reputation kept mounting. The Herald, who attended Sir John Chandos, was so filled with enthusiasm for the Prince, an admiration that he very likely got from Sir John, that he wrote a long poem on *The Feats of Arms of the very noble Prince of Wales and Aquitaine.* This poem is one of our chief authorities for the Prince's life. The Herald says: "I propose to write the life of the most valiant Prince in the world, *le plus vaillant Prince du monde,* that has been since the time of Julius Cæsar or King Arthur, the gallant Prince Aquitaine, who was the son of the noble King Edward, who had no coward heart, and of Queen Philippa, the perfect root of all honor and nobleness, of wisdom, valor and bounty. This gallant Prince, of whom I speak, from the day of his birth cherished no thought but loyalty, gallantry, valor and goodness. He was all *proece* [the qualities that become a man]. Of such high aspiration was this Prince, that every day of his life he desired to make the maintenance of justice and righteousness all his study. From infancy he fed upon such thoughts. His generous doctrines sprang from his noble and gallant character. *Jolieté et noblece* [joyousness and magnaminity] lodged in his heart from earliest childhood. *C'est chose clere* [every one knows] how noble, bold and valiant, how courteous and wise he was, how he loved unfeignedly the Holy Church, and the Most Sacred Trinity. *Noblement il usa son tamps,* nobly he spent his time, and I dare aver that since the birth of Christ was never a man more valiant than he."

And when the Herald speaks of Crécy he says that the victory was due to the Prince,

*Car par lui et par ses vertus*
*Hu li champs gaignez et vaincus.*

Such was the Prince in the popular voice; and the fame of his exploits at Crécy lived on, in uninterrupted brilliancy, until Shakespeare's time:

Edward the Black Prince,
Who on the French ground play'd a tragedy,
Making defeat on the full power of France,
Whiles his most mighty father on a hill
Stood smiling to behold his lion's whelp
Forage in blood of French nobility.

But, though the victory was won, a long road lay ahead of the Black Prince and King Edward before they could return to London to enjoy the incense of acclamation. They could hardly go home without something besides glory to show for their prowess. The King decided to take Calais. They buried the dead, and on Monday marched away from the bloody field.

They crossed several rivers on their way, and destroyed and ravaged as before. The town of Boulogne on its acropolis was too strong to take, but they burned the suburbs up to the very walls. On September fourth the King sat down before Calais and prepared for a siege. The town lay along a series of marshes close to the sea. It was surrounded by a double wall and a double ditch, which the tide filled twice a day. All around the ground was half sand and gave way under weight, so that no great engines to hurl stones could be stationed within effective range, nor movable towers pushed to the attack. Assault was out of the question; there was nothing to do but starve the garrison out. The English blockaded the port with their fleet, built themselves a little town of wood and mud to lodge in, and waited. At first the blockade was not stiff enough, and provisions were smuggled in. But with the spring the English calked the leaks, and the city soon felt the pressure of hunger. All the useless mouths, more than two thousand, were driven out. King Edward not only let them pass, but also, at least according to Froissart, gave to each a good dinner and alms. This indicated no relaxation of purpose. Calais in the past had been a refuge for privateers that preyed on English commerce; and he intended in the future to make it an English city, that should serve as an open door by which English troops could enter France or Flanders at will. The garrison's only hope lay in help from the outside. There were two possible chances. Edward might be called home to defend his kingdom from the Scots, and Philip had urged this as a happy time for an invasion. The Scots thought well of the plan. "There's not a man to hinder us," they said, "for all the warriors of England are gone to France leaving but a parcel of shoemakers, skinners and merchants behind." They reckoned ill. Earl Percy, and other northern lords surprised them at Neville's Cross, won a great victory, and deprived Calais of that chance. The second chance lay in a French army coming to raise the siege. Philip finally came with a great multitude of soldiers, but it was impossible to attack the English army, where it lay, protected by marshes and fortifications. So after many big and idle words, Philip marched away again, and left the city to its fate.

King Edward learned by chance that the prize would soon be his. The fleet had learned that the French had planned to victual Calais, and sailed westerly toward the mouth of the Somme and came upon the French "floynes, galleys and victuallers, laden with divers victuals." The French ships scattered and fled, some casting their cargo into the sea, some running ashore, but one boat was sighted out at sea by two mariners, William Roke and Hickman Stephen, and chased ashore and captured. The captain happened to be captain of the Genoese galleys and a person of some importance. Before he was taken, he had tied a letter to an ax and flung it into the sea; but both ax and letter were found at ebb-tide. It was a letter from Jean de Vienne, Commandant of Calais, to King Philip, and read as follows:

"Right dear and dread Lord,

"I recommend me unto you with all my might, as one who much desireth to know that you are in good estate, and may our Lord ever keep you in happiness by his grace. And if it please you to know the estate of our town of Calais, be certified that, when these present letters were written, we were all well and of good cheer and right willing to serve you and to do whatever might be to your honor and profit. But right dear and dread Lord, know that, although the people be all well and of good cheer, yet the town is in sore need of corn, wine and meat. For know that there is nothing therein which has not been eaten, both dogs and cats and horses, so that victuals we can no more find in the town, except we eat men's flesh. For formerly you wrote that I should hold the town so long as there should be food. And now we are at that point that we have not wherewithal to live. So we have resolved amongst us that, if we have not succour quickly, we shall all sally forth from the town into the open field, to fight for life or death. Wherefore, right dear and dread Lord, apply what remedy shall seem to you fitting; for, if remedy and counsel be not briefly found, never more will you have letters from me, and the town will be lost and we that are therein. Our Lord grant you a good life and long, and give you the will, if we die for you, to requite it to our heirs.

"Yours etc. JOHN DE VIENNE."

The die was cast. Calais must surrender. On August fourth the Commandant gave the signal that he wished to parley. Sir Walter Manny and Lord Basset were sent to hear what he had to say. He said that they had defended themselves to the best of their ability, in accordance with their Sovereign's command, that all hope of succor had been abandoned, and that they threw themselves on King Edward's mercy, begging him to be satisfied with the town and its contents and let the garrison go alive. Sir Walter Manny replied: "It is not the King's pleasure that you should go so; he demands unconditional surrender, he to be free to ransom or put to death at his pleasure, for the people of Calais have done him great mischief, and he is mightily enraged by their obstinate defense, which has cost him many lives."

The Seigneur de Vienne feared that this might mean that those too poor to pay ransom would be put to death. He answered: "These conditions are too hard. We are but a small number of knights and squires, who like yourselves have loyally served our master; but we will endure all before the meanest man in town shall fare worse than the best. Go once more, I have so high an opinion of the King's gallantry as to hope that, by God's mercy, he will change his mind." The English envoys went; it would seem that Sir Walter Manny, by birth a Hainauter, was a friend of Jean de Vienne, and spoke in his behalf. At any rate the King did change his mind, and granted a large degree of mercy.

Of this final scene in the drama Froissart has preserved a dramatic detail. When Sir Walter Manny returned, the King insisted upon a surrender without conditions; but Sir Walter Manny remonstrated and others agreed with him. Edward said: "Gentlemen, I am not so stiff-necked as to hold to my opinion against you all. Sir Walter, tell the Commandant that six of the principal citizens must come, barefoot and barehead, with ropes round their necks, and the keys of the city in their hands. These six shall lie at my mercy, the rest may go free." Sir Walter Manny reported the issue of his visit. Jean de Vienne asked him to wait, while he consulted the townsfolk. The bells were rung, and all the citizens assembled in the market-place, men and women. Vienne recounted what had passed, and announced King Edward's terms, he said that he had been unable to accomplish more and that they must answer at once. There was no physical strength left among them, and the people gave way to cries of despair; Jean de Vienne, too, wept bitterly. There was a pause. Then the richest man in town, Eustace de Saint Pierre stood up and said: "Gentlemen, it would be great pity to suffer so many people to die of starvation, if means there be to prevent it. If that were possible, such means would please our Saviour, Jesus Christ. I believe that if I die to save my townsmen, I shall find grace with God. I will be the first of the six." Then a second rich man, John Daire, stood up and said, "I will be second." Then James Wisant, a cousin of the other two, stood up as the third, and his brother Peter Wisant, as fourth. Then two others. Jean de Vienne, who was too weak to walk, mounted a little horse and rode with the six to the gate. He bade it be opened, and he and the six went out. The burghers were arrayed as the English King had prescribed. You shall see them in their gaunt and savage dignity in Rodin's statue that stands by the Jardin Richelieu in Calais. Sir Walter Manny presented them to the King. They fell upon their knees before him, offered the keys and said that they surrendered themselves to his mercy. The King, the story goes, remembered the losses he had suffered at sea from Calais pirates; his anger flared up. "Cut off their heads," he commanded. All those present entreated the King to have mercy; but he would not listen to them. Sir Walter Manny spoke out: "Let me beseech you, restrain your anger! Do not tarnish your reputation for magnanimity. If you do this, all the world will call you cruel." The King answered dryly: "Be it so," and bade them fetch the headsman. Then Queen Philippa, great with child, fell on her knees: "Gentle Lord," she said, "since I crossed the seas in great danger to see you, I have not asked one boon. Now, I ask you humbly, for Blessed Mary's Son's sake, for my love's sake, be merciful to these men." The King answered: "Lady, I wish you had been anywhere but here. I can not refuse you. I give them to you; do with them as you please." The Queen conducted them to her apartments, clothed them, fed them and sent them away in safety.

# CHAPTER VII

So CALAIS fell, and for good or ill remained in the possession of England for two hundred years. King Edward resolved to make it an English city. The French knights, who had surrendered, were held for ransom, all the other inhabitants were sent away, except a priest and two other old men, who, it was thought, would be of service on account of their knowledge of the city, and of its customs and usages. The King bestowed upon Sir Walter Manny, the Earls of Warwick and Stafford and other noblemen, very handsome houses, to induce them to establish households there, and made arrangements for repeopling the town with English families. Froissart here sounds the unfamiliar note of compassion: "We thynke it was great pyte of the Burgesses and other men of the towne of Calys and women and chyldren, whan they were fayne to forsake their houses, herytages and goodes, and to bere away nothing."

Concerning the Prince of Wales himself, in spite of the renown that he had gained from holding his ground against all the French attacks at Crécy, the chroniclers say but little. In order to obtain provisions, he conducted one particular raid on a large scale. He swept the countryside for thirty leagues, going as far as the River Somme, gathering up all the booty he could carry away, and burning villages, farms, all that fire could destroy. The old chroniclers record such facts very simply, usually without comment. Modern writers betray a

touch of national bias.  For instance, Mr. Dunn-Pattison says:
"Prince Edward was entrusted with the charge of one of these
light columns, and his raid was eminently successful.  He
swept the country right up to the banks of the Somme and returned laden with booty, well pleased with the success of his first
independent command."  On the other hand, Père Denifle says:
"There the English devastated the country round the city very
much as they had done before.  This was chiefly the doing of
Edward, Prince of Wales, a young man of seventeen, bold to
rashness, whose ferocity and taste for pillage increased with
years."  One must put oneself in the Prince's place, a lad of
barely seventeen, heir to one throne and claimant of another, the
hero of the greatest victory that men knew of, or had ever read
recorded in old books, since Cæsar or Alexander, galloping over
a flat country, with a brave array of other young fellows at his
heels, herding cattle, driving pigs—do you know Leigh Hunt's
essay *On the Arts and Graces of Pig Driving?*—catching
chickens and geese, judging captured horses, looking to see if
the girls of Picardie were pretty or no, and laying a wager as to
who could burn a grange or a barn the quicker, girding at
monks, mocking priests, drinking wine, and feeling the must of
youth rampaging in his veins.  The political causes of the war
were mere subjects of discourse, concocted by clerks in chancery,
England was poor, France was rich, and it was as much a matter
of course "for them to take that had the power," as it has been
in our day, on the Congo, or in China, for instance.  A gentleman had no other occupation than real or mimic war; and the
Black Prince ravaged the French villages and fields with the
light-hearted insouciance of boys on a spree.

By no means was everything destroyed.  When the English
army went back to England, English ships were laden with

spoils. There was not a lady of quality who did not profit by the riches of Calais, Caen and other pillaged cities, who did not wear French clothes, furs or jewelry, or lie on French mattresses and pillows, or beautify her house or castle with French furniture; and in the houses of the middle class, everywhere, were to be seen foreign table-cloths, napkins, goblets of crystal or silver, linen sheets, and trinkets of this sort and that. The English soldiers brought back to their wives and sweethearts luxuries they had never dreamed of. So when the King and Queen, the Prince of Wales, and the victorious army entered London in October, there was a mighty concourse of hurrahing people. London was all agog. A great emotion of national pride shook the city:

England my England,
Such a breed of mighty men, as come forward one to ten,
England my own.

*Jam tripudiantes, jamque laetificantes, Deum magnificantes:*
Blessed be the Most High,
Who has given such power to men,
Who has delivered great, stately, famous, brave, warlike nobles
    into the hands of the few.

"O, *dira hostilitas!* Oh, woeful bloodshed! Presumptuous pride cast Philip down! Trust in God has raised Edward up! France bewails the day of sorrow, England delights in the day of Joy and Consolation, which Our Lord Jesus Christ has deigned to grant her. Praise and honor be to him forever and ever." And, of course, as before, the corollary followed, the French were maligned:

*Francia, feminea, pharisea, vigoris idea,*
*Lynxea, viperea, vulpina, lupina, Medea,*
*Callida, syrena, crudelis, acerba, superba.*

*Anglicus, angelicus Edwardus, juris amicus,*
*Sis rex pacificus, patiens, pius atque pudius,*
*Verax, magnificus, affabilis etc.*

France, she-thing, pharisaical, a hollow show,
Cat-like, snaky, foxey, wolfish, Medea,
Crafty, false, cruel, bitter, proud.

*       *

English Edward, angel-like, the friend of right,
A peaceful, patient, pious, modest King,
Truthful, magnificent and affable . . .

Laurence Minot tuned his lyre:

Calais men, now may ze care
    And murning mun ze have to mede,
Mirth on mold get ze no mare,
    Sir Edward sall ken zow zowre crede.
Whilum war ze wight in wede,
    To robbing rathly for to ren;
Men zow sone of zowre misdede,
    Zowre care es cumen, will ze it ken.

*       *

Calais men, now you may be sorry, and mourning must be
your reward; mirth on earth ye get no more, Sir Edward shall
teach you what to believe. Formerly ye were stoutly girded for
to run speedily to robbery; mend you soon of your misdeeds,
your care is coming, you will be taught.

*       *

Lystens now, and ze may lere
    Als men the suth may understand,
The knights that in Calais were
    Came to Sir Edward sare wepeaned,
In kirtell one, and swerd in hand,
    And cried, Sir Edward thine we are
Do now, lord, bi law of land
    Thi will with us for evermare.

Listen now and ye may learn, and men may understand the truth, the knights that were in Calais came sorely weeping to Sir Edward, in tunic only, and sword in hand, and cried, Sir Edward, we are thine, do now, lord, by law of the land thy will with us forever.

The poet tells how the men of Calais used to wound Englishmen and steal their goods, but the Boar would abate their bliss, and hunt them as hound does hare; he would take up his lodging, with his soldiers, beside them. The Frenchmen made great to do, and red-hatted Cardinals tried to beguile Sir Edward. But Philip proved a coward, and fled instead of fighting. So the knights came out in their tunics, and the burgesses came out to receive what might be due to them, and the common people with ropes round their necks, complaining that Philip and his son John had left them lying in the mire, and saying that all the horses, coneys, cats and dogs had been eaten. Sir John de Vienne had been their warden, but the Boar had tamed them, and they had given up the keys.

All on this wise was Calais won;
God save tham that it is so gat wan!

And so it remained an English city till François de Guise, le Balafré, recovered it two hundred years later, leaving the image of it upon Bloody Mary's heart.

But there is a little epilogue in the Calais drama, which as it concerns the Black Prince I will now relate. Sir John Montgomery was appointed governor of the town, and Sir Amerigo da Pavia, an Italian condottiere, warden of the castle, and many English merchants, induced by a grant of privileges, had gone to try their fortunes there. A truce had been made between the warring Kings at the intervention of the Pope, and any belligerent act by either was forbidden. How far a truce between Kings bound individuals, it is not easy to say, in view of the singular privateering customs, if not rights, existent in feudal times. At any rate, Geffroi de Charny, who was French warder of the Marches there, and stationed at Saint-Omer, twenty miles away, did not feel himself bound. He said nothing to the King of France on the matter. He sounded Amerigo da Pavia and found a ready response. Communication was not difficult, because, by convention, merchants and chapmen might go from one town to the other with their wares. Charny offered twenty thousand crowns for the delivery of the citadel of Calais, and the offer was accepted; but it was not accepted in good faith. Amerigo revealed all to the King. Some think that he was a traitor, and found out, but as Edward continued to trust him, it is likely that he told of his own accord. The King bade him make arrangements to deliver the castle, but to keep him informed of the date set. The last day of the year, New Year's Eve, was agreed upon by the conspirators. Edward was told; so he, the Prince of Wales, Sir Walter Manny and other lords, with three hundred men-at-arms and six hundred archers, crossed the Channel privily, and stowed themselves about the castle. Sir Walter Manny was put in command of the enterprise, and both the King and the Prince took places *incogniti* under Manny's banner. When darkness fell on that New Year's Eve, everything was arranged. Geoffroi de Charny arrived late in the evening, and remained at the bridge of Neuillet, outside the former lines of circumvallation, and sent two squires to ask Sir Amerigo, who was expecting them, if it was time for him to advance. Sir Amerigo said that all was ready. On hearing this twelve knights with one hundred men-at-arms rode ahead in the darkness to the castle. Odoart de Ronty carried the bag that contained the twenty thousand crowns. Charny remained behind in the plain, ready to enter the town when the gates should be opened. The troop of one hundred men-at-arms came to the moat, the drawbridge was lowered and they walked in. Odoart, carrying the bag, handed it to Sir Amerigo, who took it, saying: "I suppose they are all there," and opening a door, flung the bag in, locked the door, and bade the Frenchmen follow him to the keep, for possession of the keep would give them possession of the castle. So they did, Amerigo drew back the bolt of the keep's gate, and flung it wide. Out poured two hundred men-at-arms, shouting "Manny! Manny to the rescue!" The French, finding themselves caught in a trap, surrendered with scarce a blow. They were made to enter the keep, and then locked in. The English issued forth from the castle, mounted their horses and rode out toward the bridge of Neuillet.

In the meantime Geoffroi de Charny had been waiting, his banner, three escutcheons argent on a field of gules, unfurled, impatient to enter the city. He said to the lords with him, "If this Lombard delays to open the gate, we shall all die of cold." "By God," said Pepin de Werre, "these Lombards are a suspicious folk; perhaps he is examining your florins, to see if they are the right number, and none counterfeit." While they were talking, the English came on in force, with the King and the Prince riding in disguise under Sir Walter Manny's banner. On they rode, shouting, "Manny to the rescue." The French then knew that they had been betrayed. Charny called out loud, "Gentlemen, if we fly, we lose all. Let us fight bravely and we may win the day." "By St. George!" cried an Englishman now close within ear-shot, "you are right. The devil take the man that thinks of flying." The French, for fear of confusion in the dark, dismounted, sending their horses to one side. Seeing this, King Edward halted and arrayed his men in order of battle. The French knights fought valiantly, but as their numbers diminished, and more and more English poured out of the town, the odds grew longer and longer against them. One of the French knights, Sir Eustace de Ribemont, a strong and daring warrior, was in the very front. The King, also a big man, tall and strong, who had seldom met his peer in physical combat, seeing the French knight's prowess, singled him out, and the two fought so that it was a pleasure to see them. Twice the Frenchman struck the King to his knees, but the Prince of Wales came to his rescue in the nick of time. The Herald Chandos says:

> *Et li noble Prince, son filz*
> *Qui moult fu vaillanz et hardyz*
> *La combati si vaillantment*
> *Qu'il rescoust veritablement,*
> *Par force, son père le Roy.*

[And the noble Prince, his son, who was very valiant and bold, fought there so bravely, that in good sooth he rescued by main force, his father the King.]   And no English King, Chandos goes on to say, was ever in so perilous a plight, and that many people have recorded that, had it not been for the Prince of Wales, and his *très parfite proesse,* he would have been taken prisoner.

Further resistance was obviously hopeless and the French surrendered. Ribemont, who did not know with whom he had been fighting, handed his sword to his big adversary, saying: "Sir Knight, I yield myself your prisoner, the honor of the day belongs to the English." The prisoners were led to the castle, and there they learned that the King and Prince of Wales had been present in person. They were invited to supper. Suitable robes were given them and they were seated at a great table. The King presided, while the Prince of Wales and the English knights waited on their guests till the first course was served, and then they sat down at a second table, where they were quietly waited on by their servants. After supper was over, the tables were removed, and the King and his guests remained in the great hall. The King was bareheaded, except for a chaplet of fine pearls. He went about speaking to each in turn. When he came to Geoffroi de Charny, his kindly look vanished; he said: "Sir Geoffroi, I have little reason to like you, for you tried to steal from me last night, what cost me so much money and labor to gain. I am glad I caught you. You thought to get it for twenty thousand crowns—cheaper than I did. But by God's help, you have been disappointed." Geoffroi de Charny found nothing to say. The King passed on to Sir Eustace de Ribemont, stopped before him with a friendly smile, and said: "Sir Eustace, you are the most valiant knight I ever saw. I never yet found anybody, who, man to man, gave me so much to do as you did to-day. I adjudge to you, above all the knights of my court, the prize of valor; it is justly due to you." So saying, he took off the chaplet, which was very handsome, and put it on Sir Eustace's head and added: "I present you with this chaplet, as the best fighter this day, and I beg you to wear it this year for love of me. I know that you love the company of ladies and damsels; tell them that I gave it to you. I quit you of prison and ransom. You may go to-morrow, if you wish, where you will."

It was a chivalric act. The gallant knight was rewarded,

and, as I will now tell you, the felon knight Amerigo da Pavia was punished. In due course Geffroi de Charny paid his ransom, and returned to his post at Saint-Omer as warder of the Marches; there he heard that Amerigo da Pavia was at the castle of Frethun, that lies about two or three miles to the south of Calais, and had been given him by King Edward. Here he kept a beautiful English mistress, and lived in felicity, and in the hope that the French had forgotten his trick. But when Charny learned that Amerigo was there, he made immediate inquiries as to the strength of the castle, and learned that it could be easily taken, as Sir Amerigo lived without watch or guard, as free from suspicion of danger as if he were in Calais or in London. Charny did not let the grass grow under his feet, and acted quietly. He collected a troop of men-at-arms and crossbowmen from the garrison at Saint-Omer, marched the intervening twenty-one miles during the night and arrived at Frethun at daybreak. His men surrounded the castle and crossed the moat. There was no guard. The servants rushed to Sir Amerigo's bedroom and woke him, crying out that the castle was surrounded by soldiers. He jumped up but had not time to seize his arms. Both he and the English lady were made prisoners, but not another thing was taken, out of respect for the existing truce. Geoffroi de Charny had been willing to take Calais during the truce, but not trifling booty, for he was a reasonable man; and, besides, Sir Amerigo was all he wanted. He put him to death with much cruelty in the market-place at Saint-Omer, after collecting the people from roundabout to see how treachery was punished. The English lady was let go, and she afterward made friends with a French squire.

# CHAPTER VIII

Such biographical knowledge of the Black Prince as has come down through the six hundred years since his birth, consists in the main of three martial episodes of great splendor, Crécy, Poitiers and Navarette, connected by tenuous threads of casual notices, conjectures, inference and guess. He conformed to the doctrine enunciated by Henry V:

> In peace, there's nothing so becomes a man
> As modest stillness and humility;
> But when the blast of war blows in our ears
> Then imitate the action of the tiger.

But this modest stillness and humility during the decades between triumphant victories make the biographer's task difficult.

On our hero's return to England, crowned with Crécy's and Calais' laureate wreath, his father gave form and body to an old plan of reviving King Arthur's Round Table by founding the Order of the Garter. Geoffrey Baker gives an account of this. Baker came from Swinbrook, a village in Oxfordshire not far from Woodstock. He had some connection with the great Bohun house, Earls of Hereford, and with the de la More family, and so had facilities to learn what was going on. I will quote what he says in Stow's translation, or rather adaptation [1580]. "This yeare, on Saint George's day, the King held a great and solemne feast at his castle of Windsor, where he had augmented the chappel which Henry the First and other his pro-

78

genitors, Kings of England, had before erected, of eight chanons. He added to those eight chanons a deane and fifteen chanons more, and 24 poor and impotent knights, with other ministers and servants, as appeareth in his charter dated the two and twentieth of his reigne. Besides the King, there were others also that were contributors to the foundation of this college, as followeth: 1, The Sovereign King Edward the Third. 2, Edward, his eldest sonne, Prince of Wales. 3, Henry, Duke of Lancaster. 4, Thomas Beauchamp, Earl of Warwick. 5, Captaine de Bouche [Captal de Buch]. 6, Ralph, Earle of Stafford. 7, William Montacute, Earle of Salisburie. 8, Roger, lorde Mortimer, Earle of March. 9, Sir John de Lisle. 10, Sir Bartholemew Burwash [Burghersh]. 11, Sir John Beauchampe. 12, Sir John Mahune [Mohun]. 13, Sir Hugh Courtney. 14, Sir Thomas Holland. 15, Sir John Grey. 16, Sir Richard Fitz Simon. 17, Sir Miles Stapleton. 18, Sir Thomas Walle. 19, Sir Hugh Wrothesley. 20, Sir Nele Loring. 21, Sir John Chandos. 22, Sir James de Audeley. 23, Sir Othes Holland. 24, Sir Henry Eam. 25, Sir Sechet Dabridgecourt, [d'Aubréchicourt]. 26, Sir Walter Paveley. All these together with the King, were clothed in gowns of russet, poudered with garters blew, wearing the like garters also on their right legges, and mantels of blew with scutcheons of S. George. In this sort of apparell they, being bare-headed, heard masse, which was celebrated by Simon Islip, Archbishop of Canterbury, and the Bishops of Winchester and Excester, and afterwards they went to the feast, which they named to be of S. George the Martyr and the choosing of the Knights of the Garter."

Almost all these gentlemen had fought at Crécy, and the younger among them became close friends and intimate companions of the Prince, and went with him on his later campaigns. Why a garter was chosen as emblem for the Order is not known; nor why the motto, *Honi soit qui mal y pense*, was adopted, although a similar saying is found in the English of that time, "Helhyng haue the hathell that any harme thynkes." The popularity of St. George came in with the Crusades, and so Edward III chose him as patron saint of the Order. The Prince himself adopted for his personal crest an ostrich feather or feathers, and the motto *Ich dene* [I serve], words of Low Franconian dialect such as was spoken in Gelderland. Tradition connects the feathers with the blind King of Bohemia, killed at Crécy, but the matter is involved in obscurity. The Prince had another motto, *Homout* [high spirit]; but neither is it known whence he took it. Both are carved upon his tomb in Canterbury Cathedral.

The Order of the Garter, though romantic in idea, was wholly practical in purpose. It was the keystone of the arch of the King's military organization. Edward III was essentially a soldier, and made military matters his chief care. His ordinances by which landowners should find, according to the value of their land, men-at-arms, archers or spearmen, his system of contract with the greater noblemen, who should furnish so many soldiers of such or such equipment for a certain time and stipulated wages, his encouragement of the use of the long bow, his taking tournaments under his particular superintendence, and so on, naturally led to the establishment of the Order of the Garter. This Order was a military club, composed of the most distinguished soldiers in the kingdom, which should not only serve to reward honor and success, but also to simplify the control of an army by making the higher officers acquainted with one another. This military club contained the Prince of Wales' most intimate friends and comrades, and, therefore, to help make up for the default of any personal details concerning his life, I will introduce some of its members. Henry Plantagenet, Earl of Derby and Duke of Lancaster, a great-grandson of Henry III, who, like all the nobility, had French blood in his immediate ancestry, for his grandmother was a French princess, belonged to the older generation. By this time he was nearly fifty, and the most experienced soldier in England. He preceded the Prince of Wales as the King's lieutenant in Aquitaine. Thomas Beauchamp, Earl of Warwick, was nearly twenty years older than the Prince of Wales, and so belonged to the older generation. He was really in command of the Prince's battalion at Crécy; and led the van at Poitiers. Jean de Grailly, Captal de Buch, is one of the chief characters in the story of the Prince's life. The Captalet de Buch was a barony lying between the Gironde, above Bordeaux, and the sea, a little to the south of where the great vineyards of Médoc are now. Jean de Grailly was a cousin of Gaston Phoebus, Comte de Forx, and is said to have been *"la fleur de la chevalerie de Gascogne,* well made in person, pleasant, *gallant avec une pointe de gaillardise,* and endowed with that faculty of speech, a little theatrical, which belongs to the people of Gascony."  He enjoyed a high reputation for valor :

> *Qui moult estoit vaillanz et preus,*
> *Moult hardis et moult courageus,*
> *Et moult amez de toute gent.*

Ralph, Earl of Stafford, also one of the older men, served under the Prince at Crécy. He, Warwick and Sir Walter Manny received many "fair houses" in Calais, when the King converted that town into an English city. He married a cousin of Sir James Audeley. William Montacute (or Montague), Earl of

Salisbury, was, on the other hand, just of the Prince's age; they were knighted together at La Hougue. He served at Caen, and probably at Crécy. Soon afterward he contracted a marriage, or was betrothed, or something of the kind, to the Fair Maid of Kent, Lady Joan, but this came to naught, for another Knight of the Garter, Sir Thomas Holland, proved to the Pope's satisfaction that he had been duly married to Lady Joan, and Montague's contract was declared null and void. He was then but twenty-one, and soon afterward married the daughter of Lord Mohun, another Knight of the Garter. There is no evidence, however, of ill will between the rivals. Roger Mortimer, was grandson of the famous Mortimer who deposed and killed Edward II. He, also, was of the Prince's age, and was knighted with him at La Hougue. He married Salisbury's sister. Sir John de Lisle (arms: Gules, a lyon passant gardant argent, crowned or), also a young man, was killed during the campaign prior to the battle of Poitiers. Bartholomew de Burghersh was five years older than the Prince; he served at Crécy and Calais, and accompanied the Prince in his campaigns of 1355 and 1356. The two were close friends; just before they left England the Prince gave him two silver basins enameled with the royal arms. John Beauchamp was a younger brother of Earl Warwick and carried the royal standard at Crécy. In 1348, at jousts at Canterbury, he, together with the Prince of Wales and six other knights, was presented by the King with surcoats of Indian silk, adorned with the arms of Sir Stephen de Cosington: Azure three roses or, in honor of some forgotten achievement. William de Mohun was ninth in descent from the Mohun that accompanied William the Conqueror. He married Lord Burghersh's sister, fought at Crécy and accompanied the Prince to Bordeaux. Sir Hugh Courtenay, Earl of Devon, was three years older than the Prince; he was excellent in the lists, and at twenty received from the King as a prize a hood of white cloth, buttoned with large pearls, and embroidered with figures of dancing men. He was knighted after the capitulation of Calais; arms: Or, three torteaux, a label azure, on each pendant a fleur-de-lys argent. He died soon afterward, scarce twenty-one. Thomas Holland (arms: England within a border argent) must have been ten years older than the Prince. He served at Crécy, and in the sea fight of Espagnols-sur-Mer. But he is most interesting to us as husband of Lady Joan, whom he married just before the campaign of Crécy. He had been seneschal in the household of Lord Salisbury, Montague's father, I think, and it was apparently during Holland's absence in this campaign that Montague found opportunity to persuade Lady Joan to betroth herself to him. Holland died in 1360, leaving two sons, Thomas, who became Earl of Kent, and John, who became Duke of Exeter, and two daughters, Joan who married John de Montfort, and Maud who married another Hugh Courtenay. These four, of course, on their mother's marriage to the Prince of Wales, became his stepchildren. Sir Nigel Loryng, of Bedfordshire, served under the Prince in France with distinction, so that "for the good and agreeable services that our dear and well beloved Chamberlain, Nigel Loryng, has rendered to us in Gascony, and especially at Poitiers, where he was detailed to attend upon our person, we grant to him £403, 6s, 8d." Loryng also served on the Spanish campaign. Sir John Chandos (arms: Quarterly argent and gules, a bend sable), son to the Sheriff of Herefordshire, and a descendant of Robert de Chandos, who came over with William the Conqueror, was the most famous of the English generals of his time, after the Black Prince. He is one of the most familiar figures in our story. Sir James Audeley, of Stretton Audeley, Oxfordshire, attended the Prince on the campaigns of Calais and Poitiers. He and Sir John Chandos were great friends. We shall hear of his exploits at Poitiers. During the Spanish campaign, he remained as governor of Aquitaine. Sir Henry Eam apparently came from Flanders. Arms: Or, fess sable, issuant therefrom a demi-lyon rampant gules. Sir Sanchet d'Aubréchicourt was the son of a knight from Hainaut. His choice tends to show, perhaps, both that King Edward rewarded merit where he found it, and also that he wished to bind the Low Countries to his interest. Sir Walter Paveley (arms: Azure, a cross patonce or) married a cousin of Lord Burghersh; that there was friendship as well as kinship between these gentlemen appears in that the Prince gave to each of them a clasp adorned with pearls and diamonds. And the Prince's favor did not end there; it is recorded that he granted him license to fish on the Manor of Newport, and gave him sixty live coneys from his warren at Aldebourne. Robert Ufford, Earl of Suffolk, an older man, greatly distinguished himself at Poitiers. William Bohun, Earl of Northampton, commanded the second battalion at Crécy. Others are less well known, as Sir Richard de la Vache (crest: a cow's leg ermine, bent toward the dexter, the hoof upward, or): his wife received a cask of Gascon wine from Queen Philippa in 1349.

These younger men were of the Prince's generation and composed the cream of military and fashionable society. How limited that society was, and how intimate, may be inferred both from the intermarriages I have mentioned and from a list of presents made by the Prince, on his return from the siege of Calais, and recorded in his accounts. A good number were to his friends of the Garter; a Turkish rug to John Beauchamp, a war-horse called Bayard Bisshop to Montague; another called Bayard Dieu given to Lord Burghersh's father, a distinguished old soldier; another Morel de France, to Burghersh himself, another to Baldwin de Butetourt, a neighbor at the Prince's estate at Byfleet; another, Morel More, to Walter Paveley; another, Grisel Gris, to John Mohun; a courser, Bayard Pilgrim, and also a sumpter, Grisette Dieu, to Sir John Chandos; a black courser, with a cleft nose, to Sir James Audeley; a horse's saddle to Nigel Loryng; a little palfrey to John de Lisle; a gray palfrey to Sir Walter Manny; a courser, Banzan de Burgh, to his mother, at the time of the Windsor tournament, also a palfrey, Grisel Petit Watte, given to her at Calais, and a war-horse given to her at his castle of Wallingford; a palfrey, Liard Petit Watte, to the Earl of Northampton; another palfrey, Bayard Juet, to his brother Lionel; a hobby (little horse), Dun Crump, to some German knight at Calais; a sumpter called Morel, left forefoot white, to young Richard de Beaconsfield; a gold cup to a gentleman, another to a lady, who dined with him at Calais; three casks of Gascon wine to his sister Joan on occasion of her going to Bordeaux to be married; a gold, enameled cup, for a New Year's present to his father, another present to his mother, and a bejeweled clasp to his sister Isabel, another to his sister Joan; a large beaker, ornamented with enamel and gold to his cousin, the Lady Joan, and so on; to the Dean of Windsor, Sir William Mugge, a barrel of wine, which one may hope was a pleasantry.

You see that this aristocracy was purely military, and closely intermarried, and, as it would seem, intimate and friendly, and, though it spoke French and wrote in French, was rapidly helping to create, thanks to war, a strong national feeling.

# CHAPTER IX

As WE look back, the festival that celebrated the foundation of the Order of the Garter, stands out like the Ball of Brussels. Nearer, clearer, Black Death was knocking at the door. It had come out of the east, following trade routes to the Black Sea, had proceeded to the Dalmatian coast, and, as if belly-pinched, had also come by ship to the Italian ports, and from Genoa to Marseilles, and on northward, across France to England. In Florence, the historian, Giovanni Villani, whom I have quoted, died of it, his pen scarce dry from recording a prognostication of the terrible disease: "The sun has appeared in Avignon over the Pope's palace, like a column of fire, and stayed for over an hour." In Siena, the painters, the Lorenzetti brothers Pietro and Ambrogio, died; sentimental pilgrims, heedless of sterner critics, still go devoutly to the Church of San Francesco, to gaze at Ambrogio's *Madonna del latte.* At Avignon Petrarch's Laura died, and his friend Cardinal Colonna,

*Rotta è l'alta colonna e'l verde lauro,*

Broken is the lofty column and the green laurel.

At Bordeaux, the Princess Joan, the Black Prince's sister, betrothed to Don Pedro of Castile, on her way to meet the bridegroom, met the pest instead and died. And near Paris, Queen Jeanne, wife of Philip VI, and the Princess Bonne, wife to John, Philip's eldest son, also died. I have named the illustrious.

86

Death knocked with indifference on all doors. At Narbonne, it is said, one-fourth of the population perished, at Béziers but two or three out of every twenty survived, at Saint Denis, a little city, sixteen thousand people perished; at Rouen, one hundred thousand. London is said to have lost one hundred thousand citizens; Norwich, fifty-seven thousand and so on. Sober historians believe a third of the population, or more, died.

Froissart, who loved life, its animation, its gaiety, its color, its finery, and all its flash and glitter, turns away from this unwelcome guest, this unpleasant interferer with all that he loves, and gives but three lines to it: "At this time a malady, that was regarded as an epidemic, ran all over the world, and caused the death of a full third of the whole population." But fortunately, if it be good fortune to know the black background that rolled up three times, in 1349, 1361 and 1369, close upon the brilliant drama of the Prince's life, the Latins were more ready to put their feelings into words. I will quote Boccaccio, for, of all narratives, his is the most vivid. He begins the *Decameron* with the words, "*Umana cosa è aver compassione degli afflitti* [compassion for the afflicted is due from men], and tells his tale: "I say then that the years of the beneficent Incarnation of the Son of God had reached the number of 1348, when in the noble city of Florence, more beautiful than any other Italian city, came the death dealing plague, which, by the operation of the stars, or for our sins sent upon us by the just wrath of God, having begun some years before in the East, and deprived an innumerable multitude of life, had traveled toward the West without stopping, proceeding from one place to another, and had miserably increased. Neither wit, nor precaution, was of any avail. Officials appointed for the purpose cleansed the city of dirt of all sorts, and no sick person was allowed to enter.   Many were the opinions given for the preservation of health; many were the humble supplications, not once but often, in ordered processions, and otherwise, offered to God by pious men.   And yet in the spring of that year the plague began horribly to show its dolorous effects in a manner passing nature. It was not as in the East, where a nosebleed was a clear sign of inevitable death, but, at the beginning of the disease, certain swellings, in the groin or under the armpit, showed themselves, and grew, some like an ordinary apple, others like an egg, or, usually, little lumps.   From these two places of the body the deadly lumps in short time spread anywhere about the body; and then the manifestations of the disease changed into black or livid spots, that came out on the arms, thighs, or any other part of the body, in great numbers, sometimes big and scattered, sometimes little and close together.   And as the lump was the first, so it was the sure sign of death, to whoever had them.   No physician, no medicine was of any use.   On the contrary, only a very few recovered, either because the nature of the disease prevented, or because the practitioners—of whom, beside the trained doctors, there was an enormous number, both men and women, who had never had any knowledge of medicine—did not know the cause, and therefore could not devise the right remedy.   Almost all, on the third day after the appearance of the disease, one earlier, another later, died, and most of them without fever or other adjunct.   This plague was all the worse because it was communicated to the well or the sick, as neighboring fire catches dry wood after oil is poured on.   And the evil of it was magnified, because not only talking, or any communication, with the sick gave the disease to the well and caused both to die; but also mere contact with the clothes, or anything that the sick had touched or used, seemed to carry contagion with it.   What I am going to say now will appear unbelievable.

I would hardly dare believe it myself, much less to say it, on any hearsay however trustworthy, if I and many others had not seen it with our own eyes.  I assert that this contagion not only passed from man to man, but also (which is far more difficult to believe, though frequently observed) that, if anything belonging to a man, ill or dead of this disease, touched a beast, the beast not only fell ill, but shortly died.  [He tells how this happened with pigs before his eyes.] . . . From this episode, and many more like it, or worse, those who remained alive became so frightened and apprehensive, that they all pressed to one single cruel goal—to escape from the sick, and all their belongings.  By doing so, each one believed that he would save his life.  Some were of opinion that to live moderately and to avoid all excess would be very helpful in resisting the disease." . . . So persons of this mind withdrew to houses, where no sickness was, lived upon carefully chosen food, were abstemious and would neither talk nor hear of the plague in any way.  Others, of contrary opinion, plunged into revel and riot, saying that drinking, laughing, singing, joking and doing what you will, was the best antidote.  Others had other theories.  All laws, human and divine, were flouted.  Human bonds strained and broke, brother abandoned brother, sister sister, uncle niece, the husband often the wife, and *quasi non credibile,* fathers and mothers forsook the care of their children.

Italy was so much more vocal than England in those pre-Chaucerian days that I will quote a letter of Petrarch's written to his friend whom he calls Socrates:

"Parma, June 22, 1349

"Oh! my Brother, my Brother . . . oh! dearest Brother what can I say to you?  How bring myself to speak?  Where shall I turn?  Whatever side you look, you will see nothing but horror, nothing but grief. . . . Oh! that I had never been born, dear Brother, or at least that I were already dead! And if I now so long for death, what will it be if I live on and on to extreme old age. . . . I think that no one will judge my lamentations harshly, but be indulgent and excuse, if he will consider that I mourn no light calamity. I mourn the year 1348, which has not only swept away dear friends of ours but made the whole world a desert. And if some victims escaped, lo, here comes this year following on and reaps the gleanings; with its fatal scythe it cuts down whatever survived that first visitation. How will posterity ever believe there was a time, when without fire from earth or heaven, without war or other visible destruction, not this region only or that, but the whole world was left empty without an inhabitant? When was this ever seen or heard? Where are the chronicles that tell of vacant houses and desert cities; fields full of dead bodies, and everywhere hideous solitude? . . . Will posterity believe, when we who see it scarcely believe, but think we dream, until we wake, and with wide open eyes see the horror everywhere? We walk about the city and at every step we meet a hearse; we go home, and find the house empty of our beloved. . . . Wars have some compensation, but here there is no compensation, no remedy, and the horror of this slaughter is worse from our ignorance of its cause and origin."

It was never good form in England to put into words the more intense emotions; and you have but to read the letters written about Crécy and Poitiers, or the campaigns in France, by Michael Northburgh or Richard Wynkeley, or Sir John Wingfield or the Black Prince himself, to see that convention at its best. Geoffrey Baker, the chronicler, describes the pest in

England as follows: "First it entered by the seaports of Dorset and cleared almost all the country of its inhabitants, then it went ramping into Devonshire, Somerset and Bristol. The people of Gloucester refused to let any one from Bristol enter their shire, lest the breath of those who lived among the dead and dying should breed infection. Nevertheless the pest forcibly invaded Gloucester, and Oxford and London, and finally all England, so that scarce one in ten of both sexes survived. There was dearth of burial ground; so, fields were set apart for burying the dead. The Bishop of London bought the croft, called 'Nomanneslond,' in London, and Sir Walter Manny bought that called 'Ye newe chierche hawe,' where he founded a religious house for the burial of the dead. [On this spot the Charter House was afterward built.] Lawsuits in the courts of King's Bench and Common Pleas stopped. Several noblemen died, among them Sir John Montgomery, Captain of Calais, and Lord Clisteles, who died in Calais and are buried in the monastery of Saint Mary of Carmel in London. Innumerable common people, and a multitude of monks and priests, known only to God, *migravere* (passed away). Destruction, most of all, laid hold of the young and strong, and spared the old and feeble. Hardly anybody dared touch a sick man, and the well shunned the most precious relics of the dead as infectious. To-day in high spirits, and on the morrow found dead. They were tormented by abscesses, which broke out of a sudden on different parts of the body, so hard and dry that when they were cut off hardly any liquid flowed out; but by incision or long endurance many escaped. Some had little black pustules spread over all the skin of the body; of these very very few, in fact hardly any, returned to life and health. This great pestilence, which began at the feast of the Assumption of the Virgin at Bristol, and at about Michaelmas in London, raged in England for a whole year and more, so that it emptied many country villages of almost every individual of the human race." Wyclif predicted the end of the world.

The immediate consequence of the plague was a dearth of labor, and therefore a rise in wages. There were not enough laborers to harvest the crops, nor herdsmen to tend cattle and sheep, and landlords and employers were compelled to pay far more than they had done. The gentry objected and tried to keep down wages by law, and city folk in particular insisted that food should be sold at reasonable prices, and so on. In all this the Black Prince does not stand out as an individual, until a few years later, when matters went wrong in his earldom of Chester. Other evils, too, besides the plague and high prices, had fallen upon the people of Cheshire; there was a hard winter, a furious hurricane and a drought, followed by famine. The Prince's bailiffs and stewards were put to it to collect the Prince's revenues; he urged them on; they squeezed the people and the peasants rose in revolt. The Prince himself, the Duke of Lancaster, the Earls of Stafford and Warwick, with a strong body of soldiers went there to restore order. The sinning shire compounded for forgiveness by the payment of five thousand marks. The Prince piously gave a tenth to aid in the completion of the Abbey of Vale Royal, which had been begun by his great-grandfather, Edward I. History, so far as I know, records no other action of the Prince with reference to the plague. It has been suggested that "the King and the Prince very wisely set an example to everybody by refusing to alter their manner of living." That refusal, one surmises, was part of the cause that the peasants in Cheshire rose in revolt. But one must not apply the measuring stick of modern sentiment to a hero of chivalry. Could you turn Amadis of Gaul into a socialist? The heroes of romance, whether in books or in the flesh, were no more moved by what Baker calls the *"wlgus innumerum"* who died in the plague, than by the *vulgus innumerum* that were slaughtered at Crécy and Poitiers. You might as well ask poets to be political economists, as heroes of romance to be sentimental humanitarians.

# CHAPTER X

## ESPAGNOLS-SUR-MER

PESTILENCE interfered with civil life to a high degree, but much less with fighting. The god of war, Ares, proved himself then, as now, a very great god. And the Prince of Wales, and every member of the Order of the Garter, celebrated his ritual. As there was truce with France, the next conflict was with Spain and at sea. Such a fight was necessary to complete the Prince of Wales' education. He had taken part in ordered battle-field, in siege and foray, but he had not as yet had experience of a sea-fight. At the time of the battle of Sluys he was but ten years old and he must have cursed his luck to have missed it. Now fortune brought opportunity to him. The Kingdom of Castile had felt the stimulating effect of driving back the Moors, and Castilian sailors were as good, or thought themselves as good, as the hidalgos on land. Ships from Cadiz, Seville and Coruña traded with the cities of the French coast and Flanders. And not merely merchantmen sailed the seas, but gentlemen adventurers, a little careless, when they came upon a foreign ship, as to whether there was war or peace between their sovereigns; besides, maritime cities of Castile sometimes acted for themselves in these matters without regard to their sovereign. But as to piracy, rules were not strict, and English privateers were undoubtedly quite as ready as the Castilian, or the French, to regard a defenseless merchantman as a fair prize. In the summer of 1350, a Castilian fleet under Don Carlos de la Cerda had sailed up the Channel, and had come upon some English vessels, laden with wine, hailing from Bordeaux. These they seized, killing the English seamen, and sailed on to the Flemish ports, where they unloaded their cargoes and took aboard Flemish cloth and merchandise in general. Edward resolved to punish Don Carlos on his way home. He went to the coast of Sussex, near Rye, and issued a summons for a gathering of his soldiers and seamen. A great company assembled, the Prince of Wales, his young brother John of Gaunt, a mere child still, Henry, formerly Earl of Derby, now Duke of Lancaster, the Earls of Arundel, Northampton, Hereford, Suffolk and Warwick, Sir Walter Manny, Sir James Audeley, Lords Percy, Neville, Mowbray, and all the flower of English chivalry. Never had so many noblemen joined their King, and there were also four hundred knights, including, of course, Sir John Chandos. They went aboard the fleet, and cruised between Dover and Calais.

The Spaniards heard of the English preparations and made ready to defend their cargoes. They hired mercenaries and laid in a store of crossbows and bolts, of great stones and bars of forged iron; the stones and bars were to be thrown down from a little pen, or castle, like a crow's-nest, high on the mast, upon the smaller English ships below. There were forty-four sail, large vessels, and as they sailed along, with canvas bellied out under a favorable breeze and pennants streaming, they made a fine show. In the meantime, the English fleet, which must have been far more numerous, was cruising expectant. The King himself went aboard *La Salle du Roi,* as his flag-ship, taking the guards of his household. Count Robert de Namur, an experienced soldier, was in command of the ship. The King himself sat in the forecastle, dressed in a black velvet jacket, with a small beaver hat on his head, which became him well, and showed himself as gay as ever he had been in his life. He bade his ministrels play a dance that Sir John Chandos had lately introduced, and he made Sir John sing the words. This diverted the King immoderately. Every now and again, however, he called up to the watch in the crow's-nest to ask if the Spaniards were in sight. In the midst of their jollity came the cry, "Ship in sight! It looks like a Spanish ship!" The minstrels stopped. The King called up, "Are there more than one?" "Yes, one—two—three—four! So help me God, I can't count them all!" The King bade the trumpets sound and signaled the ships to fall into line. It was late in the afternoon. Wine was fetched, the King and his knights drank and put their helmets on. The Spaniards had the wind with them, and carrying more sail might easily have avoided battle, but the Dons were no cowards and bore down on the English fleet.

Edward bade the helmsman of *La Salle du Roi* lay him alongside one of the advancing ships, which was coming on with all its canvas spread. *La Salle du Roi* was large and stoutly built, and the crash of the two vessels meeting sounded like thunder. The Spaniards lost a mast, and its crow's-nest castle fell overboard with the men that manned it, while the English ship sprang a leak, which the crew, however, managed to staunch. "Grapple with her!" the King commanded. But those about him said to let her go, that he would find a better. He did not have to wait long. Another Spaniard, also a large ship, bore down, and grappled *La Salle du Roi*. Other ships all about grappled, too. Archers and crossbowmen shot their arrows and bolts. The leak in the King's ship widened; it was conquer or sink. His men boarded the Spaniard and fought hand to hand, from deck to deck, from mast to mast, giving no quarter, and finally in triumph flung the last Spaniard, dead or dying, overboard. The King remained on the captured vessel, while Namur continued on *La Salle du Roi.*

The Prince of Wales meantime was in great peril. His ship had grappled with a big Spanish ship, and, being hurt in the shock, was leaking, with holes and gaps too wide to staunch. The ship was sinking, and unless they could board and capture the enemy's vessel, all hands must go down with it; but the Spanish bulwarks were high, and the Spanish soldiery fought excellently well. The situation was bad. The Duke of Lancaster, near by, however, perceived the Prince's danger, and luffed up to the Spaniard on the farther side, threw out the grappling chains, his mariners shouting his battle cry, "Derby to the rescue!" Attacked on both sides the Spanish crew gave way. Every man of them was thrown overboard. The Prince's ship sank almost as soon.

Elsewhere the battle was valiantly contested. A large Spanish ship bore down again on *La Salle du Roi,* grappled, set all sail, and towed the English ship off away from the others. The tow checked their speed, and as they passed another English ship *La Salle's* crew called for help, but their cries were not heard, and as evening had come on, it was too dark to see. The Spaniards were very close to carrying off their prize. But a fellow named Hanequin, one of Lord Robert de Namur's Flemish attendants, scrambled up on the Spanish ship, sword in hand, dashed to the mainmast before he could be stopped, cut the cord of the mainsail, which flopped helpless, and then with extreme agility cut four stays, so that the sail fell on the deck. Lord Robert and his men, thus encouraged, swarmed up the Spanish boat, killed every man on board, flung the corpses over and hoisted the English flag.

Other ships had varying fortunes. The great Spanish vessels loomed above the English like castles over cottages, and from their fortified crow's-nests crossbolts, spears and stones were shot, hurled and thrown, while below on deck the soldiers, with sword and lance, stood ready to defend the bulwarks. The English had the advantage of numbers, but Froissart says that they never had a harder fight. Finally, however, by sea as on land, the English archers proved their superiority. Their arrows had a longer range than the Spanish crossbows, and they forced the Spanish soldiery on deck, forecastle or poop, to pile up a barricade of boards to protect themselves, while the crossbowmen and stone-throwers in the crow's nests did not dare expose head or shoulder, or do more than lift up stones to topple down, which wrought more harm to their own men below than to the English. Under protection of this archery, the English set up their boarding ladders and swarmed over the bulwarks. One Spanish vessel after another was taken, fourteen in all; the rest fled. The darkness and the speed of the fugitives prevented pursuit. The trumpets sounded return, and the conquerors cast anchor off Rye and Winchelsea, hoping to renew the battle at dawn. But the Dons had had enough and during the night made off. In the morning nothing was to be seen but the sparkling sea. The King, the Prince of Wales, the Duke of Lancaster and other lords disembarked, took horse and rode to the monastery where the Queen was, some five miles away. The Queen had watched the fight from the downs, and was much comforted by their safe return. They had a banquet and ball that night and spent the time discoursing "of arms and amours." In this manner the Prince, aged twenty, got his baccalaureate in the arts of war.

# CHAPTER XI

THE truce that had been made between England and France after the fall of Calais had been renewed from time to time, and now, in 1354, there seemed a hope that it might be expanded and enlarged into a treaty of peace. In England the House of Commons had been asked if they wished for a permanent treaty, and they cried unanimously, "Aye, Aye." In France there was every reason for desiring peace. It was scarce five years since the terrible plague, the country had suffered incomparable calamities, the treasury was empty, food was scarce, prices had risen, King Philip had died and his son John had been consecrated in his stead, and there was little promise in his personality.

Pope Innocent VI urged a peaceable solution of the quarrels and both Kings sent ambassadors to Avignon. Edward offered to renounce his claim to the French crown, if John would grant him full sovereignty of Guienne; but these proposals were not satisfactory to John, for the English claim to the French crown was illusory, while the French rights of suzerainty were indisputable. Neither side entertained much hope, and probably not much purpose of making peace. The French envoys would not budge from their position; while, on the other hand, one of the English envoys, the Duke of Lancaster, former Earl of Derby, met the King of Navarre in secret, and discussed with him the invasion of Normandy and partition of the Kingdom of France. The negotiations came to naught. I will

99

take this opportunity of introducing two important characters who are to become connected with the Prince of Wales in this story.

Charles, King of Navarre, was closely related to the royal house of France. Through his mother he was grandson to Louis X, and, through his father, great-grandson of Philip III le Hardi, and his sister had married King Philip VI. He was small of stature, quick-witted and very intelligent. His diplomatic dexterity was extraordinary. And his rare affability marked him out from all other princes. If the title to the French crown was transmissible through women, his was the eldest title; though, to be sure, he was not born until two years after the House of Valois had succeeded to the throne (1330), and his parents had fully acknowledged the rights of Philip VI. Such obstacles, however, between a resolute man and a crown will, if he be strong enough, give way; at all events, such a claim was a good card to hold. King John was at first very kind to him, and gave him his eight-year-old daughter to wife, but he withheld the promised dowry. And John did a second thing that angered Charles; he refused him the Comté d'Angoulême, which Charles's mother had held, and bestowed it on a favorite of his own, Don Carlos de la Cerda (the Spanish Admiral in the battle of Espagnols-sur-Mer), whom he had recently elevated to be Constable of France. For this, the House of Navarre hated Don Carlos. One day in King John's presence, Don Carlos gave the lie to Philip of Navarre, Charles's brother. Both men drew their daggers. The King intervened. Philip of Navarre, as he left the room, said to the Constable, *"que bien se gardât des enfants de Navarre* [to be well on his guard against the House of Navarre]." It was no idle warning. A little later, on the eighth of January,

1353, the Constable was passing the night at an inn in the little town of Laigle, near Falaise, in Normandy. That night Charles of Navarre rode with a troop of his friends up to the town; he waited outside in a grange, while his friends went in. At daybreak, his brothers Philip, Jean d'Harcourt, a Norman nobleman, and two other Harcourts, brother and uncle to Jean, and various Norman and Navarrese knights, entered the inn, forced their way into the Constable's bedroom, and *"tant angoisseusement, vilainement et abominablement l'appareillèrent"*—in other words they gave him eighty wounds, so that he died. Charles le Mauvais, as he may now be called, and his accomplices rode to his city of Évreux, and allied himself with the Harcourts and other Norman barons, who were discontented with King John. He sent out singularly frank statements to the Great Council of the French King, and to sundry cities: "We beg leave to tell you that we put Charles of Spain to death . . . and if it chances that the King is at present a little troubled by this, for which we should be very sorry, yet we feel sure, that unless he is badly advised, he ought to be greatly pleased, when he thinks it over." Charles le Mauvais was right in his understanding that King John was troubled; for four days the King said nothing, and then he swore a mighty oath that he should never wear a light heart until he was revenged. Charles le Mauvais did not content himself with avowals; he sent a messenger to the Duke of Lancaster, then in Brabant, who at once offered him support, and he also wrote to the King of England, to say: "I possess strong castles in Normandy and elsewhere, well manned and well equipped, and if King John shall stir, I will do him such hurt as he never shall recover from. . . . Please notify your officers in Brittany to hold themselves ready to enter Normandy to help me, as soon as

I shall ask them, and I will give them as secure an entry as they may wish. And, dear Cousin, remember that, come life come death, all the noblesse of Normandy is with me."

King John, uneasy at the idea of a coalition between England, Navarre and Norman nobles, was ready to eat humble pie; he entered into negotiations with Charles, and his envoys granted such favorable conditions that they were suspected by persons not in the King's confidence of taking bribes. The murderers were all pardoned, and all sorts of baronies were given to Charles. King John also made oath that he would never, for the sake of the Constable's death, *"feroit ou feroit faire villenie ou domage* [do or cause to be done any hurt or act of harm]." So, after receiving the King's second son as hostage, Charles le Mauvais went to Paris and in the presence of the Parlement begged the King to forgive him, "for he had good and just cause to do as he had done, as he would explain to the King then or later, as he chose." He vowed that he had not done the deed in contempt of the King, and that nothing would distress him so much as the King's indignation. He was what the French call *impayable.* Thereupon, Queen Jeanne, widow of Charles IV, his aunt, and Queen Blanche, widow of Philip VI, his sister, besought the King to pardon him. So it was done; but the insolent words of Charles of Navarre did not augur well for future peace. Before the year was out, he had fled from the court. He visited Avignon secretly, where, as I have said, he held furtive interviews with the Duke of Lancaster, and then hurried on to Navarre. King John retaliated by seizing such of Navarre's Norman castles as he could. At this the secret accord between Navarre and the Duke of Lancaster was put into action. Lancaster brought a fleet from England as far as the island of Guernsey, and

Navarre led troops to Cherbourg. King John was not ready to resist them, and a second time made a humiliating peace with Navarre. Again came the hollow ceremony of Navarre's appearance in Paris, in the palace of the Louvre, before King John; again the two widowed Queens besought forgiveness for him. Again Navarre displayed his insolence, he said that some men had spoken ill of him to the King, he begged the King to tell him who they were, and he swore that, since the Constable's death, he had done nothing with respect to the King that a loyal man should not do. And again the King, by the mouth of Gautier de Brienne, Duke of Athens, forgave him *"tout de bon cuer."*

And now follows the sequel. We are in the year 1355, and war with England had been renewed. It is impossible to know just what happened, what intrigues the slippery King of Navarre had entered into. But now that there was war with England, now that the Prince of Wales was ravaging Languedoc, and there was danger of invasion in the north from Edward, himself, or from the Duke of Lancaster, it was prudent, to say the least, to close the doors into Normandy against the English and bolt them as tight as possible. The Dauphin, Charles, had been created Duke of that province, with the charge of guarding it; but there had been some misunderstanding between father and son, and unpleasant rumors had been sneaking about that Navarre, who was extremely clever and thirty-three years old, had tried to persuade the Dauphin, who was but a lad, to flee the country, and worse still, to join a conspiracy to kidnap the King, and then, and then—but Rumor does not stick at any meanness, and perhaps the King was merely a little apprehensive, without formulating any definite suspicions. Be that as it may, in the citadel at Rouen, on April 5, 1356, the Dauphin was giving a dinner to a large group of gentlemen: Charles of Navarre, the Duc de Bourbon, the young Comte d'Harcourt, who was reported to have said of the King in a rash moment, *"Par le sang de Dieu, ce roi est un mauvais homme* [By the blood of Christ, the King is a wicked man]," Harcourt's two brothers, the Sire de Biville, famous for having cut a Turc in two *"tout au long"* with one stroke of his sword, and *pluseurs aultres vaillans bacheliers,* as well as the Mayor of Rouen and other local notables, more than thirty altogether. At the Dauphin's table were seated the King of Navarre, the Counts of Harcourt, Etampes and Graville. While they were dining, the King entered the city with a hundred men-at-arms, proceeded to the citadel, strode into the banqueting hall with all his armor on. The guests all rose to greet him, and Navarre added, *"Sire, venez boire.* [Take a glass with us.]" But the King did not smile; he said, "Nothing, nothing, gentlemen, let no man leave his seat." At this Marshal d'Audrehem, at a sign from the King, drew his sword and cried: "Whoever stirs, dies." Then the King flung himself on Navarre, seized him by the collar and dragged him from the table, saying: "By the Lord, wicked traitor, you are not fit to sit beside my son. By my father's soul, I will not eat nor drink so long as you live." Navarre's squire, Colin Doublel, started up with dagger drawn. The King dropped his hold, and cried: "Seize that fellow and his master." The Dauphin broke in: "Dear Sir, what would you do? Don't you see that he is my guest and in my house?" King John bade him hold his tongue, but the Dauphin fell on his knees: "My lord, you shame me! What will be said of me? It is I that invited the King of Navarre and these lords to dinner. It will be said that I betrayed them. I never saw aught in them but loyalty and courtesy." "Calm yourself," the King answered, "they are wicked traitors and

their crimes will soon come to light. You don't know all that
I know." Then, very angry, he walked up to Harcourt, took
him by the collar so rudely that he tore his doublet to the waist.
"Proud traitor," he said, "come, get to prison. By my father's
soul, you will be clever, if you escape me. Your crimes and
treasons will soon be unveiled." Harcourt, Graville, Maubue
de Mainemares and Colin Doublel were bound, and all the
company placed under arrest. The King then sat down and ate
his dinner. Having dined, he went out, attended by his brother,
his son and various kinsmen. They mounted their horses and
rode to a field behind the castle, known as the Field of Pardon.
There the four I have mentioned were brought two by two, in
carts. The King said: "Deliver me from these traitors," and
on the spot they were beheaded. Their bodies were dragged
into the city and hanged on gibbets, and their heads stuck on
spears. Navarre was imprisoned in the Louvre, and two others
in the Châtelet at Paris. No one knew why King John had
acted so; and gossip in amazement ran riot. Some said the
King would have the two lords in the Châtelet dragged through
the streets and hanged, and that Navarre's head would be
chopped off in the night. Others said that Navarre would be
put in a mold of lead, where he would die a painful lingering
death. In Normandy Navarre's brother Philip threw himself
into the arms of the English.

The other character I shall introduce is more sympathetic.
Bertrand du Guesclin came of a younger branch of one of the
oldest and most distinguished families in Brittany, and poor.
He was ugly to look at. His complexion was dark, he had a
snub nose, green eyes, awkward movements, thick neck, heavy
shoulders, stout hands; he was not over middle height, very
compact of body and solid. He was proud, impetuous, irritable,

but his appearance expressed a high degree of masculine vigor. He was ambitious, crafty, patient, resourceful and loved fighting. Little is known of his youth, other than that he attached himself to the cause of Charles de Blois, the French candidate for the Duchy of Brittany. But legendary stories dot his path. At his first tournament, when he was seventeen, he borrowed horse and armor, entered the lists, and in full career struck his adversary's vizor with the point of his lance so stout a blow that horse and rider rolled in the dust. You will remember how, at Ashby de la Zouche, Ivanhoe made the same stroke in his course with Brian de Bois-Guilbert. Or again, his valet needed a mount. Bertrand saw an English knight riding along, with squire and valet at his heels, he dashed forward, broke to splinters the knight's lance and the squire's boarspear, left them dead and took the horses. Or, again, sick of a fever, he was challenged by an English knight, William Trussel, one of Lancaster's officers, and in the lists dealt him such a blow on the shoulder that Trussel was stretched upon the ground; and so forth. There was no better school for a soldier, who wished to study guerrilla warfare, than Brittany, for the partizans of both sides were conducting assaults, laying siege, mounting for a foray, or galloping for safety from one year's end to another. As the English supported the claim of Jean de Montfort, du Guesclin began early the struggle to drive them off French soil which lasted all his life. For he was destined, as Constable of France, to undo all that the great victories of Crécy and Poitiers had done, and by ruse, by avoidance, by patience, by *coup de main*, by the policy of Fabius Cunctator, deliver the land of France from the foreign conqueror. And this school of guerrilla warfare was all the better as the teachers were English soldiers of renown. There is no better way to improve one's game than to play against good players. Sir Walter Manny, Thomas Dagworth, Hugh de Calverley, Robert Knolles and the Duke of Lancaster, all practised the art of war in Brittany, and du Guesclin learned the art from them, and bettered it. He has become a legend in Brittany, and fact and fancy are so mixed in his biography that it would be a pity to try to untwist them. There is no end to stories of his prowess and ingenuity. He first became a provincial hero from his defense of the city of Rennes during a long siege by the Duke of Lancaster (1356-57), and later, after his famous defeat of the Navarrese at Cocherel (1364), he became a national figure. But for the present, so far as the Prince of Wales is concerned, du Guesclin is still in the background.

# CHAPTER XII

THE negotiations for peace between France and England, over which the Pope greatly concerned himself, had come to naught. The two kingdoms raised their swelling crests against each other. The old rivalries in Aquitaine, Brittany and for the crown of France galled them. And always at King Edward's elbow, like young dogs in leash on a May morning, the young Knights of the Garter chafed for adventure, honor, or the silks and jewels of France to lay at a lady's feet. King Edward thought that by confederating with the King of Navarre his time had come; and before the truce was ended he was ready with his plans. He would invade France in the north and join Navarre in Normandy, the Prince of Wales should go to Bordeaux, raid southern France and finally come to join him on the Loire. This time he might hope to achieve the crown of France.

There had been no lack of provocation. The eastern parts of Guienne had been raided by French borderers, and the population there that was loyal to the English crown was in constant alarm. The Comte d'Armagnac, lord of the county bordering on Gascony, had been appointed King John's lieutenant in Languedoc and was assaulting English and Gascon towns and castles to the best of his ability.

One of the chief Gascon nobles, the Captal de Buch, one of the Founders of the Order of the Garter, went to England to lay the political situation in Gascony before King Edward and to ask for help. He was warmly welcomed in London, and the Prince in particular was very glad to see him. The Prince undoubtedly desired a government away from his father's tutelage and saw an ally in the Captal. He was not mistaken. The Captal represented to the King the political advantage of having the Prince of Guienne as a sort of viceroy; such an appointment would increase the loyalty of the provincials. This sounded like good sense. The King laid the matter before Parliament, and the plan was approved. The Prince's high renown fully justified the responsibility put upon him; and a group of eminent soldiers was selected to accompany him, the Earls of Warwick, Salisbury, Suffolk, Oxford and Stafford, Sir Bartholomew de Burghersh, Sir John Montague, Lord Despenser and others, and in particular as his chief advisers, his dear friends, two knights of experience and reputation, Sir John Chandos and Sir James Audeley.

The Prince was formally appointed the King's Deputy and Captain General in Aquitaine, with full powers of sovereignty,— authority to administer justice, to promote to ecclesiastical benefices, to garrison towns and castles, to punish or pardon, to supervise officials, and so on. A fleet of three hundred ships was assembled at Plymouth, and an army of one thousand men-at-arms and two thousand archers, together with a considerable number of Welsh spearmen was also mustered there. The ships were loaded with all the equipment necessary for a campaign, portable bridges for crossing rivers, fascines for making a road over a swamp, all sorts of military stores, and so on. As a matter of fact, the expedition had been decided upon months beforehand, as appears from the Prince's register:

"London, March 24, Order to Robert de Eleford, Steward
and Sheriff of Cornewaille [Cornwall], John de Kendale, Receiver there, John de Skirbeck, and Thomas the Havener,—
Inasmuch as John who calls himself King of France has broken
the covenants that were drawn up at Caleys between the King
and the French, for which reason war has broken out, and the
Prince has prayed the King to grant him leave to be the first
to pass beyond sea, which thing the King had granted him, so
that he must needs be at Plymmuth at the octave of Midsummer
next with eight hundred men-at-arms on his way to the ports of
Gascony,—to arrest all the wines that can be found in the towns
of Plymmuth, Dertemuth [Dartmouth] and Fowy [Fowey],
and in all other towns on that seacoast in Cornewaille and
Devenshire purvey 300 quarters of oats and 100 quarters of
wheat pending the arrival of the Prince's officers in those ports,
as well as brushwood in a place as near to Plymmuth as possible and where least damage will be caused, have the same
carried to Plymmuth, cause the wines of prise, if they have
not been sold in pursuance of the late order, to be preserved and
certify to the Prince by their letters and by the first messenger,
how much wine he can be assured of having in those parts, and
touching all the other matters ordered in this letter."

The Prince took leave, blithe and glad at heart, rode to
Plymouth in hot haste long before the sailing and saw to the
putting on board of the military stores and provisions.   The
fleet sailed on September eighth, and arrived at Bordeaux on
the twentieth.   The Prince was welcomed *cum omni gaudio et
honore*.   The Lord of Albert, whose lands marched with the
Captalet de Buch, and many of the Gascon noblemen came to do
him honor.   That evening was gaily spent, the Prince and Sir

John Chandos played at "odd and even." The ceremony of presenting the King's warrant of authority to the local authorities took place the next day, in the Cathedral of Saint Andrew. The Constable of Bordeaux read aloud the oath for the Prince to take; and the Prince, with one hand on the gospels and the other on a cross, swore to observe the rights, franchises, liberties, customs and privileges of the citizens of Aquitaine. Then the Mayor and other officials of the city took an oath, in which all those in the cathedral joined, that they would be true and loyal subjects. Indeed there had never been any doubt about the sentiment of the citizens of Bordeaux. They had been under the English allegiance for a longer time than we have been American citizens, and many English had settled there. The rich men of the city were wine-merchants and their trade was mainly with England. Even to-day traditions of wines and wine-growers date back to the English occupation; for instance, Château Issan, over whose portal is inscribed *Regum mensis arisque Deorum,* and Château Talbot, which is named after an English Talbot. Another wine, known as the Cru de Canolle was named after Sir Robert Knolles, a gentleman adventurer of whom we shall hear; and the district of Saint Émilion, which lies eastward from Bordeaux just north of the River Dordogne, was first defined by a charter of King Edward I. Gascon wines were imported in great quantities to England. During the twelfth century they were sold in London for from three farthings to twopence a gallon. It was a thriving trade. Most of the nobles owned vineyards. So it is not strange that not only the merchants of Bordeaux but the Gascon lords, also, were enthusiastic subjects of the English King.

And quite apart from the ties of commerce that bound Guienne to England, apart from the political union during six generations, there were larger causes that tended to keep the province separate from that France whose center was Paris. Southern France, the *midi*, had always been different from northern France. If you draw a line from the mouth of the Garonne via Limoges, Clermont-Ferrand and Grenoble to the Alps, you will have approximately the boundary between the people to the north, who spoke a language in which *oil* is yes, and those to the south for whom *oc* is yes. In the fourteenth century the two languages had still marked differences, although *Provençal*, for so we usually call the *langue d'oc*, as a language of literature had been rudely trodden down in the religious and political wars of the thirteenth century that had ended with the annexation of the *midi* to northern France. The two regions differed in speech, in traditions, habits and tastes, they held separate *États Généraux*.

These differences ran back to difference of race, for in ancient days the southern half of France was inhabited by people of Iberian stock, whereas in the north the inhabitants were of Celtic stock; whatever those ethnological words may mean. National sentiment at this time, as I have said, was still rudimentary; a man's political duty, such as it was, lay toward his feudal superior and when we find Gascon lords, like the Captal de Buch and Lord d'Albret, fighting under the English banner against the French, they were doing their political duty. It was natural therefore that Aquitaine, or Guienne—the words are used interchangeably—should be loyal to England, especially on the coast, where the population was subject to mercantile influence; but as you went away from the sea the reasons for such loyalty were not so clear, and on the French border there was a great deal of confusion and contradictory thought on the subject. I find it hard to discover just where that boundary ran and the border barons appear to have been in considerable uncertainty.

By the treaty between Saint Louis and Henry III in 1259, this boundary started on the Bay of Biscay, at the mouth of the River Charente, wandered eastward to take in the Limousin, Quercy, Périgord and the Agenais, and then southwesterly to the Pyrenees; it included the cities of Limoges, Angoulême, Périgueux, and Cahors, as well as the two important seaports, Bayonne and Bordeaux. But from that time on, it is difficult to follow the boundary. When Edward II was deposed and together with his crown ceded the Duchy of Guienne to his son, Edward III, the province seems already to have shrunk. At all events, each country appears to have claimed places that the other thought belonged to it; and, as I have said, the Comte d'Armagnac was assaulting towns and castles which the English and Gascons insisted were theirs. So, all things considered, the Prince of Wales had good right to cling to the motto, *Dieu et mon Droit,* and to take steps to assert his rights.

As to how this had best be done, several plans lay open. The Prince might retake the towns and castles that Armagnac had taken, and set the east boundary of Aquitaine where he thought it should be; or, he might take other towns and castles elsewhere; or he might make a devastating raid wherever it should be most profitable. In favor of the last plan were the considerations that a wide destruction would deprive King John of the rich contributions that he received from the *États Généraux de Languedoc,* and teach the inhabitants not to let their rulers infringe English rights. And there was a happy precedent.

Ten years before, the Duke of Lancaster, then Earl of Derby, had proved how easily this might be done. He had taken, or recovered, the regions roundabout the lower reaches of the Garonne, the Lot and the Dordogne. He had looted to his heart's desire, and had been magnificently liberal with the booty. *Erat tam liberalis, tam profusus in donativis,* that every man deemed it sweet to be one of his soldiers. Whenever he captured a village, he took little or nothing for himself but gave everything to his men. At Bergerac he promised every man that captured and took possession of a house, that he should have the house and everything in it. One soldier found a great sum of money, and, as he did not believe treasure trove included in the promise, reported it; but the Earl said that he had not promised *modo puerorum,* and that the finder should keep the money.

But one must not think the Earl of Derby inhumanly self-forgetful; he built the palace of the Savoy in London out of his winnings. No wonder that the English and Gascons were eager for another raid. It was, therefore, decided to make a foray all through the province of Languedoc, from the Bay of Biscay to the Mediterranean Sea.

There was no reason for delay, the season was growing late and the army was ready. And so, on October fifth, they set forth at daybreak, following the Garonne on its left bank, marching through what are now the vineyards of Barsac and of Château Yquem, the glory of white wines, past Langon, past Bazas, where the traveler still sees the *ecclesia cathedralis,* which the chronicler speaks of, and the Porte de Gisquet through which the troops entered, and on until they reached the territories of the Comte d'Armagnac. Since the battle of Crécy the French commanders had had a wholesome respect for the English in the field and avoided a pitched battle. The Comte d'Armagnac, having called every man over fourteen years of age to military service, warned the peasants to take their families into fortified towns, and retired himself within the city of Toulouse. It was as well for him, for the Prince of Wales had now his first experience as commander-in-chief, his was the responsibility, his would be the honor, and his officers were admirable soldiers, the Earls of Warwick, Oxford, Suffolk and Salisbury, the Captal de Buch, Lord Cobham, Bartholomew de Burghersh, and others from England and Gascony, all men of valor and repute. The army consisted of probably seven thousand men, all mounted. They spread out in three parallel columns in order to devastate as wide a stretch of country as possible. Their route led them across the Garonne just above Toulouse, to Carcassonne and to Narbonne on the Mediterranean. I will let the Prince of Wales tell his own story. But one would have liked a personal element in this dry, modest, manly letter. He believed that King John had usurped the crown of France from his father, and from him as his father's successor; that King John had committed ferocious acts of cruelty; that the French had violated the truce; and, yet, as he went through the lovely country of Languedoc, watered by its crystal rivers plashing down from the forest-clothed flanks of the Pyrenees, and spread destruction with fire and sword, did he not sometimes think of his England and of what makes England lovely, of its pleasant valleys and short grass on the hills, of larks singing up in a blue sky, of farmhouses tucked under bunches of elm trees, of cows in the water meadows, knee deep in buttercups, and how, as a boy, he would lie on a hilltop in the morning and see the sun and clouds chasing shadows over the kindly land, and muse how English forefathers had worked and fought, and sweated, and sorrowed, over every inch of it, and feel a thrill of tender pride over his incomparable inheritance? I think that he probably did; and Sir John Chandos, as well, he thinking of Herefordshire, which "would scorne to be considered seconde to any other county throughout all England for fertilite of soile," and Sir James Audeley, too, he thinking of Oxfordshire; but no one of the three let the others guess his thoughts. They talked of horses, armor, roads and fords, of filling moats and escalading walls and so on. But here is the Prince's letter after he got back to Bordeaux.

To the Bishop of Winchester

Bordeaux, Christmas Day, 1356

Reverend Father in God and right Trusty Friend,

In respect of news of these parts, please you to know that, since the writing of our last letters, which we sent unto you, it was agreed by advice and counsel of all the lords and barons of Gascony, by reason that the Count of Armagnac was leader of the wars of our adversary and his lieutenant in all the land of Languedoc and had more oppressed and destroyed the liegeman of our most honored lord and father, the King, and his land than any other in those parts, that we should draw toward his land of Armagnac. So, in regard thereto, we went through the land of Juliac, which yielded to us with the strongholds which were therein. So we rode afterward through the land of Armagnac, harrying and wasting the country, whereby the lieges of our said most honored lord, whom the count had before oppressed, were much comforted. And from thence we passed through the land of the viscounty of La Rivière. So we rode afterward through the county of Astarac, and from thence through the midst of the County of Commingues, even to a town called Samartan, which was the best town of the said county, and which those which were within deserted at the coming of our people. And then we passed by the land of the Count of Lisle, till we came to a league's distance of Toulouse, where the said Count of Armagnac and other great men of our enemies were gathered; and there we tarried two days. And from thence we took our march and crossed in one day the two rivers of Garonne and Ariège, one league above Toulouse, which are very swift and strong to pass, without losing scarce any of our people; and we lodged the night a league the other side of Toulouse, where were many goodly towns and strongholds burnt and destroyed, for the land was very rich and plenteous; and there was not a day but towns, castles and strongholds were taken by some one of our battles or by each one. And from thence we went to the town of Avignonet, which was very great and strong, and it was taken by storm; and therein were lodged all our battles. So we went from thence to Castelnaudary, whither we came on the eve of All Saints, and we abode there the day of the feast, all the host being lodged therein. And from thence we took our road to Carcassonne, which was a fair city and great, and great chieftains were therein and men of arms and commons in great number; for all the greater part of the people of the land of Toulouse were fled thither, but at sight of us they forsook the city and fled to the old city, which was a very strong castle. So we stayed there two days, all the host being lodged therein, and the whole of the third day we remained for burning of the said city, so that it was clean destroyed and undone. And then we rode through all the land of Carcassonne until we came to the city of Narbonne, which was a noble city and of fair size, greater that Carcassonne; which the people of the same did forsake and betook them to the castle, wherein was the Viscount of Narbonne with five hundred men of arms, as was said; and there we abode two days, all the host being lodged therein.

And at this time the Holy Father sent to meet us two bishops, which sent unto us to have safe conduct, which we would not grant unto them. For we would enter into no treaty, until we should know the will of our much honored lord and father the King, and specially by reason we had news that our lord was passed the sea with his power. But we sent back word to them by our letters, that, if they should wish to treat, they should draw toward him, and that which he should command us, we would do it; and in such manner they turned back. And then we took our counsel whither we might best draw; and by reason we had news from prisoners and others that our enemies were gathered together and were coming after us to fight us, we turned again to meet them, and thought to have had the battle in the three days next following. And on our turning back toward them, they turned again toward Toulouse. So we pursued them in long marches near to Toulouse; where we took our road to pass the Garonne at a town called Carbonne, at three leagues from Toulouse, where we tarried a day and the night following. Before midnight there came word unto us that the enemy with all their power, to wit, the Count of Armagnac, the Constable of France, the Marshal Clermont, and the Prince of Orange, were come from Toulouse and were camped at two leagues distance from our rear-guard; and there they lost some of their men and wagons at their camping. And upon this news we drew toward them, and therein we sent forth, my lord Bartholomew de Burghersh, my lord John Chandos, my lord James of Audeley, my lord Baldwin Botour, my lord Thomas Felton, and other of our

men, to the number of thirty lances, to certify us of the certainty
of the said enemy. And they rode toward them, until they
came to a town where they found two hundred men of arms
of their side, with whom they fought and took of them five
and thirty men of arms. Upon which doings the enemy hasted
sore afraid to their quarters, and held their road right to the
cities of Lombez and Sauveterre, which towns were distant
the one from the other only half an English league; and before
them we encamped that same night so near to the enemy
that we could see their fires in their quarters. But there was
between them and us a great deep river, and on the night before
our coming they broke down the bridges, so that we might not
pass over until on the morrow we sent our people on before to
remake the said bridges. And from thence the enemy drew
to the town of Gimont, whither we came the day that they
came; and, before that they could enter that said town, our
people took and slew full plenty of them. And on that same
night we camped before the said town and abode there on the
morrow the whole day, thinking to have battle. And the same
day we stood in arms, with all our battles, in the fields before
sunrise; where there came unto us the news that before daylight
the greater part of their host had gone away, but the leaders
remained in quiet in the said town, which was great and strong
to hold against much people. And after the news we returned
again to our quarters and took counsel what were best for
us to do. And, for as much as we perceived that they would
not have fighting, it was agreed that we ought to draw toward
our marches, in manner and according as my lord Richard of
Stafford will know how to tell you more at large than we could
write unto you; to whom please you, in these matters and in all
others which he shall tell and show as from us, to give faith

and credence.   Reverend Father in God and right trusty Friend, may He who is almighty have you in his keeping.

Given under our privy seal, etc.

So ended this highly successful raid from Bordeaux to Narbonne and back.

# CHAPTER XIII

THE next summer a more ambitious plan was devised; for in the spring the Bordeaux sun dances on polished armor and Gascon horses pull on the bit. An English army should come down from Normandy to the River Loire, and the Black Prince should go up from Bordeaux, and they should meet in the neighborhood of Tours. Possibly their united forces might march on Paris, possibly they might hope to meet King John in the field and a second Crécy. At this point Geoffrey Baker drops into a singularly sentimental mood, as I did in the last chapter. He is my excuse and justification. He says that the Prince heard a report that his father was coming himself to France, and that the thought of his father's undergoing care and trouble without his being there to help, or that his father's health might suffer in the campaign, touched the dutiful young man's bowels, and that he wished to go north *"cupitis osculis paternis se presentare* [to receive the longed for paternal kisses]."

At all events the Prince left Bordeaux in July with an army of English and Gascons. He felt his oats and was in high feather. He had sent the Captal de Buch to capture Périgueux, which he claimed as a part of the Duchy of Aquitaine. The Pope wished to ransom it, for its immediate lord was the Comte de Périgord, brother to the Cardinal de Périgord, a friend of the Pope and a correspondent of Petrarch, and sent to make proposals. The Prince was in a Plantagenet mood; "My father,

121

the King of England," he answered, "is, by God's grace, very rich, and has supplied me so abundantly with gold and silver that I neither need nor wish, by tolerating things like this, to procure more gold and silver. It is my purpose to do in all respects what I have come here for—to punish, to discipline, and subdue, by force of arms, all the inhabitants of the Duchy of Aquitaine, now in rebellion against my father, and bring them back to their old allegiance, and keep them in their proper obedience."

He was obliged to send certain troops to garrison towns and fortresses and provide for the defense of Guienne in his absence, and then with the rest, probably about the same numbers as the year before, seven or eight thousand men, began his march northward. He left Bergerac on August fourth, accompanied by the same experienced officers that had served in the *chevauchée* through Languedoc. It is not necessary to follow his march with nicety. He went to Périgueux where the English flag was already flying. There the Englishmen saw the strange cathedral of Saint-Front, such as they had certainly never seen in England, with its domes, pendentives and colossal piers, and loiterers would have found remains of a Roman amphitheater, built by conquerors of a thousand years before, in the castle of the displaced Counts of Périgueux. The Duc de Berry, one of King John's younger sons, might have been curious about these things, but not a Plantagenet, or any of his bulldog Englishmen. The Prince then marched to Brantôme, a delightful town on the charming little River Dronne, with an island, an abbey, a great belfry and a church, where the Prince should have stopped, for there the Angevin style of vaulting had triumphed over the domes of Périgord. It is such a pleasant land, that the memory of those clanking

Englishmen and Gascons, ravaging and ravishing as they went, lies like a shadow on one's path. They arrived at Lesterps on a Sunday, August fourteenth; and there some attempt at defense was made, but the town was obliged to capitulate, and the chronicler makes note of the exceptional fact that both the church and the inhabitants were spared; and, so, to-day the twelfth-century belfry still exists. From there, on and on, northward, passing near Lussac, hard by the place where fourteen years later the famous Sir John Chandos was to meet death, past Châteauroux, once part of the dowry of Eleanor of Aquitaine, past Issoudun, where the Prince's Plantagenet ancestors had left bellicose memories, to Vierzon, where a noble abbey was completely burned down. That day, Sunday the twenty-eighth, Sir John Chandos and Sir James Audeley, inseparable as Roland and Oliver, with ten knights and two hundred common soldiers, came upon a French leader, known as Gris Mouton, with eighty knights. The English took eighteen prisoners, killed others and put the rest to flight. Gris Mouton was the first to run away. A detachment in the meantime had ridden to Bourges, but the city was too strong to take, and the raiders were forced to content themselves with burning the suburbs. So the monotonous story goes: "the fiery pillar glided slow" and destroyed most of what was destructible.

But after getting as far north as Romorantin the face of affairs changed. King John and the Dauphin had collected their power. Great numbers of the French nobility had come to his standard, he had hired German mercenaries, and various adventurers. Sir William Douglas and a band of Scots, Don Enrique of Trastamara, bastard brother to Don Pedro of Castile, had also joined him. With a large army he was approaching the Loire. The Prince was still hoping to unite with the Duke of Lancaster and then confront King John in a pitched battle. But the Duke, having been obliged to withdraw in order to reintegrate his army, had kept to the west near Angers and was unable to cross the river. The Prince tarried a few days near Tours, ravaging the neighborhood on the south bank of the river, which must have been singularly beautiful at night, as flames from burning houses and hay-ricks flashed across its silvery surface. But when news came that King John with vastly superior forces was crossing the river higher up, at Meung, Blois and Amboise, and also at Tours, there was nothing to do but retreat southwardly.

The Prince broke camp, on Sunday, September eleventh, crossed the Rivers Cher and Indre, and stopped for the night at Montbazon. Here the Cardinal of Périgord came with exhortations from the Pope to make a truce. The Prince distrusted the Pope, Innocent VI, a Frenchman, and therefore fobbed off the Cardinal, and proceeded in a southerly direction until he reached Châtellerault on the River Vienne, where he stayed for two days, September fifteenth and sixteenth. It is difficult to surmise why he did this. Perhaps he wished to rest his men and his horses, so that, if need were, they would be equal to forced marches. Perhaps he feared to hurt the morale of his army, or encourage the enemy, by the appearance of flight; and Plantagenets disliked very much to quicken their pace with an enemy at their heels. The armies were scarce a dozen miles apart. King John passed the night of September fourteenth at the place where the English had camped the night before. Then, instead of pressing on the Prince from behind, he made a rapid sweep, in a half-circle, to his left, passed the Prince while he was at Châtellerault, went south to Chauvigny, crossed the Vienne there and proceeded toward Poitiers. Poitiers, you remember, was in the hands of the French, and King John had given careful orders for its safety; only three gates of the city should be open, and at each of the three there should be an inspection post of ten notable citizens to stop and examine all who wished to go in or out; no shop or tavern might hold a soldier's weapons in pawn; and every householder must keep a cask of water before his door, and maintain a lighted candle during the night. Nevertheless, it looks as if he had been fearful lest the Prince should take it by a coup de main, or by treachery. Perhaps he merely wished to bar the Prince's road of escape to Bordeaux, and thought Poitiers would be a good base of operations. When the Prince learned that the French army was not north, but south, of him, he appreciated his danger. He sent his baggage train across the Vienne that Friday night, and early on Saturday morning crossed with his army, and marched due south, by a route that passed about midway between Chauvigny and Poitiers, through the fields, by what Froissart calls *les chemins des bruyères*. He probably did not know just where the French army was, and hoped to slip by. It chanced that he came upon a laggard troop of the French on its way from Chauvigny to Poitiers, near a croft called La Chaboterie, close to the hamlet of le Breuil l'Abbesse, and captured several prisoners of importance. At last each of the two armies knew just where the other was. On getting the information King John moved his army back from Poitiers to the southeast, and encamped on a plateau a little west of the village of Nouaillé, very near the road that the Prince would be likely to take. And on the next day, on Sunday morning, the Prince of Wales did take that road and halted his army a couple of miles to the east of the French position.

The two armies that confronted each other offered a marked contrast. One thinks of the contrast between the trained and disciplined Macedonian phalanx under Alexander the Great, and the indefinite, incoherent heterogeneity (as Herbert Spencer would have called it) of the Persian army under Darius. The English army was a well organized unit, under the command of officers of large experience, who were ready to command those below them and obey those above; the men were trained soldiers, disciplined under a definite system, the flower of English manhood, while the Gascon troops were very nearly, if not quite, as good. In numbers there were some seven thousand; Froissart says two thousand men-at-arms, four thousand archers and fifteen hundred spearmen, Geoffrey Baker says four thousand men-at-arms, two thousand archers and one thousand *sirvientes* which Stowe translated "armed souldiers," presumably Welsh or Cornish spearmen.

The French army outnumbered the English, I suppose, three to one, perhaps more. Froissart shifts the numbers he gives according to his mood, in one place he says forty-eight thousand, in another fifty thousand, in a third sixty thousand, and again he reckons them at five times as many as the English, and elsewhere, at seven times. Geoffrey Baker says eight thousand men-at-arms, without counting *serviencium numerus* (by which he means, I suppose, the various bodies of footmen), and contrasts the *multitudo* of the French with the *paucitas* of the English. Sir Bartholomew de Burghersh, writing home, puts the French figures at eight thousand men-at-arms and three thousand foot, an estimate that does credit to his modesty, and we suspect that he must have got such moderate numbers from the Prince. Matteo Villani says fifteen thousand men-at-arms and a great number of *sergenti in arme*. Apart from these various estimates, it is apparent from the story of the battle that the numbers were extraordinarily unequal. I think that we may safely conclude that the French were three times as many. Even the brilliant Froissart could hardly make a legend of seven or nine to one, out of whole cloth. But this French army was very similar to that at Crécy, a mob of gentlemen who fought with brilliant valor and dazzling stupidity.

# CHAPTER XIV

LET me repeat. King John, when he heard that the Black Prince was near, turned back from Poitiers and marched down to interpose his army between the English and their direct road of retreat, which road of retreat led to a village, Roche-Prémarie, and on, past Villedieu and Gençay, to Limoges, Périgueux or Angoulême. John encamped on Saturday night on a plateau, some seven miles southeast of Poitiers, to the east of the brook Miosson and somewhat less than two miles northwest from Nouaillé, a village that you will find on the map. The next morning the Black Prince, having spent the night at La Chaboterie, or rather in a forest near it, marched down by a converging route and halted opposite the French army. The land there lies after this fashion. There is a little valley, extending roughly northeast and southwest. To the west of it rises the plateau on which the French army was encamped, and to the east of it the plateau on which the English army had halted. At the north end of the English plateau was a fortified grange, or something of that sort, called in old time Maupertuis, and more recently la Cardinerie; and from this grange a road ran along the flank of the plateau due south, over various inequalities in the ground, to a ford across the brook Miosson, and thence proceeded on to the village of Roche-Prémarie, where it gained the main road from Poitiers down to Périgueux. The distance from the grange to the ford is about a mile and a quarter. The breadth of the little valley between the two plateaus is some six hundred yards. The armies may have been a couple of miles apart.

On that Sunday morning, September 18, 1356, it looked as if a battle would begin at once. King John held a council of war. The question was, should they march straight upon the English and attack, or should they avoid a pitched battle, and instead block the Prince's path of escape, cut off his supplies, surround him and force him to surrender or to fight under most disadvantageous conditions. The more experienced officers, and probably all who had been present at Crécy, advocated the policy of prudence, but the hot-heads had their way, and it was decided to advance. Orders were given, the trumpets blared, Geoffroi de Charny unfurled the Oriflamme. The Constable of France, Gautier de Brienne, Duke of Athens and the two Marshals, Jean de Clermont and Arnoul d'Audrehem, superintended the falling into battle array. Following tradition, they divided the army into three battalions, the first under the nominal command of the Dauphin, a lad of eighteen, the second under the Duc d'Orléans, the King's brother, and the third under the King.

While the battalions were forming the King sent Lord Eustace de Ribemont, the knight who had fought so valiantly against King Edward at Calais, and two others, to reconnoiter. "Ride forward," he said, "as near the English army as you can, note their appearance and their numbers, and see whether it will be better to attack on horse or on foot." The three nobles galloped off to do as they were bid; and the King, mounted on a white courser, rode to the head of the army, and made a brief speech: "When you were at Paris, Chartres, Rouen and Orléans, you were full of threats against the English and wished that, helmet on head, you had them before you. Well, you have your wish. I will show them to you, and you can show your wrath, and avenge the wrongs they have done to you. For most certainly we shall fight them." Those within hearing answered: "Sire, by God's help, we will do so gladly." The three noblemen, having made their inspection, pushed their way up to the King. Lord Eustace de Ribemont spoke for them: "Sire, the English amount to about two thousand men-at-arms, four thousand archers, and fifteen hundred foot. We do not think that they make more than one battalion, but they have drawn it up exceedingly well. They have posted themselves along a road thickly protected with hedges and bushes and they have lined the hedges with their archers." As I think that Froissart has confounded the position occupied by the English on Sunday with that occupied by them on Monday, at the time of the battle, and by so doing has caused much confusion, I have omitted the latter part of the speech he puts into Ribemont's mouth. The King then asked whether they had better attack on horse or on foot. Sir Eustace replied: "Sire, all on foot; except that there should be a body of three hundred men-at-arms, the boldest, bravest and most venturesome in the army, and well mounted, to break through and scatter the archers, and then your battalion of men-at-arms will quickly follow on foot to attack their men-at-arms hand to hand. That is the best advice I have to give; if any man have a better let him speak up." The King approved Sir Eustace's advice, and the two Marshals rode through the ranks to pick out the three hundred best knights.

It was at this point, with the French all ready to advance, and the English drawn up across the valley, that the Cardinal de Périgord came riding up at full gallop. It was he who had attempted several days before at Montbazon, without success, to lay the Pope's mediation before the Prince of Wales. He begged King John to listen to him for a moment, and began with an appeal to the King's magnanimity: "You are here with the flower of knighthood of all your kingdom, and the English are but a handful. You can get them by other means than a battle, and so to do will be more honorable and more profitable than to hazard the lives of all these noblemen. I beseech you in all humility and in God's name, to permit me to go to the Prince and expound to him the dangerous situation in which he lies; for it is certain that he that is in the wrong must needs render an account before God on the day of doom." The King assented and the Cardinal rode across the intervening plain, and found the Prince on foot, in the thick of a vineyard. The Prince received him politely. The Cardinal dwelt upon the great size of the French army, and hoped that the Prince would accept his mediation. The Prince replied that he could not discuss any matter that touched his honor, or that of his army, but otherwise he would listen to any reasonable proposal. He agreed, he said, that it was a Christian duty to prevent a battle, if it might be. "But we maintain that our quarrel is just and true. You know well that it is no idle tale that at the time that King Philip of Valois was crowned, my father, King Edward, was the rightful heir, entitled to hold and possess France; nevertheless, I do not wish it said that so many goodly young men should die here through my pride. I will not set myself against peace. If it can be made, I will further it with all my power. But I can not make a final treaty of peace without my father, all I can do is to agree to an armistice. I do not fear; our quarrel is just, and I am ready to abide God's will. But to prevent this sin of bloodshed, I will agree to terms, subject to my father's ratification."

The Cardinal thanked him and hurried back to the King of

France; and, pointed out that, in the position where it was, the English army could not possibly escape, he asked the King to consent to a truce till sunrise the next morning, so that in the meantime they might come to terms. The King hesitated and many of his nobles opposed the suggestion, but the Cardinal appealed so earnestly that he consented. All that day the Cardinal spent riding to and fro, carrying proposals and counter-proposals; and the Black Prince kept his men busy throwing up mounds and digging ditches in front of his position. At one time commissioners from both armies met in the open ground between. On the French side there were the Comte de Tancar-ville, the Archbishop of Sens, Lords Charney, Bouciquaut and Clermont; on the English, the Earl of Warwick, the Earl of Suffolk *au poil gris,* Bartholomew de Burghersh, Sir John Chandos and Sir James Audeley. But they could not agree, although the Prince (according to Froissart) went far. His provisions had run very low, and, unless for some highly im-probable happening, he would be obliged either to throw himself on King John's mercy, or fight on the ground and under con-ditions chosen by the enemy. He offered to give up what towns and castles he had captured during the campaign, to set his prisoners free without ransom, and not to take arms against France for seven years. The French rejected these terms. Then King John proposed that the Prince and a hundred of his knights should surrender unconditionally. Neither the Prince nor his army would listen to this. He said: "I have but one death to die, and I had rather put it to the hazard than live in disgrace." Finally Geoffroi de Charny proposed that one hun-dred knights from each side should decide the quarrel. But War-wick waved the proposal aside, perhaps he did not trust them: "What do you wish to gain by this?" he asked, and pointing to the plain between the armies, said, "There is the place to settle this matter; let each man do his best, and may God uphold the right."

It chanced after this that Sir John Chandos and the Maréchal de Clermont, each *jone et amoureus,* riding out in front of their lines, met, and both were astonished to discover that each had the same device on his surcoat, the outer garment that covered the corselet: the Virgin Mary embroidered in blue, surrounded by the sun's rays. Maréchal Clermont called out: "Chandos, since when have you taken upon yourself to wear my device?" Sir John replied: "It is you that have mine; at least it is as much mine as yours." The Maréchal answered: "I forbid it; and if it were not for the truce, I would soon show you that you have no right to wear it." "Indeed!" Sir John retorted, "to-morrow you will find me in the field ready to prove that it is as much mine as yours." The Maréchal: "English arrogance! You can invent nothing new, so you take what belongs to others." Then they rode back, each to his lines, to find definitely that no terms could be agreed on, and that the Cardinal, admitting failure, had ridden back to Poitiers. That night the French had a good dinner, while the English were obliged to content themselves with short rations; both were in accord in blaming the well-meaning Cardinal for his interference.

That evening the Prince of Wales held a council of war. There could be little doubt that the French meant to fight; but it was prudent to guard against the chance that they would try to surround the English and starve them out. The road of escape, as I have said, was that which ran from the fortified grange of Maupertuis south across the Miosson, by the ford, the Gué de l'homme, to the hamlet, Roche-Prémarie. It was agreed that the line of retreat should be secured, and an attempt made to profit by it; and, accordingly, that the more cumbrous booty should be burned, and at earliest dawn Warwick should go first with his battalion and convey the baggage train across the brook Miosson, while the Prince with the second battalion should follow, and old Salisbury bring up the rear-guard. The battalions should keep the battle formation as nearly as possible and, if a retreat could not be effected, take position to the east side of the road, which would protect their front with a hedge and a ditch.

The truce ended at sunrise on Monday morning, the nineteenth, and Warwick was already on his way southward with the baggage train. The ground about the ford was marshy and the causeway narrow, so that even after an hour he had not fully crossed. In the meantime the indefatigable Cardinal de Périgord, who was really acting as became a Christian, made one last effort to procure an armistice, but nobody heeded him and so he rode away. And, as I understand it, the Prince with his battalion and Suffolk with the rear-guard at once started southward, following Warwick, along the slope of what I have called the English plateau, toward the ford across the brook Miosson. This plateau sloped, you remember, down to the little valley that separated it from what I have called the French plateau to the west. The English could not have kept wholly in the road, that ran from the grange to the ford, as their lines would have been far too much extended; the two battalions, six abreast, would have strung along almost its entire length, and, besides, they endeavored to maintain, as best they could, their fighting formation. They must have marched through the fields. The land is uneven, and rises here and there to higher elevations. There must have been much more forest than there is to-day, especially on the French plateau, for the

armies could not see each other.  That part of the English
plateau not covered by forest, was partly wild, full of briars and
thorn bushes, and partly cultivated, with vineyards or other
crops, or left as fields for grazing, and, in places, it seems, to
mark private ownership or to keep cattle from passing, divided
up by hedges and ditches.  The road to the ford, as I understand
it, was ditched and hedged on the east side all along, except in
one place where there was a gap made by carters for convenience
of harvesting.  The course of the battle, and the sites of the
various encounters, make a capital matter for guessing.  Froissart had not been on the battle-field and his description is a
mixture of hearsay and fancy.  Neither Geoffrey Baker nor
the Herald Chandos had been there, and Baker evidently lies
under grave misapprehensions.  If you are interested in various
interpretations, you may look at the maps of the battle in Longman's *Edward III*, in the *Chronicon Galfridi le Baker*, edited
by E. Maunde Thompson; in *The Black Prince*, by R. P. Dunn-
Pattison; in the *History of the Art of War*, by Charles Oman;
or in the *Entwickelung des Kriegswesens*, by General G.
Köhler.  So, drawing such inferences as seem to me reasonable
from the statements of chroniclers and from general prob-
abilities, I proceed.

The English on breaking camp marched southward, as I say,
with the French on their right, *"en costeant par devant eux,"* to
quote the Prince's words, "passing sidewise in front of them."
The French army was however hidden by wooded uplands, and
the Prince dispatched two knights to reconnoiter, Sir Eustace
d'Aubréchicourt, from Hainaut, a gentleman adventurer, and
Petiton de Curton, a Gascon.  Both went too far forward and
were taken prisoners.  Sir Eustace was foolhardy.  He behaved like a French knight, and helps one to understand the

lack of discipline in the French army; an English knight would not have put romance ahead of orders. No sooner did he see an advanced body of the enemy's men-at-arms than he galloped toward them. A German knight, perceiving him come on, rode out, lance in rest. The shock of their encounter was so great that both were hurled to the ground. The German, wounded in the shoulder, found it hard to get up, while Sir Eustace leapt nimbly to his feet, recovered his breath and was rushing upon his adversary, when other Germans, coming to their comrade's assistance, struck him down and made him prisoner.

The Prince was impatient for the information which did not come. In the direction of the enemy was a plat of rising ground covered by a thick wood and surrounded by ditch and hedge. He dashed the rowels in his steed, leapt ditch and hedge; his men followed and drove out the French soldiers that they found there. From the farther side of the wood the Prince could see the enemy still at a considerable distance, drawn up in three great battalions. Obviously they would soon attack. By this time the Prince's battalion and the rear-guard had proceeded some way from the grange toward the ford, and Warwick had actually crossed the brook. It is now time to see what the French were doing; but that I leave for the next chapter.

# CHAPTER XV

THE French army, as I have said, was drawn up in three battalions. The men-at-arms were dismounted, and had shortened their spears and taken off their spurs, so that they might fight more commodiously on foot. A cavalry squadron consisting of the three hundred picked men, together with the foreign mercenaries, under the command of the two Marshals, Clermont and Audrehem, were stationed in front, so that they might charge first and scatter the English archers. It was then that they perceived that the English army was in motion, but the view was so much obscured, so fragmentary, that it was difficult to say which way it was going. Some thought, among them Marshal Clermont, that they were advancing to attack. Others thought they were trying to retreat, and shouted out to pursue or the English would escape. One of these was Marshal d'Audrehem, who cried out angrily: "We shall soon lose them, if we do not set on." Clermont answered: "You are in too great haste. Do not be so impatient. We shall surely be there in good time. The English are not fleeing, they are coming on, and faster than a walk." D'Audrehem retorted, "Your delay will make us miss them." Clermont lost his temper. "By Saint Denis, my lord Marshal, you are brave but not so brave as to follow me close enough for the point of your spear to touch my horse's rump." And, both angry, they galloped forward, followed helter-skelter by their division of cavalry, over the plateau, down across the little valley, and up on the eastern plateau to charge the English.

The distance was so great and they rode so fast that they left the Dauphin's battalion, which was on foot, far behind. As they came, they perceived the opening in the hedge, made as I have said by harvesters, and rode for that point.

The position of the English at this point, I conceive to be about as follows: The vanguard had reached the ford, the baggage train had crossed, but on account of the narrow causeway, the greater part was still on this side, and as soon as it was known that the French were coming on, Warwick turned and led his men back up on the English plateau, and stationed them so that they, as well as the rest of the army, would be protected by the hedge and ditch that bordered the road from the grange to the ford. His battalion, then, was to the south of the gap in the hedge. The Prince's battalion was stationed higher up on the plateau and more to the east, and was at first held as a sort of reserve; while old Salisbury's rear-guard, which had marched lower down, nearer the valley, following in the footsteps of Warwick's battalion, took its station along the roadside just before coming to the gap. The three battalions, then, stood in such manner that when they turned right face toward the French, Warwick's constituted the left wing, Salisbury's the right wing, with the gap in the hedge between them, and the Prince's the center, but back, to the rear. With the battle imminent, the Prince walked out in front of his men-at-arms, who, according to the English tactics on the defense, were all dismounted, and made a brief speech. He said that the obstacles in their way could only be removed by the sword, flight could not save them, that they were going to fight enemies they had often beaten, that they must remember their honor and renown, and that only if victorious could they achieve peace with glory and return to a happy old age with their wives and children.

"I also reflect," he said, "that this ground, where we are about to fight, belonged to my ancestors, Kings of England, by ancient hereditary right, and ought to belong to us.  So, all motives conspire together—the justice of my Father's cause; desire to avoid death, prison, shame and poverty; your English custom (*vestra virtus assueta*) to overcome many with a few, and blithely to bear the yoke of war—these give me great hope to triumph over these French epicures, no matter how many, and ought to breed like hope in you.  And bear in mind, that as we prosecute a righteous cause, whether we live, or whether we die, we are servants of God, and he that shall persevere in the service of God unto death shall inherit eternal life, for whosoever shall suffer for righteousness' sake, theirs is the Kingdom of heaven."

He then walked out in front of the archers and made a speech to them: "Your courage and loyalty have been well proved to me.  In many wild times you have shown that you are not degenerate Englishmen, but flesh of their flesh and bone of their bone, who under the lead of my father, and my ancestors, Kings of England, found no task unconquerable, no plot of land too rough to cross, no mountaintop inaccessible, no towered castle impregnable, no hostile ranks impenetrable, no enemy in arms formidable.  Their lively courage tamed Frenchmen, Cypriotes, the men of Syracuse, of Calabria, of Palestine, it subdued the stiff-necked Scotts and Irishmen, and the Welsh, too, men that can endure all hardships.  Occasion, time and danger make the timid brave, and dull-witted men imaginative.  Moreover, honor, love of country, and the rich spoils of France, more than any words of mine, exhort you to tread in your father's steps.  Follow your banners; keep your bodies and your wits intent upon the orders of your officers, so that, if life and victory come hand in hand, we may long maintain our fellowship, one in mind and one in will. Or, if envious Fate, which God forbid, should in this present task drive us upon the last road of all flesh, no unpaid debts to heaven will stain your names; and these gentlemen, my comrades, and I, will drink of this same cup with you. There is danger in fighting the nobility of France, but a danger wrapped in glory; there is danger of defeat, which God forbid, but it is a danger free from shame and makes a man's soul tingle."

Then men fell into line. The archers were drawn up in front, for, as at Crécy, the first rule of tactics was to bring the whole force of the archery to bear upon the charge of the French cavalry. Then Sir James Audeley—he and Sir John Chandos were the Prince's chief staff officers—turned to the Prince and said: "Sir, I have served your Father and you loyally and I shall continue to do so all my life. But let me tell you a vow, made long ago, that, if ever I was in a battle where your Father was, or any of his sons, I would be in the forefront. I beg you dearly, in recompense for any services I have rendered to your father or you, to grant me permission to leave you, for honor's sake, and to perform my vow." The Prince nodded assent, held out his hand, and said: "Sir James, may God grant to you this day to outshine all other knights in valiancy," and Sir James went to the front rank, attended by his four squires, Dutton of Dutton, Delves of Doddington, Fowlehurst of Crew and Hawkeston of Wainehill.

The French men-at-arms were galloping up, as I said, toward the gap in the hedge, meaning to ride through the gap and take Warwick's men in the flank, but old Salisbury, seeing them coming, moved his battalion out to protect the gap. He cried to his men: "Forward, gentlemen, for God's sake. Since it pleases Saint George that we, who were hindmost, should become the front rank, let us bear ourselves in a manner to win honor." This maneuver was performed just in time. Then came the shock and clash of armed men, who laid on load with sword and spear and battle-ax, while from behind the hedge the English archers shot horse and rider and did more hurt than the men-at-arms. As at Crécy, the horses wheeled, reared, stampeded and dashed into one another, throwing their riders. Warwick and Salisbury fought in fierce emulation to see "which of them should dung the land of Poitiers most with Frenchmen's blood," and gloried to see their armor total gules. As the Herald Chandos says, had there been an indifferent spectator to look on, it would have been a glorious sight:

> *Mais, certes, granz pitez estoit*
> *Et merveilleuse chose et dure,*
>
> But, indeed, great pity was it,
> A wonderful, cruel thing.

The confusion of frantic horses and helpless riders was hideous. The French showed reckless courage, but it was of no avail, the Constable Gautier de Brienne was killed, so was the Marshal de Clermont, and the Marshal d'Audrehem was wounded and taken prisoner. It is too bad that the actors in these famous dramas say nothing afterward. You shall read the Prince of Wales' report of the battle; his modesty was as great as his valor. But a hand-to-hand fight with battle-axes must have left memories. Winston Churchill says of the charge of the twenty-first Lancers at the battle of Omdurman: "I remember no sound. The event seemed to pass in absolute silence. The yells of the enemy, the shouts of the soldiers, the firing of many shots, the clashing of sword and spear, were unnoticed by the senses, unregistered by the brain. Several others say the same. Perhaps it is possible for the whole of a man's faculties to be concentrated in the eye, bridle-hand and trigger finger, and withdraw from all other parts of the body."

However that may be, the first encounter was over. The French mounted battalion was a confused mass of infuriated fugitives. The English kept the same formation except that Warwick's and Salisbury's division closed up, and it seems that the Prince's joined them, too, and that the whole army formed one line along the roadside. The first French division, commanded by the Dauphin, came on, but disordered and somewhat dismayed by the maddened horses that had dashed about in front of it. The first ranks bore themselves *très chivalrousement*, but the rear ranks quickly began to thin out. Nevertheless it was a far harder fight than with the men-at-arms—*grant mervilles fu a veir*. Cries of Saint George! Saint Denis! Guienne! Montjoye! sounded among the clash of arms and the groans of the dying. The struggle at the hedge was very severe. It was at this point, according to Froissart, that the Prince directed a flank attack, which had been planned beforehand. The Captal de Buch with sixty men-at-arms and a hundred archers, all mounted, rode off to the right, winding round some higher land, through woods, and fell upon the Dauphin's left flank and rear. The French noblemen to whom the Dauphin had been entrusted, when they saw the flag of Saint George in a new quarter, feared lest he be surrendered and captured, so they hurried him away to safety, and raced along the road to Chauvigny. At the same time the Prince's battalion came into action in front. The tactics appear to have been admirable. This was the real crisis of the battle, for if the English could not defeat the Dauphin's battalion before King John's battalion came up, the field would be lost. Sir John Chandos, who stayed beside the Prince when the Captal's flag was visible, said: "Sir, the day is ours, push forward. God will give them into your hands." The Prince replied: "John, get forward. You will not see me turn my back to-day. I shall be among the foremost." The Prince issued the order to his standard-bearer, Sir Walter Woodland: "Advance, Banner, in the name of God and Saint George," and they charged. The Dauphin's crumbling battalion gave way, and also the Duc d'Orléans' battalion, without stopping to strike a blow, frightened by the Captal's flank attack. As Geoffrey Baker puts it: "After enormous slaughter those wise Frenchmen adopted that prudent policy which, *ore invincibiles*, they are wont to call, not a flight, but a handsome retreat."

By this time, as I understand it, the English had fought their way considerably west of the road from the grange to the ford, and were approaching an open stretch (to the south of a little hamlet that is there now, les Bordes), known as the Champ d'Alexandre. The Prince's order was strict not to pursue the fugitives but to keep the ranks, and this order, with scarce an exception, was obeyed. There was reason enough for it, as King John's battalion, by itself outnumbering the English army, was coming on. Why he had remained so far in the rear that he could not support the other battalions is difficult to understand, unless it was that he was haunted by the battle of Crécy, where all the French battalions seem to have got in one another's way. He had kept at such a distance that he could not see what was going on. An officer reported to him that the Dauphin "had withdrawn and that the English were in possession of the field." The King turned to the man and vowed, on his sacred word of honor, that he, the King, would not quit the field that day, unless killed, or captured, or taken off by force, and bade the standard-bearers advance. At this the battalion marched up across the little valley, to which I have referred (*a valle secedens*), on to the broad plain where the English were.

In the meantime the English soldiers had been dragging their wounded under bushes and hedges out of the way, and some, whose swords and spears had been dulled, picked up sharper ones on the field, and the archers drew out arrows from the dead or wounded. But the recess was not for long. On came the royal battalion, fresh and formidable, men from Picardie and the Bourbonnais, from Burgundy and Auvergne and the Limousin, led by their feudal lords, in all the bravery of banners, pennons and heraldry. The rank and file of the English despaired of victory, for many were wounded, and all were tired, and the supply of arrows short; nevertheless holding life as nothing, they commended themselves to God, and resolved not to die alone, or unavenged. Some one, standing near the Prince, a man of high courage withal, groaned: "Ah, we are doomed to defeat." The Prince turned upon him, and shouted out: "You lie, you lily-livered dastard; it is blasphemy to say that we can be defeated, so long as I am alive!" And looking up to heaven, he prayed: "Father Almighty, inasmuch as I believe that Thou art King of Kings, and that Thou didst endure death upon the cross to redeem us all from hell, O Father, very God, very Man, be pleased by Thy most holy name, to keep me and my people from evil, even as Thou knowest that my cause is good." Then he straightway gave the order, to his standard-bearer: "Advance, Banner, and let every man look to his honor." On both sides, horns, trumpets, clarions burst into uproar, until, as Geoffrey Baker says, you would have imagined that the mountains were bellowing to the valleys. The English fought like bulldogs. Sir John Chandos won great praise that day, so did Warwick, Suffolk, Salisbury and Oxford, Despenser, Mohun, Basset, Cobham, Bartholomew de Burghersh, *qui moult fu hardis en ses fes,* and the Gascon Lords, Pommiers, d'Albret, Lesparre, Fossard, Couchon and Montferrant, and among the foremost, the Black Prince, "pressing on in fury, carving the Frenchmen with his sharp sword, and teaching them how terrible is desperation with its armor on." Geoffrey Baker's pen leaps like a grasshopper at mere mention of the Prince's name. Sir James Audeley, with his four squires, Dutton, Delves, Fowlesworth and Hawkeston, was in the thick of it; he was wounded in body, head, and face, but while his strength lasted he fought on, and then his squires took him and laid him under a hedge as gently as they could and took off his armor, dressed his wounds and sewed up the gashes.

Long and doubtful was the struggle, *la avoit moult grande bataille,* so that even the bravest felt dismay, but the Black Prince kept shouting: "Forward, gentlemen! For God's sake!" The French gradually gave way and took to their heels, except the guardsmen about their king, who fought valiantly, falling where they stood; none of them attempted to escape. King John kept his vow, and swung his battle-ax like a valiant soldier, "and showed in every act that he had not degenerated from the royal blood of France." But the shouts of Montjoye, Saint Denis, died away, and Saint George! Guienne! resounded on all sides; there was a great scattering and a bloody pursuit. In the mêlée where swords meet shield and helmet, wounds and death are comparatively few, but where the conquerors pursue fugitives and strike and stab them in the back, and no one defends or strikes back, the carnage is terrible.

Fortune had carried the Black Prince and Sir John Chandos,

who was always by his side, to another part of the field from
where King John was. The tumult and shouting flowed off
toward Poitiers. Chandos suggested: "It will be well to halt
here, and fly your flag from the top of some tall tree so that we
may gather together our scattered soldiers. I do not see any
French pennons, nor any units still resisting. You are much
heated; you need to rest a while." So the Prince's flag was
hoisted on the tallest tree and the trumpets sounded a recall. A
tent was pitched. The Prince went in and ordered wine; and
little by little, many knights, returning with their prisoners,
stopped there. It was now high noon. But not until vespers did
the soldiers all straggle back. The city of Poitiers had, out of
abundant prudence, shut its gates against both fugitives and
pursuers, and let in no man. Up to the very walls the French
were butchered, or made prisoners. All the field was littered
with broken armor, helmets, swords, shields, lances, knives,
flung away in the desperate flight, dead horses, dead men, dying
men, pennants, trumpets, arrows, saddles, and Welshmen wandering about with their long knives giving the quietus to soldiers
not worth the ransoming, or picking up what might seem
valuable enough to take away. Jehan le Bel, a contemporary
historian, muses on the battle thus: *"Qu'en faut-il longuement
faire procès? Fortune voloit les ungs aydier et les aultres
fouler; si ne se poeut plus tenir, ainsi fist sa roe tourner.* [What
is the use of long discussion about it? Fortune willed to aid
the ones and cast the others down; she can not stay still, and so
she turns her wheel.]"

# CHAPTER XVI

KING JOHN had wielded his battle-ax long and well. His faithful friends fell where they stood. The list of noblemen and knights whose bodies lie buried in the convent of the Frères Mineurs in the city of Poitiers reads like a peerage: Gautier de Brienne, Duke of Athens, Constable of France, Regnaud Chaveau, Bishop of Chalon, Sir Geffroi de Charny, Sir Ansiaulme de Hois, Yvon du Pont, Seigneur of Rochecheruière, Sir Bonabes de Roges, Sir Macé de Grosbois, Sir Simon Oynepuille, Sir Henry his brother, M. le Vidame de la Roche Dagon, Sir Guiscard de Chantylon, and scores more. Likewise in the church and cloisters of the Frères Prescheurs another list is as long. There the Duc de Bourbon lies to the right of the great altar, the Maréchal de Clermont on the left, lower down Sir Aubert d'Anger and the Viscount of Rochechouart, in the middle of the choir Aymer de la Rochefoucault, and so on, Sir Ymbert de Saint-Saturnin, Sir Wm. de Digoyne and his son, Sir John de Montmarillon, and his son, Sir Gourard Guenif, Sir Vipert Beau, and many, many another. It is pleasant to know that, on a later day, honorable obsequies in memory of these illustrious dead were performed in all the churches and convents in Poitiers at the cost of the good citizens of that town.

But on that Monday, as the sun was drawing near high noon, most of those bodies were lying bleeding on the ground, and many heaped about the Champ d'Alexandre, where King John was in great danger. Geffroi de Charny had just been slain with the banner of France in his hands, and there was a great press crowding up, in eagerness to capture the King. Those nearest cried out: "Surrender! Surrender! or you are a dead man!" Just behind was a young Frenchman, Denis de Morbeque, who was serving in the English army because he had had to fly from France for killing some one in a fray. This young man, who was very strong, pushed through the King's assailants, and speaking in very good French, cried out, "Sire, surrender yourself." The King asked: "To whom shall I surrender? Where is my cousin, the Prince of Wales? If I could see him, I would speak to him." "Sire," Denis replied, "he is not here. But surrender to me, and I will bring you to him." "Who are you?" the King asked. "Sire, I am Denis de Morbeque, a knight from Artois; but I serve the King of England, because I can not stay in France, as I am under ban." The King gave him his right glove, and said, "I surrender to you." But there was great crowding and pushing, for every man wanted to capture the King.

It was just at this time that the Prince, assured of victory, had taken off his helmet and had ordered wine for himself and his companions. He asked if any one had any news of the King of France. He was answered: "Not with any certainty. We believe that he must be either killed or a prisoner, for he has not left his battalion." The Prince then turned to the Earl of Warwick and Lord Cobham and said: "I beg you to mount and ride over the field, so that you may bring me some certain intelligence." The two noblemen rode to the top of a small hillock and saw a great crowd of men-at-arms on foot, advancing very slowly. In the midst of them was the French King, evidently in great danger, for the Gascons and English had wrenched him from the young Frenchman, and were disputing who should have him. Bernard du Troy, a Gascon squire, was elbowing in, swearing that he had made the capture, and many others likewise claimed a part in it. One bawled, "He is mine." "No," others shouted, "he belongs to us." The King protested: "Gentlemen, gentlemen, I beg that you will bring me and my son in a civil manner to my Cousin, the Prince, and don't make such a riot over my capture. I am sufficient of a person to render you all rich." What he said quieted them a little, but soon they began again and disputed at every step. The Earl of Warwick and Lord Cobham, seeing that something was happening, spurred their horses to the spot. They asked what the matter was, and were told that the King of France was there, a prisoner, and that a dozen and more knights and squires were brawling as to which had captured him. The two lords forced a passage through the crowd, and bade everybody give way. They spoke sharply, "In the Prince's name stand back, under pain of instant death; keep your distance, and only come forward when ordered." The crowd fell back; the two Lords dismounted, and approached the King with profound reverence. And they then conducted him to where they had left the Prince.

In the meanwhile, the Prince asked those about him if any one had any news of Sir James Audeley. "Yes, sir," somebody answered, "he is very badly wounded and is lying on a litter only a little way off." "By my troth," the Prince said, "I am sorely grieved that he is so wounded. I beg you to see if he is able to be carried here; otherwise I will go to visit him." Two knights carried the message to Sir James. "I thank the Prince a thousand times," he said, "for his condescension in remembering so poor a knight as myself." He called his attendants, and eight of them carried him on his litter to the Prince's tent. When he was brought in, the Prince bent over him, embraced him and said: "Sir James, you deserve to be honored very much. This day you have won more glory and honor than all of us; your prowess has proved you to be the most valiant knight." Sir James answered: "My Lord, you have a right to say whatever you please; and I wish it were as you say. If I have been forward to serve you to-day, it was in order to accomplish a vow, and that is not to be thought much of." The Prince replied: "Sir James, I, and all the rest of us, deem you the best knight on our side. And out of respect for your renown, and to provide you with means to pursue the career of arms, I retain you as my knight, with five hundred marks a year, to be charged upon my estates in England." "Sir," the wounded man replied, "God grant that I may deserve the honor you bestow upon me." That was enough; his strength was exhausted; his attendants picked up the litter and carried him back. He had scarcely gone, when the Earl of Warwick and Lord Cobham arrived, escorting the King of France. But I must first finish the episode concerning Sir James Audeley. On getting back to his tent he sent for his brother, Sir Peter Audeley, Lord Bartholomew Burghersh and others, his kinsmen, and for his four squires, Dutton, Delves, Fowlehurst and Hawkeston. Turning to his kinsmen, he said: "The Prince has been pleased to grant me five hundred marks a year; for which gift I have done him very trifling bodily service. Here are these four squires, who have always served me most loyally, and especially in to-day's fight. What honor I may have gained has been their doing. So I wish to reward them. I therefore make over to them, in the same manner as it was given to me, the five hundred marks that the Prince was pleased to give me. I grant it to them absolutely." The knights replied: "May the Lord God remember you for this. We will bear witness of this gift, wheresoever and whensoever they may ask for our testimony." So they left Sir James on his litter and those invited repaired to the Prince's tent for supper.

There is an epilogue to this story. On the march to Bordeaux, the Prince heard how Sir James had passed on his gift to the four squires. So he sent for him. The wounded knight was carried into his presence. "Sir James," the Prince said, "I have been told that after taking leave of me and going back to your tent, you made a present to your squires of the gift I had made to you. If this is true, I should like to know why you did so. Was not my gift agreeable to you?" "Yes, my Lord, most agreeable," Sir James replied, "and I will tell you my reasons. These four squires have long and loyally served me on many dangerous occasions, and until that day I had never rewarded them for their services, and never were they of such service to me as then. I am much bounden to them for what they did at Poitiers. I am but a single man, and can do no more than my powers permit, but by their aid I have accomplished my vow. By their help I was foremost in the fight, and my life would have paid for it had they not been near me. So, when I consider their courage and the love they bear me, I should not have been courteous or grateful had I not rewarded them. Thank God, I have enough to maintain my rank; wealth has never failed me, nor do I believe it will. If I acted contrary to your wishes, please forgive me, for I and my squires will always serve you as loyally as heretofore." The Prince answered, "Sir James, I do not find fault; on the contrary I confirm your gift to them. But I insist on your accepting six hundred marks on the same terms upon which I gave the others to you."

In the meantime, when King John was introduced, the Prince gave him a right hearty greeting, and was fain to help take off his armor. But the King expostulated: "Fair sweet Cousin, for God's pity, forbear. It is not fitting, for by my faith you have to-day won more honor than ever a prince won in a single day before." The Prince replied: "It was God's doing, not ours. And we ought to thank Him for it, and with humble hearts pray Him to grant us salvation, and to forgive this victory." So in this manner they talked, *doucement ensamble parloient,* and the Prince ordered wine and spices to be brought. And when evening came, the Prince gave a banquet in his tent to King John, to the English and Gascon nobles and to their distinguished prisoners. The food and wine, of course, came from the French stores. A special table was set for King John, his son Philip, Jacques de Bourbon, Comte de Ponthieu, Charles d'Artois, Comte de Longueville, Jean de Melun, Comte de Tancarville and a few other great nobles. The Prince himself waited upon them, and resisted every entreaty to sit with them, saying that "he was not worthy of such an honor, nor was it fitting for him to sit at table with so great a King, or of so valiant a man as he had shown himself that day." And he added: "Dear Sir, do not make a poor dinner because God Almighty has not gratified your wishes in the issue of this day. Rest assured that my lord and Father will show you every honor and kindness in his power, and will set your ransom so reasonably that you shall ever after be friends. To my thinking, you have reason to be glad that the issue of this day was not as you wished it, for you have acquired such high renown for gallantry that you have outdone all the knights on your side. I do not, Sir, say this to flatter you, but all on our side who saw and observed what was done on either side, are all agreed that this praise is your due, and award to you the prize and coronal for it." All present murmured hearty assent. And both French and English said that the Prince had spoken nobly and to the point; and the general voice affirmed that he was a very *gentil seigneur*. King John in his turn said: "Regrets are inevitable, nevertheless we have tried to keep them within becoming bounds, for although by right of war we be in the power of my princely Cousin, we were not captured like rascals or faint-hearted runaways taken in a corner, but like stout-hearted gentlemen, ready to live or die in a just cause. By the fortune of war, we have been brought from the battle-field, where many rich men were taken, and spared for their ransoms, where cowards and dastards fled, and many, the stoutest and worthiest, laid down their noble lives."

A rumor had gone about, rightly or wrongly, that King John had issued an order to his soldiers to give no quarter, and afterward the story went that the Prince, alluding to this, said to him, "Good Cousin, had you made me prisoner, as I, by God's mercy, have made you, what would you have done with me?" But the Prince was a good fellow, and very much of a gentleman, and he was in capital spirits with victory and wine and a good dinner, after very scant rations for several days, and I feel sure that there was no bitterness in the question. Words, said with a smile and a glass in your hand, have a significance other than that in print. That night the English were right merry, *les Englois fesoient grant deduit,* and it was late when the Prince retired to his tent pitched on the battle-field, with dead bodies lying all about.

The most interesting matter to the Gascons and English was the ransom of the prisoners, for besides the King and his son Philip, there were seventeen counts, and unnumbered barons, knights and squires. There were too many to carry with them, so a great number were set free on parole. And in spite of what

Froissart says, the ransoms were probably high; for in one aspect these raids were daring business ventures, and an English archer who captured a rich French gentleman, as Pistol did at Agincourt, might exact enough to go home, marry Dame Quickly and set up as landlord of the Boar's Head in Eastcheap, or an English knight might with the ransom of a duke buy great estates in Essex or Westmoreland. The Earl of Warwick, for instance, received eight thousand pounds, an enormous sum, for the ransom of the Archbishop of Sens. And the Gascons, so the English thought, were always greedy. The Prince was well content with his prisoner, for the ransom to be exacted was half a kingdom. The city of Poitiers could not be taken; it was too strong, and the Dauphin had had presence of mind enough to send a hundred lances from Chauvigny to garrison it. Besides in King John the Prince knew he possessed the key to the city gates. So on the morrow the English took their prisoners—they were already loaded with gold, silver, jewels, such finery of all kinds as provincial towns and feudal castles had contained—and started on their way to Bordeaux. What with baggage and prisoners, they proceeded slowly. The Prince took the precaution of sending five hundred men-at-arms ahead, to guard against attacks, but they met no enemy; the inhabitants were so thoroughly frightened that not a soldier ventured outside of the fortified places. The Prince continued through Poitou, Angoumois and Guienne, via Ruffec, La Rochefoucauld and Libonne, where they stayed several days, in order to allow enough time in Bordeaux to prepare proper lodgings for their illustrious prisoner. That done, the Prince entered his provincial capital, like a conquering Cæsar. Bordeaux was a loyal English city, and the citizens welcomed the triumphant army and their brilliant young Prince with cheers and jubilation. Everybody turned out to greet them, old men, children, ladies, girls, servants, processions of priests, with cheers, prayers and hymns of thanksgiving. The Prince conducted his royal prisoner, guest I think he would have said, to the monastery of Saint André, next to the city walls, beside the cathedral, where the great choir begun under the Archbishop, Bertrand de Got, afterward Clement V, was still unfinished, but the noble statues of the north portal were already older than the memory of any living man. Here the King was lodged in one side of the monastery and the Prince in the other. The Prince wrote an account of the battle to the Bishop of Worcester in England. The original is in French.

Bordeaux, October 20, 1356
Reverend Father in God and very dear Friend,

I thank you very very much, as I have heard how kindly you have behaved toward us, praying to God for us and for our success. And I am sure that it is due to your pious prayers and those of others, that God has succored us in all our need. For which we must thank Him always; and beg that you, too, will for your part continue in your attitude toward us as you have done, for which we are much beholden to you. And, Reverend Sir, as to my condition of which I think you are kind enough to wish good news, I may say that, at this time of writing, I am well and happy in every respect. Thanks be to God who granted this. And may I hear the same of you. Please inform me of this by your letters and by travelers as often as you can conveniently, in exchange for our news here. I wish to tell you that on the Eve of the Translation of St. Thomas of Canterbury I started upon a campaign with my army into French territory, chiefly because I expected the arrival of my very honored lord and Father, the King, in that country.  So I proceeded to the regions round Bourges (in Berry), Orléans and Tours, and had news that the King of France with a great army was coming there to fight us.  We came so close together that a battle took place in such fashion that the enemy was discomfited, thanks be to God, and the King aforesaid and his son, and many grandees were captured or killed.  I send you their names by the bearer, my beloved squire, Roger de Cottesford.  And may, Reverend Father in God and dear Friend, the Holy Ghost have you ever in his keeping.

The Prince naturally wished to make a triumphal entry into London as soon as possible, but there was much that hindered. The Pope, Innocent VI, had his heart set on peace; no doubt, being a Frenchman, he had French sympathies, but besides that, Europe was in a mess, the Turks were rising into menace, and he believed war between Christians contrary to the precepts of Christianity.  The persistent Cardinal de Périgord, with another, came again, but this time the Prince refused to see them. The trouble was that after the Cardinal's last failure on the eventful Monday morning, several knights of his suite had slipped away and fought on the French side.  But the Cardinal was in nowise responsible, and after two weeks' waiting the Prince accepted his excuses and received him.  The Pope welcomed this as an entering wedge, and wrote the Prince with ecclesiastical unction:

Our reverend Brother, Talleyrand, Cardinal of Périgord, Nuncio of the Apostolic See, has written us that you have confirmed and enhanced the nobility of your breed by your magnanimity, and virtuous conduct, and have entertained him with such honor and favor as becomes a son to show to his Father in Christ. And more than that, he says that, with a mind prepared for any event, not puffed up by prosperity and success, but humble in the sight of the Lord God, you attribute it all to Him, from whom you received it, and that you, in all courtesy, show our dear son in Christ, John, the illustrious King of France, the honor due to so great a prince. Therefore, we send to your Highness, our well deserved praise, and hope that Almighty God, who respecteth the lowly but humbleth the proud afar off, will bestow upon you the full grace of His benediction.

Dated, Avignon, October 3, the 4th year of our pontificate.

The effect of this unction upon the Prince is not quite certain. In England, in various towns, placards were posted after news of the battle: "The Pope is French, but Jesus is English. The world may now see which is the stronger, the Pope or Jesus." At all events, there were reasons enough for peace, quite apart from the attitude of the Pope, and the negotiations dragged along; but interest in peace was far superseded by interest in ransom. The Gascons wanted to settle the business at Bordeaux and go home to their castles. So the Prince of Wales bought the greater part of their French prisoners of high rank and paid cash. But the question as to who had captured the King was more difficult. There were many claimants, Gascon and English. Denis de Morbeque insisted on his right; and Bernard du Troy insisted on his. After a great dispute, a challenge passed between them, but the Prince placed both under arrest, and bade nothing more be said on the subject till they had laid the matter before King Edward. King John, whose testimony was important, supported Denis as against the others; but the matter was delicate and it was prudent to refer its solution to King Edward, so the Prince who seems to have made up his own mind between the claimants, gave Denis twenty pounds and conferred upon him the duty of carrying the news of King John's capture to London. King Edward displayed a prudence equal to his son's: he gave to each of the two claimants an annual pension in reward for the capture, but before he rendered his decision, both claimants had died.

The Prince of Wales' diplomatic postponement of the particular issue between the French and Gascon squires solved but one part of the difficulty. The Gascons, as I have said, bore among the English the reputation of being grasping, but there was considerable merit in their contention that the capture of the King of France was not due to Denis de Morbeque or Bernard du Troy, for it was mere chance that had brought them to the right spot at the nick of time, but to the combined forces of England and Gascony, and that therefore the King of France was to be regarded as a sort of joint treasure trove. This feeling found articulate expression when it transpired that the Pope was unable to bring about a peace, and that the Prince proposed to take King John to England. A delegation of Gascons waited upon him. "Dear Sir," the spokesman said, "we owe you all honor and obedience, to the utmost of our power, but it is not our intention, since we have labored so hard to put him in his present situation, to let you carry the King of France away from Bordeaux. Thank God, he is at present well and in a good city, and we are well able to keep him in spite of any force that France may send to take him from us." The point, barely hinted at, that it was not fair to them, granted their joint ownership, to expose their joint treasure to the perils of the sea and the possible insalubrity of London, sounds well taken. The Prince replied: "My dear Lords, I agree, of course, to all you say, but the King my father wishes to have him and to see him. We are very sensible and grateful for the services you have rendered both to him and to myself, and you may depend on being handsomely rewarded for them." But the Gascons did not propose to give up their security in reliance upon King Edward's generosity; they had heard how the great Florentine bankers, the Bardi and the Peruzzi, had been forced into bankruptcy by Edward's failure to pay his debts to them, upheld though those debts were by all the trappings of signatures and seals. The Prince was also known to have many unsatisfied creditors. The Gascons refused to let the King go. The Prince consulted with Sir John Chandos and Lord Reginald Cobham, who advised him to treat the matter purely as one of business. The Prince offered them sixty thousand florins. The Gascons rejected the offer. They compromised on one hundred thousand florins, and the Prince was permitted to take the King.

In the meantime Bordeaux had been very gay in celebration of the victory, there were jousting, dancing, feasting, great revelry and making merry. Roundabout the city lie the best vineyards in the world, and they had been under cultivation since the time of the Romans. Finally, in March, 1357, though the negotiators were not able to bring about a treaty of peace, and indeed that did not lie in the Prince's power, they did, however, *pour la révérence de Dieu, de notre Saint-Père et de la Sainte Eglise Romaine,* procure a truce to last until Easter 1359. The Prince was then at liberty to sail. He let many of the prisoners go upon parole in order to raise their ransoms. He appointed four Gascons, headed by Lord d'Albret, to govern in his absence. The Captal de Buch and many others went with him. The King of France was given a ship to himself. They sailed at the end of April and landed at Sandwich on the fourth of

May, at that time still maintaining its reputation as *omnium Anglorum portuum famossissimus*. There they stayed two days, while suitable preparations were made to receive them in London and en route. Then they went on to Canterbury. In the Cathedral they said their prayers at the shrine of the martyr, Thomas à Becket. From Canterbury, following the road the pilgrims took, now lined with cheering crowds, they proceeded to Rochester, Dartford, Greenwich and so to London. The city was wild with pride and joy. The guilds appeared in their liveries, the masters donned their best finery, nobles, and commoners, ladies, men servants, maid servants, varlets and children, crowded the streets or stared from windows. Never had London had such a day. David, King of Scotland, was already there, a prisoner, and also Charles of Blois, deposed Count of Brittany. The procession crossed London Bridge, and turning westward, past Blackfriars and Whitefriars, along Fleet Street, past St. Clement Dane's, proceeded to Westminster Palace. It was a gallant sight. First a thousand citizens on horseback, followed by men-at-arms and archers, next the Gascon nobles and their retainers, and then the King of France on a great white charger, richly caparisoned, with the Black Prince riding at his side on a little palfrey, as became the lieutenant of the Duchy of Guienne, beside his suzerain lord, and after them a brilliant troop of French knights attendant upon their King. At the palace of Westminster the august prisoner was warmly welcomed by King Edward, and then escorted to the palace of the Savoy, and afterward, as Jehan le Bel relates, he was put *"en ung beau chastel qu'on clame Vindessore* [in a fine castle called Windsor]," and there he stayed, while he and King Edward held conferences from time to time as to the terms on which the two kingdoms might make a lasting peace.

# CHAPTER XVII

THE Dauphin had ridden hard from his broken battalion on the lost field of Poitiers, and saved himself at Chauvigny. There was various criticism of his safe escape. Some said that he had obeyed a direct command from the King; some, that old soldiers, men of high rank and distinction, attendant upon him to advise and guard, had obliged him to go; others said that in either case disobedience would have been more consistent with his honor. Others, still, like Matteo Villani, who probably received an unfavorable account from the Italian Savoyards that had served in the French army, did not mince their words: "The Dauphin and the Duc d'Orléans ran away like the vilest cowards." At all events the Dauphin was at large.

The military power of France was crushed, the King a prisoner, the feudal nobility in great part killed or captured, the Dauphin a lad of eighteen; if theories of modern strategy had been in men's minds, the Black Prince could have marched on Paris. The country was terrified and indignant. Burghers and peasants denounced the incompetency and cowardice of the princes and nobles, they suspected treachery. Harsh words were spoken, and bitter songs sung:

*Dieu veuille comforter et garder nostre roy*
*Et son petit enfant qu'est demoré o soy*
*Et confonde traistres qui par leur grant effroy*
*Ont tray leur seigneur à qui il devoient foy.*

161

Please God, comfort and keep our King
And his young boy who stayed by him,
And confound traitors who in their great fright
Betrayed their lord, to whom their faith was plight.

The circumstances which the Dauphin confronted were not
pleasant. Nobody knew what would happen. Would the English cross the Channel and invade again? How about the King's
ransom? What terms would the conquering English exact for
peace? The Dauphin convoked the * États Généraux* of northern
France. The nation must decide for itself what to do. So the
* États Généraux* met in angry mood, and though the Dauphin
spoke *moult sagement et moult gracieusement*, they appointed
what might be called a Committee of Safety, that met in the
very Convent of the Cordeliers destined to ring four hundred
and thirty odd years later with still more revolutionary speeches.
The leader of this Committee of Safety was Étienne Marcel,
*Prévôt des Marchands,* an office virtually equivalent to a modern
mayoralty.   Visitors to Paris will remember the equestrian
statue erected in his honor on the river side of the Hôtel de Ville,
a tribute to the theory that he represented the cause of democratic
liberty and constitutional government. Under his leadership the
radical party assumed many royal prerogatives, and made common cause with Charles le Mauvais, who had just come out
of the castle, where he had been imprisoned by King John, *sans
prendre congé de son hôte,* as he himself said.   The Dauphin
was obliged to yield, and accept both what the radicals and
Charles of Navarre demanded.   Needs must, as Étienne Marcel
said: *"Sire, faites amiablement au roi de Navarre ce qu'il vous
requiert, car il convient que cela soit fait.* [Sire, be so good as
to do what the King of Navarre asks of you, for it is very fitting
and necessary that that should be done.]" So the Dauphin and

Charles met at the hotel of Charles's wife, the Dauphin's sister, for the first time since the memorable banquet. Navarre was reinstated in all his towns, castles and strongholds, and a full pardon was granted to him and his partizans, and the bodies of Harcourt, and the other three, still swinging on gibbets in Rouen, were to be *dépendus publiquement* and buried in consecrated ground. That was not all.

On the wall that surrounded the Abbaye de Saint-Germain, there was a sort of opera box from which royalty was wont to watch the jousts that took place in the Pré-aux-Clercs hard by. From this box Charles le Mauvais addressed ten thousand Parisians from nine to eleven o'clock on the text: "For the righteous Lord loveth righteousness, his countenance doth behold the upright." He harangued on his innocence and unjust imprisonment and, it seems, had his audience with him. He spoke *sagement et bellement,* complained of the wrongs that had been done him, said that nobody should be suspicious of him, for he wished to live and die in defense of the Kingdom of France, and that he would do both well, for he was descended from the royal house on both sides, and argued that if he wanted to claim the crown, it would be found that he was nearer of right than he who was in an English prison, or than the King of England. He said nothing openly against King John or the Dauphin, but insinuated *assez de choses deshonnestes et vilainnes* (many mean and nasty things) concerning them.

The Dauphin was obliged to put up with it all. It was humiliating; but under a meager and uncomely appearance, the Dauphin possessed great political astuteness, long patience and rare foresight; Petrarch called him a young man of great spirit. Before his reign was over, he had proved these qualities to the full; and in spite of his shrewdness and subtle policy, he was not a bad fellow, as you can see in the admirable statue, once at the portal of the Church of the Célestins, and now in the Louvre. But at this time his fortunes were low, and matters were made worse because news came that King John had agreed upon terms of peace, and that meant his return, and if he returned, what would become of Étienne Marcel and of Charles le Mauvais? It happened at this untoward time that a fellow belonging to the faction of Marcel and Navarre, Perrin Marc by name, met the Dauphin's treasurer in the street and dunned him for some payment or other. The treasurer put him off. At this Perrin Marc lost his temper and stabbed the other in the back, then, taking to his heels, sought sanctuary in the church of Saint-Merri near by. The Dauphin, on hearing of the murder of his treasurer, sent an officer, Robert de Clermont, to the church. Clermont had the door broken in and seized the murderer. The next day the murderer's hand was cut off on the spot where he had stabbed his victim, and he was then taken to the Châtelet and hanged. This punishment angered the radicals; and the Bishop of Paris, who inclined to that faction, complained of the breach of the ecclesiastical right of asylum and excommunicated Clermont. The mob was so threatening that the Dauphin was obliged to allow him to cut Marc's body down from the gibbet, and conduct it back with honor to Saint-Merri. That afternoon two funerals were held; the Prévôt des Marchands and a great crowd of burghers followed the bier of Perrin Marc, while the Dauphin and his partizans followed that of the murdered treasurer.

The revolutionary party was becoming savage. And Étienne Marcel was prepared to make use of terror as a political weapon; he said it would be a good thing, if some of those about the Dauphin *should be removed*. Other versions give the credit of the idea to Charles le Mauvais.  There was need of a bold stroke, for rumor persisted that peace would soon be made, King John would return and the plans of Navarre and the radicals go to pot.  On February 22, 1358, the Prévôt des Marchands assembled the guilds of Paris in arms at the priory of Saint-Eloi in the Cité (the island on which Notre-Dame and the King's palace stood), about three thousand men, decked out in parti-colored caps, red and blue, the city's colors.  The story reads for all the world like a passage in the Revolution of 1789; for the people of the Faubourg Saint-Antoine have shown themselves more times than once to be a savage people.  They marched upon the King's palace, just as the Jacobins on June 20, 1792, marched on the Tuileries.  On their way, the revolutionists caught sight of an unpopular official, Regnaut d'Acy; they howled, "Kill him!"  He darted into a pastry-cook's shop, but unluckily for him the shop had no back door.  He perished under innumerable blows.  On to the palace.  The Prévôt with some armed followers mounted the stairs to the Dauphin's apartment.  The Dauphin was in his bedroom with several of his officers, Robert de Clermont, who had violated the sanctuary of Saint-Merri, and was Marshal of Normandy, son to the Marshal of France killed at Poitiers, and Jean de Conflans, Marshal of Champagne, and others.  These two Marshals were thought to oppose the popular movement, and Clermont was said to have spoken very ill of the people, when he was dragging Perrin Marc from Saint-Merri to the Châtelet.  The Prévôt spoke insolently to the Dauphin, bade him look better to the business of the Kingdom and to stop the brigands who were overrunning the country and doing great mischief.  The Dauphin replied that he would gladly stop the brigands if he had the means, but that the task more properly belonged to the man that raised and received the taxes, and that that man could do it if he would. Hot words followed. Marcel said: "Sir, don't be dismayed whatever you may see; for it has been so ordained, and so must be." At that Conflans was murdered on the spot; his blood spattered the Dauphin. Clermont, too, who escaped from the room into a closet, was pursued and murdered. The Dauphin begged to be spared. Marcel clapped a red and blue bonnet on his head, taking the Prince's in exchange, and told him that his life was safe. The two bodies were dragged out into the palace court, while Étienne Marcel harangued the crowd. He said that the murdered men were wicked traitors and that what had been done was for the good of the Kingdom. Then he went back into the palace, told the Dauphin that the Marshals had been put to death by the will of the people in order to prevent something worse, bade him ratify what had taken place, grant full pardon to the murderers and generally do what the people wanted. He then went to his warehouse and sent the Dauphin two bales of cloth, one red, the other blue, to make hoods of the city's colors for his household. The great nobles, too, were obliged to wear those colors.

The Dauphin had made submission, but it was evident that there must be a fight to the finish between the royal authority and the revolutionary pretentions. Outside factors added to the danger of the situation. There were the brigands and freebooters, soldiers disbanded in consequence of the truce between England and France, who went about pillaging at will. To this gentry I must return in a later chapter. Étienne Marcel had used their depredations as an argument that the monarchy, as it stood, was a failure and must be altered. And so, in a manner, the freebooters helped the revolutionary cause. On the other hand there was also *les Jacques,* poor peasants, infuriated by taxation and pillage, who had risen in revolt. They attacked the castles and manor houses of the landed gentry, and committed frightful retaliations. The nobility defeated the Jacques in the field, and in their turn took prodigal vengeance. As the Parisian radicals, or some of them, had made common cause with the revolted peasants, they had still further alienated the conservative classes, and to that extent the rising of the peasants helped the Dauphin against the radicals. At this juncture, Étienne Marcel made a grievous error; Charles le Mauvais was at Saint Denis, the Dauphin was away collecting an army, and Marcel introduced a band of English soldiers, the national enemy, into Paris to strengthen his military power; the citizens would not bear this, and the English had to go, but in a fracas many citizens were killed or wounded. So fortune shifted, until Marcel's only hope seemed to lie in close confederation with Charles le Mauvais; perhaps there was a plot to put Charles on the throne. At any rate, while the warders of the city gates were under the Dauphin's authority, Étienne Marcel made an attempt to admit Charles of Navarre into the city.

On the night of July 31, 1358, certain distinguishing marks were seen on many houses, and, as observation noted, only on the houses of people opposed to Navarre. It was afterward believed that Providence was on guard that night. The next morning Étienne Marcel, attended by some of his partizans, went round to the city gates, asking that the keys be delivered into his own hands. At the Porte Saint Denis, the guards refused. While they were disputing, up came the captain of that city district, Jean Maillart, a man of loyalist sympathies, one of those whose suspicions had been aroused. A violent dispute arose. Maillart said to the Prévôt: "Étienne, what are you doing here?" Marcel answered: "Jean, why do you ask? I am here to take care of the city; it is in my charge." "By God," John answered, "things shall not go on so. You are not here for any good, as I shall show." And turning to those about him, he said, "See how he has tried to get the keys of the gates, in order to betray the city." The Prévôt broke in, "Jean, you lie." Maillart replied, "Étienne, it is you who lie," and mounting his horse, grabbed a royal banner and galloped through the streets, shouting, "Montjoie! Saint Denis! For the King! For the Dauphin!" The loyalists, who seem to have been forewarned, gathered in troops and hurried to the Porte Saint-Antoine, where the Prévôt had already arrived, demanding the keys. The loyalists ordered him to cry, "Montjoie! For the King and the Dauphin!" Marcel refused, but seeing his danger, changed about and cried, "Montjoie! Hurrah for the King and the Dauphin!" It was too late. Accusation and passionate words were interchanged. Some one cried out, "This Prévôt has betrayed us!" All was soon over. Étienne Marcel and one or two more lay dead.

The Dauphin entered Paris and showed a wise clemency. Charles le Mauvais withdrew, and soon there was open war between him and the Dauphin.

Such was the state of France as the result of the Prince of Wales' victory at Poitiers. Only a prophet could have guessed that, within a dozen years, Fortune would turn her wheel so far as to roll the English down and the French up.

# CHAPTER XVIII

THE Prince of Wales was a gay and gallant fighter, but he was also a good fellow and liked pleasure. On his return to England from his great victory he was twenty-six and might well have been intoxicated by the praise and admiration of England. The Herald Chandos says that he and his comrades were escorted to London by more than twenty earls, that they were greatly fêted by the ladies, and that there never was (so might God gladden his heart) such rejoicing as was made at that time. Besides the King and Queen who held him very dear, there was many a dame, many a damsel, *très amoureuse,* lively and beautiful; there was dancing, and hunting, and hawking; there were banquets and tournaments, as in the time of King Arthur. And in those days it was not the fashion for a prince to be a Puritan. When he was a lad of eighteen, he presented a pony, named Lyard Hobin, "to his own little son Edward"; and now two other sons make their appearance. One, whose mother is said to have been Edith de Willesford, was destined to become Sir John Sounder and to be honorably mentioned by Froissart; and the other, to become Sir Roger de Clarendon, to receive a silk bed by bequest from the Prince, and, under suspicion of treason, to be executed by command of his cousin, Henry IV. There is no other evidence that the Prince trod the primrose path, and the only woman who seems to have been of consequence in his life was the lady who became his wife. He and his cousin Jeannette had been babies together in the care

169

of Queen Philippa, and when Jeannette grew to womanhood, they seem to have remained good friends, for when he was eighteen and she twenty, he gave her an ornamented silver beaker, though at that time she was already married, but whether to Sir Thomas Holland or to William Montague, the Pope had not then, I think, definitely decided. Had she not been married, it seems likely that there would have been no Sir John Sounder nor Sir Roger Clarendon.

The Prince's principal princely quality, after his valor, was his extravagance. As I have said, his budget was never balanced, he was always in debt. He always was in need of money, and never thought of the peasants and artizans who produced the means for his princely generosity; nobody did. I mean nobody in attendance upon the court, for William Langland, a Shropshire lad, was, indeed, already meditating the *Vision of Piers Plowman,* but the Prince of Wales and his friends were not aware of it. Business did not interest him. His principalities, baronies, estates were, as with almost all the rich people of the time, merely sources of income. Even Queen Philippa, whom everybody praises, after begging mercy for the six burgesses of Calais, accepted the confiscated houses of John Daire, the second of the six. Business was business. Stewards, bailiffs, keepers and such, took charge of the Prince's estates. Sir John Wingfield, to whose letters I have referred, was one of the chief of these. I will show you a sample of their business administration:

"London, February 18. Order to R. de Eleford, steward and sheriff of Cornewaille (1) with reference to the ship which is arrested at Plummuth according to his certificate to the Prince's council, to join with the Prince's havener there in disposing of it as shall seem most profitable to the Prince; and (2) with reference to the wines of prise which are not sold, to join with the havener in putting them in cellar and marking them to be kept safely, so that they be not moved until further order."

"London, March 8. Order to Robert de Eleford, steward and sheriff of Cornewaille,—notwithstanding the Prince's late order that all his wines of prise in Cornewaille be kept safely until further order,—to join with the Prince's havener in selling the said wines, as the Prince has learned that wines in those parts are now dearer than they were, to wit, 10 marks the tun.

"By advice and ordinance of Sir John de Wengefeld."

"London, March 28. Order to Thomas Fitz Henry, havener of Cornewaille,—notwithstanding his report that the Prince's wines of prise could not now be sold at 10 marks the piece (as the Prince, when he lately ordered them to be sold, was given to understand that they could), since wines are now much cheaper in the parts of Cornewaille than they were,—to sell the said wines quickly at as high a price, and in as profitable a manner, as possible.

"By advice and command of Sir John de Wengefeld."

The entries that bear the subscription of the Prince's personal attention almost always, I think, concern his own generosity. For example:

"1359 January 1, Berkhampstead Castle. Order to John Dabernoun, steward of Cornewaille, to deliver to the Prince's clerk, Sir Thomas de Madefrei, as a gift from the Prince, twelve dry and leafless oaks in the Prince's wood of Coispost for fuel during his stay at his prebend of Penryn. And whereas Sir Thomas has given the Prince to understand that there is a great lack of laborers and workmen at his said prebend, the steward is to help him as far as possible to get such and as many laborers and workmen as he needs, paying them suitably for their labour in accordance with the statute of labourers. And whereas Sir Thomas has also given the Prince to understand that there are many debts still due there to the Prince's clerk, Sir John de Gippeswiz, deceased, the steward is to give assistance in every possible way so that the said debts may be levied speedly and paid to Sir Thomas.

"By command of the Prince himself."

"London, June 5, 1359. Order to John Dabernon, steward of Cornewaille,—in pursuance of an inquisition taken before him showing that the parsons of the church of Stoke in Clymeslond, time out of mind and without interruption, have been in possession, as in right of their church, of the right to take 'housbote,' 'haybote' and 'firbote' in the Prince's woods outside the Park of Clymeslond by view and livery of the Prince's ministers of the manor there; and that they never have been in possession of tithes of the agistment in the said park, but were in possession, in name of the said tithes, of the right to have ten oxen at pasture in the said park every year from the feast of the Holy Cross until St. Peter's Chains, and always had that right without interruption until the time when Peter de Brompton and Richard de Wolveston were parsons of the church; and that they have always been in possession of the tithe of honey produced in the said park and the Prince's foreign woods there,—to allow the said parsons henceforth to have the aforesaid rights in accordance with the finding of the inquisition, unless he has good information favourable to the Prince and contradictory to the inquisition.

"By the inquisition endorsed and by command of the Prince."

"London, July 30. Order to the Prince's bachelor, Sir John de Sully, keeper of the Prince's game in the parts of Cornewaille and Devenshire, or his lieutenant to deliver to Sir John de Cheveneston, Sir Edward Sauvage, Master John de Stretely and William de Wakefield four bucks of grease each, to be taken from such places in his bailiwick as he considers best for the preservation of the Prince's game.

"By command of the Prince himself."

"Byfleet, June 30, 1361. Grant and commitment for life to Nicholas Pego, yeoman of the Prince's chamber, in consideration of his past and future good service, of the offices of controller of the Prince's prises of wines, 'wrek' of sea, and 'coket,' and clerk of the statute, in the duchy of Cornewaille, with 3d a day by the hands of the Prince's receiver of Cornewaille for the said office of controller. Grant to him, also, for life, of the office of bailiff of Blackmore, in the said duchy, free of rent to the Prince or his heirs.

"By command of the Prince himself."

"Be it remembered that on sixteenth of February, John de Kendale, constable of Rostormel and keeper of the park there, was ordered to deliver to Serle de Cornewaille, who has decided to lead a hermit's life, two oaks fit for timber in the said park for the building of a hermitage at the end of the town of Bodmyn."

His generosity is the more marked because he was always pinched for money. You find in his registers such entries as these:

"Order to John de Kendale, receiver of Cornewaille, to be at London at the quinzaine of Martinmas with all the moneys of the issues of his bailiwick which he has in hand or can quickly raise, and with full information on all matters concerning his bailiwick; as the Prince wishes to have full personal knowledge of the state of all his affairs."

"Be it remembered that on twenty-third of May a letter was made out to John de Kendale, receiver of Cornewaille, ordering him to send to Sir Peter de Lacy, the Prince's receiver-general in London, all the moneys of the issues of his bailiwick which he has in hand or can in any way lay hands on quickly."

The phrase "at as small a cost as possible" is the usual concomitant to orders of building or repairs.

As to his social relations we do not know very much. Toward his father, Geoffrey Baker speaks of him as *piissimus*, most dutiful, and all the evidence bears this out; he was always exceedingly careful never to infringe upon his father's authority. As his mother was in every way worthy of his affection, it is likely that he was also *piissimus* toward her; the Prince's register for 1348-49 shows several gifts to her. As to his sisters, Isabella and Joan, we know nothing of their mutual relations apart from his presents to them. His next brother, Lionel, who lived to man's estate and became Duke of Clarence, left little trace in the Prince's life. He was eight years younger, and married Elizabeth, daughter to the Earl of Clare and

Ulster, a marriage that is of interest, because by the time the Black Prince came back from Bordeaux after the battle of Poitiers, there was in Lionel's household, attendant upon his wife, a young man of eighteen or nineteen perhaps, the son of a London vintner, Geoffrey Chaucer. Lady Elizabeth was present at Windsor at the celebration of the Feast of Saint George, in 1358, and also at Woodstock for the Feast of Pentecost, and also at the funeral of the Queen Dowager Isabella at London. On all these occasions Chaucer must have seen the Black Prince, even if the Black Prince did not take much notice of him. Perhaps, too, the Black Prince saw him later, in the campaign of 1359, when the three princes, he, Lionel and John of Gaunt, accompanied King Edward, and Chaucer was also there serving as a soldier. Chaucer was taken prisoner, and King Edward paid, perhaps for Lionel's sake, or John's, a ransom of sixteen pounds, a sum said to be equal to eight hundred dollars to-day. The Prince's brother John, known from his birthplace as John of Gaunt (Ghent), was ten years younger than the Prince. One associates him with King Edward's political ambitions in Flanders, for Jacques van Artevelde was his godfather and held him at the font; John's nurse, Isolda Newman, like the Black Prince's, received ten pounds a year. He went on the Prince's ship for the battle of Espagnols-sur-Mer. Again we hear of him, at seventeen, spending Christmas at Hatfield in Yorkshire with Lionel; and it seems that then the friendship between him and Chaucer began. The Prince of Wales may have been there, too. John seems to have had a taste for literature, absent in his great brother.

At nineteen he married Blanche, younger daughter to Henry of Lancaster, a lovely lady. In his poem, *Boke of the Duchesse,*

Chaucer makes John describe how he first saw his bride:

> Hit happed that I come on a deye
> Into a place, ther that I seye
> Trewely the fayrest companye
> Of ladyes, that ever man with eye
> Hadde sene togedres in oo place.
>
> Amonge these ladyes thus echone,
> Sothe to seyne, I saugh oone
> That was lyke noon of the route;
> For I dar swere, withoute doute,
> That as the sommerys sunne bryghte
> Is fayrer, clever, and hathe more lyghte
> Than any other planete in hevene,
> The moone, or the sterres seven;
> For al the worlde, so hadde she
> Surmounted hem alle of beaute,
> Of manner, and of comelynhess,
> Of stature, and of wel sette gladness;
> Of godleyhede, and so wel beseye;
> Shortely what shal I seye?
> By God, and by his halwes twelve,
> Hyt was my swete, ryghte al hir selve,
> She hadde so stedfaste countenance,
> So noble porte and meyntenaunce.
> And Love, that hadde wel herde my boone,
> Had espyed me thus soone,
> That she ful sone, in my thoughte,
> As helpe me God, so was I kaughte
> So sodeynly, that I ne toke
> No manere counseyl, but at hir loke,
> And at myn herte.

The wedding was celebrated on May 29, 1359, in Reading and was followed by three days of jousts at Reading, and three more at London, under the auspices of the City. Twenty-four knights wearing the heraldic arms of the City entered the lists, and, to the delight of the citizens, they proved to be the

King, his sons, Edward, Lionel, John and Edmund, and nineteen other gentlemen. It is pleasant to think that the Black Prince's sister-in-law was so charming, debonair, good and glad, and also able to dance in comely fashion and to sing sweetly. One may feel confidence in Chaucer's eulogy of Lady Blanche, for Queen Philippa makes one sure that, with herself as a model—"decked and adorned with all noble virtues, and beloved by God and man"—the sons would choose admirable wives. It was not until after the Queen's death that the old King became infatuated with Alice Perrers, and not until after Lady Blanche's that John of Gaunt fell in love with his children's governess.

On his father-in-law's death John of Gaunt became Duke of Lancaster, and very rich. Part of his inheritance was the Savoy, the finest palace in London, where King John was lodged for a time, and where the Duke entertained the Kings of Denmark, Scotland and Cyprus. The Prince himself, on his return from Calais, when in London, lived in Pulteney House, sometimes called the Manor of the Rose, in or near Candlewick Street, in the parish of Saint Lawrence Pountney, which had been built by Sir John Poulteney. It was called, I think, The Manor of the Rose because Sir John had rented it for the rent of a rose to be paid in midsummer. The Prince hired it from the estate. It was a handsome mansion, with grounds extending to the Thames, where the Prince kept a goodly number of swans. He was obliged to give it up in 1359, because Sir John's widow was going to marry Sir Nicholas Loveyne and wished to live there; so the Prince stored his furniture in his *garderobe* for a time. After that, perhaps, he moved to Fish Street where he had "a great house, for the most part built of stone." But probably he liked the country better. In addititon to the Castle of Berkhamstead, which lay on the eastern slope of the Chiltern Hills, in Buckinghamshire, he had a country place at Wallingford, on a pleasant stretch of the silvery Thames, another at Northbourne, near Sandwich, another at Byfleet, and also Kennington Manor just out of London.

Another young man, of about Chaucer's age, who did far more than anybody else to preserve for us a record of the Prince's exploits, Jean Froissart, must certainly have been known to the Prince. He was a fellow countryman of Queen Philippa, and came, as she did, from Valenciennes. He followed her to England in 1361, and presented her with a poem he had written on the battle of Poitiers, and stayed in attendance upon the court for five years. A man like Froissart, who buttonholed every man of distinction, must have hovered about the Prince when he could. He also saw him later at Bordeaux at the beginning of the Spanish campaign. Froissart was already a poet, and his youthful poems, *Paradys d'Amours, L'Espinette amoureuse Li Orloge amoureux,* if not works of genius, give a romantic, a charming, idea of young society at Valenciennes and at Queen Philippa's court. It has a touch of Victorian propriety, that would have made a young Tennyson feel quite at home there. There is an innocence, as of apple blossoms and fringed gentians, in his *Espinette amoureuse:*

> *Et quant on me mist à l'escole,*
> *Où les ignorons on escole,*
> *Il y avait des pucelettes*
> *Qui de mon temps erent jonettes;*
> *Et je, qui estoie puceaus,*
> *Je les servoie d'espinceaus,*
> *Ou d'une pomme, ou d'une poire,*
> *Ou d'un seul anelet de voire.*

And when I was first put to school,
Where they teach each little fool,
There were pretty maidens there,
Young as I, and very fair;
And I, a youthful hobbledehoy,
In fealty offered them some toy,
A pin, pear, apple, trifling thing
Or perhaps a beaded ring.

And then came the episode of the garden party where She, aged
fifteen, picked five violets, gave him three, and kept two for
herself. Or, when a little older, he continued, and more fer-
vently, to do homage to love!

> *Mieuls ne poet employer le tems*
> *Homs, ce m'est vis, qu'au bien amer;*
> *Car qui voelt son coer entamer*
> *En bons mours et en nobles teches,*
> *En tous membres de gentilleces,*
> *Amours est la droite racine.*

It is impossible, he says, to do better than to be in love, and
more than half anticipates Tennysonian ideas that there is no
more

                    Subtle master under heaven
Than is the maiden passion for a maid,
Not only to keep down the base in man,
But teach high thoughts, and amiable words
And courtliness, and the desire for fame,
And love of truth, and all that makes a man.

In fact, *mutatis mutandis,* one perceives a similarity of ideas,
standards, usages and social dogmas in Philippa and Queen
Victoria.

The Black Prince also certainly knew the famous William
of Wykeham, who was appointed Surveyor of the King's works

at the Castle and Park at Windsor on October 30, 1356. Even then the King recognized Wykeham's great abilities; for it is said that he was persuaded by Wykeham to pull down a great part of Windsor Castle and rebuild it. Wykeham's patent gave him authority to impress, like a crimp, all sorts of workmen, and they were not allowed to leave Windsor without his permission. For salary he received a shilling a day while at Windsor, and two when he went elsewhere. In 1359 he was made Chief Warden and Surveyor of the Castles of Windsor, Leeds, Dover and Hadlam. He was at Calais in 1360, where he was one of the witnesses to the Treaty of Bretigny. By this time Wykeham stood high in the King's favor, and rewards began to be showered upon him. A common method of rewarding faithful services to the monarch was to bestow ecclesiastical appointments, especially at this time, when the plague had swept away many clerks. Wykeham did not become even a subdeacon till 1361, nor priest till 1362, but he had taken the elementary orders and wore a tonsure, and was able to accept prebends. In 1360 he was made Dean of Saint Martin le Grand in London, perhaps in recognition of his services at Calais. In 1361 he received the following prebends, two-thirds of them from the King; July twelfth, in the Church of Hereford; July sixteenth, in the Collegiate Church of Abergwilly and in that of Llandewy Breys, both in Saint David's diocese; July twenty-fourth, in the Collegiate Church of Bromyard, in the diocese of Hereford; August sixteenth, the prebend of Yatmonster Overbury in the Church of Salisbury; October first, that of Oxgate in the Cathedral of Saint Paul's, London; October ninth, of Bedminster and Ratcliff in the Church of Salisbury; October fifteenth, that of Totenhall in the Church of Saint Paul, London. In 1363 he became Warden

and Justiciary of the King's forests this side Trent; in 1364,
Keeper of the Privy Seal and Bishop of Winchester; in short,
as Froissart says: "Wykeham was so much in favor with the
King of England that everything was done by him and nothing
without him." But by that time the Black Prince was in his
principality of Aquitaine. Richard, the Black Prince's son, said
that his father had a great affection for Wykeham.

The remaining great figure of that epoch, John Wyclif, was
Master of Balliol about 1360, studying philosophy and theology,
and did not enter the service of the crown till 1372, and could
hardly have met the Black Prince till after that. Wyclif
certainly did not belong to those joyous days between the battle
of Poitiers and the recurrence of the plague in 1361, when the
French prisoners added to the general gaiety: the King, four
royal French dukes and a great retinue of counts, barons,
knights, squires, and distinguished burgesses, sent as hostages
from the chief cities of France. These prisoners, at least the
nobles, were given great liberty; they went hunting and hawking
and took part in all the gaieties. "I could not tell nor recount
[Froissart says], no, not in a whole day's talk, those noble
dinners and suppers and feasts, those joyous meetings, those
gifts and guerdons and jewels that were freely given." Those
were the happy days when the Prince was still young and well,
at the height of his renown, universally admired and beloved,
as he deserved to be. The Herald Chandos says: "From the
day of his birth this noble Prince cherished no thought but
loyalty, nobleness, valor and goodness; all the days of his life
he set his whole intent on maintaining justice and right; gaiety
and nobleness were in his heart from boyhood; his bounty
came from his generous and noble disposition; he was noble,
bold, valiant, so courteous, so wise and very religious minded."

As you see *noble* is the adjective that stands out, like the ostrich plumes that tradition says he got on the field of Crécy.

*Noblement il usa son tamps*

Nobly he used his time.

Indeed the Herald is right to say that "in his person Chivalry was nurtured." Wherever he went there was "gaiety, noblesse, courtesy, goodness and largesse."

# CHAPTER XIX

KING JOHN fared well in his captivity. In the later years, after war had broken out again, he was kept more strictly at some inland stronghold, Hertford, or Somerton, and, for a time, in the Tower of London. But in the earlier days he lived at Windsor. The French lords, prisoners likewise, were free to keep him company. He attended the tournaments and great festivities. He had an excellent table, and received wines and dainties from France. He was fond of music, and kept minstrels. He was amused by cock-fighting, and kept fighting cocks. He is said to have been delighted with a portable watch. He read romances, consulted his astrologer and jested with his fool. He took a personal interest in the health and welfare of his servants, paid their doctor's bills, their apothecary bills; and, being of a kindly disposition, he liked to give money away. But his allowance from France was limited, so he tried to eke it out; he imported wine from Languedoc and sold it, and he also sold horses. But he was thoroughly bored and tried to come to terms with Edward.

One of the great difficulties in the way of a treaty of peace was that there was no stable government in France to make one. The Dauphin was acting as regent, but even after the death of Étienne Marcel, his rod of authority was very fragile; no considerable body of people was ready to obey him. Charles of Navarre had openly defied him. In Brittany and Normandy, the adherents of England had as much or more power than he. Roundabout Paris and almost everywhere the freebooters wandered here and there, pillaging and destroying, until, as one reads the chronicles, it seems as if all trace of organized government had disappeared. However, King John was tired of imprisonment, he was homesick, and bored by his limited diversions, and wished to be King again; so he came to terms with King Edward, that is, he was ready to accept King Edward's conditions. Edward demanded all the western half of France from the Channel to the Pyrenees, and an enormous sum of money (March, 1359). One must remember that on the east France extended only to the Meuse and the Rhone; beyond those rivers lay the Holy Roman Empire. But the *États Généraux* rejected the treaty; they said that, rather than diminish and defraud the noble Kingdom of France, they were ready to endure to the utmost, and so they resolved to wage war stoutly against the English.

King Edward had not expected his terms to be accepted. He had already begun preparations for a renewal of hostilities on the expiration of the truce, and now he hurried them on. He intended to strike a decided blow; he would be crowned King of France at Rheims, and enforce his will. The armament and its equipment were to be admirably adequate. As he could not expect to find in the ravaged and devastated provinces of France the various materials he would need, let alone comforts and luxuries, he took an enormous quantity of artizans as well as of supplies. Carpenters, masons, mechanics, workmen of many kinds, were called out. Mills were taken to grind corn, ovens to bake bread, forges for blacksmiths, little collapsible boats, made of leather, large enough to hold three men, for catching fish, and an incredible number of carts and horses to drag all this. He also took thirty falconers with their hawks and their horses, sixty couples of hunting dogs, and sixty couples of greyhounds for coursing. He did not expect much opposition in the field, and wished to be able to drive dull care away.

The truce agreed upon at Bordeaux, was to end on April eighteenth, and though Sir Walter Manny had gone to France to negotiate an extension, the preparations were not relaxed. The Prince of Wales did his share, ordering bows, bowstrings, sheaves of arrows to be got ready and shipped by sea from Cornwall to Sandwich. An entry in his register shows that Henry Skuryn, Master of the Ship, *Le Seinte Maribot* of Fowey, made such a trip, carrying victuals, for one hundred shillings. All the noblemen, all the sheriffs and other county officers, were likewise collecting supplies as well as men-at-arms, archers, hobilars and spearmen. Also mercenary adventurers of all sorts from the states of Germany and the Low Countries flocked to Calais to meet the King on his arrival. The truce was extended until June twenty-fifth, but it ended then.

On the morning of October 28, 1359, the great expedition sailed from Sandwich and arrived at Calais that evening. Europe rang with stories of England's might. The Florentine, Matteo Villani, said that the army exceeded one hundred thousand men. The King's four sons were there, and all the flower of English chivalry. But the wary Dauphin would not, or could not, attempt to stop the invaders; he had read the lessons of Crécy and Poitiers aright. King Edward marched south from Calais, through Artois, Picardie and Champagne to Rheims, where he hoped to be anointed King of France; but the walls of the city were too strong to be carried by assault, and the country roundabout had been too much ravaged to support a great army during a long siege. Besides bad weather interfered with military operations. So the English King marched on, making a great red welt across the northeast provinces, very much as the Black Prince had done in Languedoc. On he went, down past Bar-le-Duc and Troyes, into Burgundy where he took two towns by assault. He had to secure some plunder for his troops, especially for the mercenaries. The Duke of Burgundy, in alarm, bought immunity for the rest of his dukedom with a great sum of money. Then the English marched north to Paris. The Dauphin burned the suburbs to deprive the enemy of provisions, and Sir Walter Manny, riding up to the city gates, rode over devastated fields. Petrarch, who saw it soon afterward, says: "Even the neighborhood of Paris manifests everywhere marks of destruction and conflagration. The streets are deserted; the roads overgrown with weeds; the whole is a vast solitude." The Dauphin refused to give battle, but he was ready to treat seriously of peace; the country was in sore need, with the power of England threatening to lay waste the valley of the Loire, and Charles le Mauvais making cruel war in Normandy. Indeed, as Froissart says, "the whole noble kingdom was so grievously oppressed it did not know which way to turn."

At last, however, King Edward modified his pretensions; he had declared that he would conquer the whole kingdom, but he had not had much luck. Rheims he could not take, Paris he could not take, the Dauphin would not meet him on the field; the good understanding between France and Scotland was disquieting, and French ships had raided some of the Channel ports, the risks, possibly, were not all on one side. And then happened what appeared to be a portent. "A storm of thunder and hail descended upon the English army, as if the world was coming to an end, hailstones fell so large as to kill men

and beasts, the boldest were frightened." All the chroniclers
agree on the fierceness of the storm; "Man's nature could not
carry the affliction nor the fear." The weak perished, horses
and men. Carts and baggage were abandoned. Old men could
not remember, of themselves, or from tales told to them, of
such wind and storm and cold. For a long time that Black
Monday was remembered. There was something in it more
than natural. Many of the soldiers doubtless had heard their
parish priests discourse on prophecies that foretold how the end
of the world was coming soon, how Isidore of Seville, that
most learned man, had made the computation based upon Holy
Writ, how Abbot Joachim of Calabria (whom Dante said was
endowed with prophetic gifts) had made similar predictions.
King Edward, himself, felt that it was eerie. He was then at
the little town of Bretigny, near Chartres. He went on a
pilgrimage to the great cathedral of Notre-Dame, all glorious
with statues and glass, to the sacred image of the Virgin and
vowed that he would make peace. And, accordingly, the Treaty
of Bretigny was signed on the eighth of May, 1360; of which
the substance was that King Edward abandoned his claim to the
crown of France and King John ceded to him, in absolute
sovereignty, the whole region from a little south of the River
Loire to the Pyrenees, including Poitou, the Limousin, Périgord,
Quercy, the Rouergue, Guienne and Gascony, in all nearly a
third of the Kingdom, and to pay three million crowns in gold.

# CHAPTER XX

## MARRIAGE

THE treaty made, King Edward and the Black Prince went back to England. The meeting with King John was very friendly. King Edward now gave him the title of King of France, and said, *"Beau frère de France, moy et vous* [the putting *moy* before *vous* may be attributed to the fact that they were in England] *sommes, la mercy Dieu, en bon accort."* They kissed and did each other obeisance and made most affectionate mutual demonstrations. The ransom was to be paid by instalments, delivery of cities and castles should be made as soon as might be, King John should be released, and the multitudinous company of hostages, chief of them John's younger sons, Louis Duc d'Anjou, Jean Duc de Berry, and Philippe (afterward Duc de Bourgogne) and his brother the Duc d'Orléans, were to be surrendered to the English in John's stead till all obligations had been fulfilled. King Edward and the Prince of Wales accompanied their royal guest to Calais, where the exchanges were to be made. At Calais there were more banquets and entertainments and also more reconciliations. These reconciliations were accomplished, at least as far as words went, in accordance with that chivalric etiquette which the two Kings and the Prince of Wales delighted to observe. King John was dining with King Edward. John asked a boon. Edward replied: "Beau Frère, there is nothing that I would deny you, saving my honor and my realm." John replied, "What I am asking does not touch those." King Edward said: *"Beau*

*Frère, je le vous donne."* John then asked that Edward be reconciled with Louis, Count of Flanders, the gallant, who, after a formal betrothal, had run away from marriage with Edward's daughter Isabel. The next day King Edward dined with King John, together with the Prince of Wales and the royal princes of France. Edward said: *"Beau Frère de France, il faut que vous me donnes ung don,* and I ask it of you." John replied: *"Beau Frère,* say it." Edward asked that he be reconciled with Philippe de Navarre, brother to Charles le Mauvais. King John answered: *"Beau Frère, pour l'amour de vous je le veux."* So Philippe was brought up, and Edward presented him to John, *"Beau Frère,* I give you the most loyal gentleman that ever crossed the sea to come to my court." These hypocrisies accomplished, and part of the first instalment of ransom paid, and the hostages delivered up, and after a last grand dinner, *un moult grand souper et bien ordonné,* King John left Calais on October 25, 1360, a free man. He started, on foot as a pilgrim, to render thanks to Our Lady of Boulogne, so the Prince of Wales, and his two brothers, Lionel and John, also went, out of courtesy and piety blended. At Boulogne the Dauphin met them; they all repaired to the church, made their offerings, and then went to the abbey for the night. The Prince of Wales returned to Calais the next day, and on the vigil of All Saints (October thirtieth) he and his brothers sailed for England, taking with them the French hostages.

One of the English commissioners appointed by King Edward to help in the transfer of certain places under the treaty was Sir Thomas Holland, husband of the Fair Maid of Kent. He was taken ill at Rouen and died on December twenty-eighth, and his body was buried in the Franciscan Church there. His widow, now thirty-two years old, was not only beautiful, but also one of the richest ladies in England. Everybody was agreed that she was *une dame de grant pris qe bele fuist plesante et sage*. You remember that she was a cousin of the Prince of Wales, and that they had always been good friends; he had stood as godfather to her eldest son Thomas. Her earlier history is not well known. She was extremely pretty, so very pretty, that when she was over fifty and had been taken prisoner by the Kentish rebels in her son's time, Richard II, they set her free for the ransom of a few kisses. She was also probably a great flirt. When a girl in her teens, she was betrothed to Holland and they regarded themselves as married, without waiting for the formal solemnization of a full wedding ceremony. It was probably a war marriage, just before he went off on the Crécy campaign. There he distinguished himself; at Caen he took prisoner the Constable of France, the Comte d'Eu, for whom (it is said) King Edward gave him eighty thousand florins. While he was away, young Montague appeared upon the scene, and she betrothed herself to him. At any rate, when the matter came into the ecclesiastical courts, and was submitted to the Pope, Clement VI, he decided in favor of the marriage *de facto* (November 13, 1349), and there is no memory of any criticism passed upon the lady. Sir Thomas Holland, now Earl of Kent, held honorable offices in the English possessions in Brittany, Poitou and Normandy, and his wife seems always to have accompanied him. They had three children.

The widow, as I say, was a great catch, and, as in those martial days there was little time for the more delicate hesitations and diffidences of life, suitors very soon gathered round. Many gentlemen, knowing that she and the Prince were not only cousins but good friends, went to him and asked him to say a few words to her in their favor. The most importunate of these was Lord Brocas, a very gallant nobleman of high rank, who had served the Prince well both in war and peace. The Prince, accordingly, accepted the commission and went to see the Countess of Kent several times on the suitor's behalf. The chronicler states that he went very willingly; for which, apart from the commission, there were reasons enough. First, she was his cousin; second, he took notice of her very great beauty and of her gracious manner that pleased him wonderfully well; and third, the time passed agreeably. On one occasion, when the Prince was speaking to her of the said gentleman, she answered that she should never marry again. She was *moult soubtille et sage* and repeated this to the Prince several times. The Prince replied, "Heigh ho! *Belle Cousine,* in case you do not wish to marry any of my friends, the great beauties, of which you are compact, will be wasted. If you and I were not of common kin, there is no lady under heaven whom I should hold so dear as you." And the Prince was taken unawares by love for the Countess. And then, like the subtle woman, and skilful in ambush, that she was, the Countess began to cry. Then the Prince tried to comfort her; he kissed her very often, and felt great tenderness for her tears, and said to her: *"Belle Cousine,* I have a message for you from one of the gallant gentlemen of England, and he is besides a very charming man." The Countess answered, still weeping: "Ah, Sire, for God's sake forbear to speak of such things to me. I have made up my mind not to marry again; for I have given my heart to the most gallant gentleman under the firmament, and for love of him, I shall have no husband but God, so long as I live. It is impossible that I should marry him. So, for love of him, I wish to shun the company of men. I am resolved never to marry."

The Prince was very desirous to know who was the most gallant gentleman in the world, and begged the Countess insistently to tell him who it was.  But the Countess the more she saw his eagerness, the more she besought him not to inquire further; and, falling on her knees, said to him: "My very dear Lord, for God's sake, and for His mother's, the sweet Virgin, please forbear." The Prince answered that, if she did not tell him who was the most gallant gentleman in the world, he would be her deadly enemy.  Then the Lady said to him: "Very dear and redoubtable Lord, it is you, and for love of you no gentleman shall lie beside me." The Prince, who was then all on fire with love for her, said: "Lady, I swear to God, that as long as I live, no other woman shall be my wife." And soon they were betrothed.  A story went about that King Edward was greatly displeased, for the Prince might have looked much higher, for no emperor, king or prince under heaven but would have had great joy to marry his daughter to the Prince of Wales.  It may be that King Edward thought that a prince's wife should be chosen from considerations of political expediency; he had once proposed to Philip VI, when the Prince was one year old, to make a match between him and Philip's daughter, and again, when the Prince was nine, he had proposed to the Duke of Brabant to marry him to the Duke's daughter, but now the Prince was a grown man, famous throughout Christendom, and it is not likely that the King opposed the marriage.  He might have done so effectively, for a dispensation from the Pope was necessary as the young people were cousins, and an objection from the King would surely have been listened to.

Joshua Barnes, the romantic-minded historian of Charles II's time, says: "A glorious torch of Hymen lighted up at court this year.  He who was all along unconquerable in war, laid aside now his Lion's skin, and began to be softened with the warm fires of love." The object of his affection was "that incomparable paragon of beauty," the Fair Countess of Kent. "He, the glory of his sex for military performances and other princely virtues, and She, the flower of hers for a discreet and honorable mind, sweetened with all the delicacies of a most surprising beauty," and so forth. But traditions of this sort are not to be lightly disregarded, especially in the absence of any conflicting evidence. The only criticism that I have come upon is that she was extravagant, but it seems likely that it was her husband who was to blame for that. Barnes also says, and I believe he was right, that the Prince easily got his father's consent. The espousals took place on October sixth, in the presence, among others, of Sir James Audeley and Sir Nicholas de Loveyne, the gentleman then living at Pulteney Manor on the Thames, and the wedding, celebrated by the Archbishop of Canterbury, on October tenth. And the royal family came to the Prince's castle at Berkhamstead for Christmastide. Froissart was there, too. The marriage was a great success; it is reported by the Herald of Chandos that he loved her *durement*, very tenderly as we would say, and that was natural, for he was a charming, well-bred person, *tant fuist gentils*.

Political considerations determined that they should live in Aquitaine. The Treaty of Bretigny had provided that great strips of France, with cities, villages and castles, should be delivered up to the English, but the Kings had not consulted the inhabitants of those places, and many of them were loath to change their allegiance. The able, moderate and vigorous Sir John Chandos, who was one of the English commissioners appointed to receive keys and so on, met with difficulties, hesitation, delays, fobbings off; he said, *"ces choses lui semblaient*

*bien étranges* [he found their behavior very extraordinary]."
He complained because they made him *"tant muser en oisiveté*
[stay about kicking his heels]"; however he slowly progressed,
going from city to city. But there was so much discontent and
unrest that it seemed wise to make the Prince of Wales what we
should call Governor-General of Aquitaine. So he went, as the
poet says, to Gascony *"pour prendre la possession de sa terre et
de son pais* [to take possession of his duchy]," and with him
went his wife. They landed at La Rochelle, where they stayed
a few days. Sir John Chandos, who had been acting as governor in the Prince's absence, rode up from Niort to greet them
with a troop of knights and squires, and showed the greatest
hospitality, I presume at the expense of the city. From La
Rochelle the Prince and Princess proceeded to Poitiers and
thence to Bordeaux.

Sir John Chandos and the Earl of Warwick were to be his
chief advisers. The task of taking the new oath of allegiance
began in the Cathedral of Saint-André at Bordeaux. Each
vassal came up before the Prince, knelt bareheaded, put his
joined hands between the Prince's hands and declared himself
his man and King Edward's man; the Prince then gave him the
kiss of peace upon his mouth and lifted him up. After he had
received the homages to be rendered in Bordeaux, the Prince
made the circuit of his dominions, Bergerac, Périgueux, Angoulême, Cognac, Saintes, Saint-Jean d'Angély, La Rochelle,
Niort, Saint-Maixent, Poitiers and Agen. This journey lasted
from August, 1363, to April, 1364. In all he received homage
from ten hundred and forty-six vassals. That was the easiest
part of his duties, although a number of vassals annexed conditions to their allegiance. After that his personal business, in
the main, was to superintend the working of the government.

It does not appear that he did this with much success, nor with much show of interest. Complainants wrote to London of wrongdoings by seneschals, bailiffs and other officials, they alleged that these officials laid burdens on them *countre droit et raisoun et custume de paiis*. King Edward was obliged to look into some of these matters himself, and, among other measures of redress, he finally established a new court of last resort, *Curia superioritatis Aquitaniae*.

As for the Prince's revenues and expenses, his budget was never balanced. You might as well have asked Achilles to do such a mercantile thing. Unfortunately, as I have said, the Prince and the Princess were very extravagant. Their retinue was very large: chaplains, clerks of the counting house, gentlemen-in-waiting, squires, pages, varlets, hawkers, huntsmen, maîtres-d'hôtel and so forth; and they squandered a great deal of money on furnishings, trappings and personal apparel. There were cloths of velvet, cloths of gold, damasks, fabrics domestic, fabrics foreign. The Princess affected delicately woven stuffs of iridescent hues and wore most sumptuous gowns not merely at fêtes and ceremonies, but at home and on the street. For instance, she introduced a new fashion of a bodice embroidered with ermine, and there was some criticism, I believe, of the cut below the neck. She delighted in silken girdles, decorated with gold and enamel; in furs; in veils of linen or silk, fetched from Lyons, Aleppo or Alexandria; in great head-dresses glowing with pearls. Then there were the expenses of hunting parties, of tournaments, of traveling from place to place and so on. A prophetic economist could have foretold that these courses would create a larger and larger deficit, followed by attempts to fill the deficit by the imposition of new taxes, and, following the taxes, a popular discontent that might prove disastrous. And another

cause of discontent among the nobles of Aquitaine was furnished by the Prince's preference of his countrymen in appointment to office. It was proper enough that the Prince's
chief officers should be Englishmen. No one could reasonably
find fault with the appointment of Thomas Felton as seneschal,
John Chandos as constable, or John Harewell as chancellor,
but the Prince also filled all his stewardships and bailiwicks with
Englishmen, and these kept up, at the expense of the inhabitants,
much greater state than those inhabitants cared to pay for.

But the English, and other foreigners, such as the Herald
Chandos, who came from Hainaut, saw only the radiant ob-
verse of the coin. The Herald, who was there, says: "He
reigned seven years in Gascony in joy, and peace, and pleasant-
ness, all the princes and barons of the land held him to be a good
lord, loyal and wise, and they were right, for since the time when
God was born, never was open house kept so handsomely and
so honorably, as under him. Every day he had at his table more
than four score knights and full four times as many squires.
In Angoulême and Bordeaux there were revels and tournaments. There was the home of lordliness, of joy and jollity, of
lavishness, aristocracy and honor. All his subjects, all his men,
loved him with true affection, for he did them a great amount of
good. Those who dwelt about him bore true respect and love,
for liberality was in his hand, high purpose governed him, and
good sense, moderation, righteousness, reason, justice and restraint. A man could truly say that you might search the whole
world round, and you would not find another such Prince.
Neighbors and enemies had great fear of him; for so high was
his courage that his power prevailed everywhere. In what we
say and what we do, we should never forget what he did."

*Si qu' on ne doit mye ses faiz*
*Oblier en diz ne en faiz.*

But the Prince possessed one quality inherited from his Plantagenet ancestors, that the Herald passes over. Cuvelier, the poet who celebrated the exploits of Bertrand du Guesclin, says:

*Prince de Galles qui cuer ot de lyon*
*Qui estoit a Bordeaux en dominacion:*
*De Guienne tenoit le pais environ,*
*Où le pais tenoit en tel subjection,*
*Cone ne chevalier ne prisoit un bouton,*
*Bourgoises ne bourgois, ne nul homme de non.*

The Prince of Wales, who had the heart of a lion,
And over Bordeaux held domination,
And over all the land of Guienne roundabout,
Held that region in such subjection
That he did not value a knight at one button,
Nor burgher, nor burgher's wife, nor any common folk.

And Cuvelier goes on to speak of this Plantagenet pride of his: "Not since Alexander has any man borne himself so proudly, for he values no man but himself, he deems himself the best in Christendom, and does not give a peeled onion for the King of France, not a red cent (*un denier nonnoré*) for the Duc d'Anjou." And finally his pride (so this poet says) brought him down. His pride may have helped, but the primary cause was the indebtedness piled up by the Spanish campaign.

# CHAPTER XXI

BEFORE proceeding further, I must introduce the Free Companies to your better acquaintance. If I wished to convey in shortest space an idea of what these picturesque rascals were, I should say that they were all more or less like Long John Silver, clever, dissembling, valiant, ruthless ruffians. But as they, or some of them, were the cause of the Black Prince's third exploit, a worthy sequel to Crécy and Poitiers, I will introduce them at greater length.

The nobility, whether of England or France, as I have said, had no serious occupation apart from war; but they were not the only ones to be bored by a quiet life. There were many landless resolutes, yeomen or artizans, or younger sons of the gentry, wild-hearted, high-spirited fellows, eager to drink the cup of life, who, when war was afoot, thronged to the banners of well-known captains. A campaign with King Edward from Caen to Calais, or with the Duke of Lancaster, or the Black Prince, or with the local chiefs in Brittany or Normandy, gave these fellows the excitement that they craved, and when the Kings of England and France made a truce or a treaty, and they were thrown out of employment, they had no mind to go back to their homes and become plowmen, masons, carpenters, underskinkers, weavers, shopkeepers, or, if of higher rank, bailiffs or seneschals, or stewards, on the estates of great nobles, so, when the order to disband came, they kept their arms and joined some bandit baron, or condottiere, who, under a claim of not

198

having his pay in full, or such like pretext, or none, seized a town, or castle, and raided the region roundabout, or, more ambitious, marched through France pillaging, robbing, raping, murdering and burning to heart's content. Sir Thomas Gray in his *Scala-chronica* describes them in these words: "They so acted that all Christian people were filled with astonishment. And yet they were but a gathering of the commons, young fellows who had been hitherto of but small account, and now became exceedingly rich and skilful in war, wherefore the youth of many parts of England went to join them." The English, though predominant in certain places, were by no means all; there were bands of mercenaries, now out of a job, from the states of the Empire, from Hainaut, Brabant and Flanders, from Navarre and Spain, and many Bretons and Gascons as well. To quote Shakespearian language, the neighbor confines purged them of their scum, and sent ruffians that would revel the night, rob, murder and commit the oldest sins the newest kind of ways, in great multitudes to make a hell of France.

The evil existed after Crécy, but it had come on a rush with the truce after Poitiers. Let me quote M. Coville, in Lavisse's great *History of France:* "The leaders were knights, squires, bastard sons of great families, or valets, peasants, artizans, riff-raff, with names of robber chiefs, *Espiote, le Petit Meschin, Hogre l'Escot, Bras-de-Fer, Brisebarre, Guillampot, Trous-sevache, l'Abbé de Malepaye.* They pillaged churches, robbed monasteries, laid hands on bishop and priest, chased the monks into the woods, drank from the sacred vessels of the altar. They violated the women of the people, took high-bred ladies along with them or up into their strongholds, they forced young gentlemen to be their pages and wait upon them. They led prisoners, like dogs, on a leash, they broke their teeth with stones, cut their hands off, whipped them, shut them up in sacks or cupboards, squeezing them into pitiable shapes. What they liked best, were fat ransoms from individuals or towns. From merchants they took what money they could, or cloth, or wine, furs, spices, fish or forced labor, anything was grist to their mill." The only safeguard against them was occasional divine interposition such as happened at Ronay in Champagne, as Froissart reports. Here an English squire entered the church while the priest was celebrating high mass, he walked up to the altar, took the chalice in which the priest was pouring the sacred wine, emptied it on the floor. The priest remonstrated. The squire struck the priest with his gauntleted fist so hard a blow that his blood spurted upon the altar, and then went out, mounted his horse and started to ride away. The horse plunged, reared, leaped and, as if mad, fell to the ground, horse and rider breaking their necks, and both immediately turned into dust and ashes.

These Free Companions had been trained in the practice of war by the best captains. They were expert veteran soldiers, they had raised the foray to a fine art. They took with them smiths, saddle-makers, tanners, butchers, coopers, tailors, washerwomen, surgeons, doctors, bookkeepers to keep their accounts, and priests to invoke blessings upon them. They were also accompanied by women of the camp; the English, with traditions of respectability, often brought their wives. The chiefs lived in great style, with every luxury. Sometimes these brigands traveled in small bands, sometimes, if there was danger, or a greater object in view, several bands united. They roamed all over France, but they preferred provinces, like Normandy, where there was good pasture for their horses, or Burgundy, where the wine was of the best. I will name some of the leaders more particularly.

Sir Hugh de Calverley, *qui volontiers fiert de l'espée* (who enjoyed drawing his sword), a sort of Saxon giant, son to Sir David de Calverley, was an English gentleman adventurer, a soldier of fortune. He had excellent training in Brittany, where the partizans of Montfort, supported by the English, were always fighting the partizans of Blois, supported by the French. He fought on the English side in the famous tournament between English and Bretons, thirty knights in each band, at the half-way oak tree between Josselin and Ploermel, on the fourth Sunday in Lent, in 1351. For a time he led a freebooter's life; then served under Sir John Chandos in Brittany, and then again went back to freebooting.

Croquart, such another, apparently a Breton, had originally been a poor boy and began life as a page; when he grew up, he went to the wars in Brittany, in the service of a man-at-arms. He showed such prowess that when his master was killed his companions elected him their leader. He acquired the reputation of being the most expert man-at-arms in the country. His business was to capture towns, villages or individuals, and set them free for a ransom. He became very rich, worth, it was said, about forty thousand crowns. He was particular in the selection of his horses, which he liked of a deep roan color; of these he owned twenty or thirty, very handsome stout beasts. King John tried to attach him to the French side, but Croquart refused knighthood, a rich marriage, and two thousand livres a year. He, too, was one of the famous Thirty who fought by the midway oak tree. He died while riding a young horse that he had just purchased for three hundred crowns; the horse ran away, stumbled into a ditch and Croquart broke his neck.

Sir Eustace d'Aubréchicourt, who came from Hainaut, had been one of the most distinguished officers in the Black Prince's army, and his brother was a Knight of the Garter. He fought at Crécy and Poitiers. A band of English and German free-booters selected him for their leader, while he was a prisoner. They all contributed cheerfully, each man his share, to pay the necessary ransom; and also, it seems, the sum necessary to re-cover his war-horse and his hackney, which had been given to him by the Lady Isabella de Juliers out of affection. All sorts of rascals enlisted under his banner; and he led them into a part of Champagne, which had had the good luck to be unmolested till then. They stormed the town of Attigny, where they found more than a hundred butts of wine, and therefore decided to make it their headquarters. Poor Attigny! It had once been the residence of Carlovingian Kings, and during the Great War it was occupied and reoccupied. It lies on the Aisne. They raided Epernay, nowadays visited for its cellars, that make an im-mense labyrinth of galleries. That town, which lies on the Marne, was also to be occupied and reoccupied in the Great War. They captured Damery, where Adrienne Lecouvreur was to be born three hundred and thirty years later, and Vertus, which the church of Saint Martin could not protect, where they found so much booty that they quartered a garrison there.

Sir Broquart de Fenestrage had fought for the French against the English and Navarrese in Champagne, but the money for his hire had not been paid. He sent his bill to Paris, but did not receive a satisfactory answer; so Sir Broquart hurled de-fiance at the Dauphin and at all France, and seized the town of Bar-sur-Seine. Broquart could not take the castle, but he burned all of the town except the walls and carried away five hun-dred prisoners. He then went to Conflans, where he committed

more atrocious acts than ever the English and Navarrese had
done; but he collected enough spoil to pay his men their full
wages, and provide a fortune for himself. Then he withdrew to
Lorraine, whence he seems to have come.

Sir Robert Knolles came from Cheshire, and was probably
a half-brother to Sir Hugh de Calverley. He served in Brittany, that hothouse of freebooters, under the Duke of Lancaster. When formal war had ended, he led an army of some
three thousand English up the Loire, through Berry. He had
heard what good fortune had attended the Archpriest, Arnaud
de Cervolles, another of these brigands, who had blackmailed
the Pope at Avignon, and thought that he would follow so
laudable a precedent. But, obstacles arising, he prudently slipped
off in another direction, and in due course took service again
under the Prince of Wales, acquired vineyards near Bordeaux
and went upon the Spanish campaign. He was very liberal
with his men, as he could afford to be, and was cheerfully obeyed.
Report said that he had gained upward of one hundred thousand
crowns. He went home to die, and his honored bones were
buried in Whitefriars.

The Archpriest, Sir Arnaud de Cervolles, who had had the
wit to aim at the Papal treasury, had marched about Provence
and ravaged the country up to the gates of Avignon. The Pope
was frightened and offered to treat. Having received proper
hostages, the Archpriest went into Avignon, where he was
treated with as much respect as if he had been the King's son; he
dined many times with the Pope and Cardinals. They came to
terms, the Pope gave him forty thousand crowns and absolution
for all his sins. Another of these fellows was a Welshman,
named Ruffin, who took for his bailiwick the country between
Paris and Orléans, exacting toll, where he accumulated "such

immense riches as could not be counted." So they went, marking their journeys on the map of France with fire and sword, with blood and tears. In a letter written in February, 1360, Petrarch compares the state of France with what it had been when he saw it as a young man: "Everywhere is solitude, ruins, misery; the fields are deserted, the houses dilapidated and empty, except in walled towns; everywhere you see the cruel tramplings of hostile feet, everywhere scars still bleeding from the English swords. And royal Paris, the capital, up to the very threshold of her gates shamed by devastation, and within by fear and terror. The very Seine flows sadly through the town as if it felt the sorrow of it, and wept, and trembled for the fate of the whole land." And again, "Where is now that Paris, which, though famed beyond its deserts, was a great city? Where are the crowds of students, the colleges overflowing, the great riches? Where is the gaiety and content on every face? In place of philosophy, of literary discourse, of peaceful conversation, you hear the cries of arms, the bellowing of battering rams beating the walls, and the alarm of soldiers fills the streets with tumult and fear!" Even Petrarch could not exaggerate the horrors of it all.

Various solutions of this problem were attempted. The Pope tried to get the Free Companies off on a crusade against the heathen, but his plan was not very successful; another suggestion diverted some, notably Sir John Hawkwood, into Italy (you may see his portrait in the Duomo at Florence); another idea, more valiant, was to subdue them by force, but the army of law and order was defeated. At last a plan of delivering the country, by sending an army of them into Spain, was put into effect. As this plan is the link that connects the fortunes of our hero with the Free Companies, I must explain it at some length.

Don Alphonso XI, King of Castile, who died in 1350, had neglected his Queen for Doña Leonor de Guzman, and had left several illegitimate sons, Don Enrique, Count of Trastamara, Don Tello, Don Sancho and others. The lawful heir, Don Pedro, known to his enemies as the Cruel, and to his friends as the Stern Judge, quarreled with his bastard brothers. This could hardly be helped; the dowager Queen was jealous of Doña Leonor and had had her poisoned. Whether Don Pedro was privy to the murder or not, I do not know, but Don Enrique and his brothers believed that he was and sought safety in flight. Don Enrique went to France, and for a time was in the service of King John. Don Pedro, whatever his real character, had a knack of making enemies. He quarreled with his neighbor, the King of Aragon, and the two were at war; he alienated many Castilian noblemen by his neglect of them and by prodigal gifts to favorites. Added to that, he had married a princess, Blanche de Bourbon, sister to the Dauphin's wife, on a Monday (I think it was) and had left her on Wednesday and gone back to his mistress, the beautiful Maria de Padilla, a lady so beautiful, it was said, that the subservient courtiers lapped up the water from the fountain in which she had bathed. The whole affair was very indelicate, and English respectability was shocked. The English chroniclers were ready to believe anything of him; one says Don Pedro married a Saracen, another that he married a Jewess, others charged him with having Saracen and Jewish concubines. Finally, poor Blanche died (1361) and rumor said that her husband had poisoned her; and afterward, when Maria de Padilla was also dead, Don Pedro (in order to legitimize Maria's children) declared that she had been his lawful wife before the ceremony with Blanche. In these ways, then, Don Pedro had made enemies of the King

of Aragon, the Dauphin, his half-brother Don Enrique, and
of many Castilian lords. And more dangerous than any of
these, he had made an enemy of the Catholic Church. He was
accused of keeping priests in prison and seizing the revenues
of churches. He certainly had put Jews in high office; he
probably believed that the Mohammedans of Granada were more
civilized and pleasanter acquaintances than many of the Christians he knew; and he certainly had made treaties with the Mo-
hammedan rulers, enemies of God. Complaints on these matters, emanating from various malcontents, were brought to the
Pope, who sent a fatherly command for the King to come to
Avignon and clear himself of these imputations. Don Pedro
received the Pope's envoys very rudely. Thereupon at Avignon,
in full consistory, on June 9, 1365, Urban V excommunicated
"the wicked King who persevered in his sin," he declared him
unworthy to hold the title of King, and his Kingdom vacant,
and, having first conferred legitimacy on Don Enrique, he
handed the Kingdom of Castile over to him.

In consequence of all this, it occurred to Pope Urban, as
it did to Charles V (for King John had died, and the Dauphin
had succeeded to the crown of France), that this provided an
admirable solution of the terrible problem of the Free Companies. They should go into Spain with Don Enrique, where,
it was to be hoped, they would be killed, or if not killed, lured
on into war with the Moors of Granada, or of Africa, or anywhere in the world, out of France. The best man in the country
to lead them was Bertrand du Guesclin, but unfortunately he
had been taken prisoner in the war in Brittany by Sir John
Chandos and was held for one hundred thousand florins ransom. The ransom was paid, and du Guesclin set at liberty. It
was important, however, to conceal the real purpose of the

expedition; so it was given out that there was to be a crusade against the Moors of Granada.

How carefully the attempt was made to mislead the public appears in the report of the official speech by du Guesclin to King Charles: "Sire, it is a fact that the Prince of Wales, who lords it with more pride than Nebuchadnezzar ever showed, is planning night and day how to take Normandy from you, and to make you hold your own kingdom, as a fief from him, which shall never happen, please God. You know well, Sire, that neither his father, King Edward, nor he, has kept the promises they made to your father, the good King John, whom God assoil; but that, in true English fashion, they have acted disloyally. Be sure that these Free Companies are kept in France by their doing, for, if it had suited them, the Companies would have gone away long ago. Now you must drive them out. Nevertheless, Sire, to give my opinion, I do not advise you to make war on them, for they could wage war in terrible fashion, they are so strong and there are so many of them. You would find it exceedingly troublesome. But, for the honor of the Christian faith, if you should please to make me commander-in-chief of an army against the Saracens of Granada and Benemarin, who are very close neighbors to us, it seems to me that you should pay a sum to these Companies to induce them to join my army, and that you should also procure absolution for them from the Pope, who has excommunicated them. They then might well be willing to leave their strongholds and, once out of the Kingdom, no force that they could ever bring, nor King Edward, nor the Prince of Wales, could put them back in possession again."

It was not easy, however, to persuade these bands of freebooters to leave the comfortable lodgings where they had established headquarters. Finally they agreed to go, but it was necessary to pay them well. Bertrand du Guesclin, accompanied by Marshal d'Audrehem, and other veteran soldiers, assumed the command. They took their way to Spain by Avignon, ostensibly to obtain the Pope's absolution, really to extort more money from him. The army halted on the farther side of the Rhone and sent word of their presence. The Pope dispatched a cardinal to hear what they had to say. Sir Arnoul d'Audrehem, Marshal of France, *homme sage et desert,* spoke for them: "Your Reverence, these gentlemen, Hugh Calverley, the Green Knight, Scott, Jean d'Évreux, Walter Hewet, and others of this army, who have been carrying on war in France, who have violated churches and women, have burned, killed and pillaged, now present themselves to the Holy Father, who once excommunicated them at the request of the King of France. The King has pardoned all their offenses, and they have come here in company with Messire Bertrand du Guesclin and of the Comte de la Marche, who are leading this army against the Saracens, in defense of Christendom. They have come this way in order to obtain absolution. It is in their name that I make this statement and present this request, which you will please take to the Pope, and say besides, in the name of all the army, that, according to the custom of employing the Church treasury for the service of Our Lord and the maintenance of the faith, our Holy Father the Pope will please send here, together with his absolution, two hundred thousand florins from the Church treasury for this enterprise which will be of such great service to the interests of Our Lord." The Pope was looking out over the plain from the window of his palace, and saw bands riding fast here and there for pillage. *"Mon Dieu!"* he said, "those fellows work hard to get to hell." Even at that, du Guesclin was obliged to borrow ten thousand francs from the citizens of Montpellier to satisfy his hungry followers. Many more English and Gascon condottieri came flocking in. Some, like Sir Hugh Calverley, Sir Walter Hewet, Sir Matthew Gourney, Bertucat d'Albret, Sir Eustace d'Aubréchicourt, the Bégue de Villaines, may be regarded as gentlemen adventurers; but most of them were mere robber chiefs, John Cerneille, Naudon de Bageran, Robert Briquet, La Nuit, le petit Méchin, le Bour [bastard] Camus, le Bour de l'Esparre, Battiller, Espiote, and such. Of course it was impossible to hide the army's real object. Nevertheless du Guesclin uncovered that object with extreme delicacy. "Seigneurs," he said, "King Charles has sent me to you, to uphold our religion, for he has raised this army against the Saracens. He had proposed to send us to Cyprus to the aid of good King Peter there; but that good King has been miserably murdered by his brother. On the other hand, very bad news has come across the mountains. Pedro, King of Castile, who had married Blanche de Bourbon, sister to the Queen of France, has put her to death, quite without right. However, the King of France is advised to send this army against the Saracens in Granada. From there we could go to Cyprus, and *perhaps* the army will march into Castile to fight Don Pedro, a very irreligious man, who trusts so wholly to Jews and Saracens that they govern the kingdom." And so he goes on with a very smooth speech. Hugh de Calverley spoke for the assembled chieftains: "Bertrand, *beau frère* and comrade, I am with you, one of your men, because of your honest dealing and your valor, for to-day you are the mirror of chivalry. I am ready to aid you under all circumstances, and so are my companions. I speak in the name of all in asking permission to join you as a comrade in arms."

The King of Aragon, being in the conspiracy, admitted them into his realm. Then, they wrote to Don Pedro asking that a free passage through his country be granted to them and that provision might be made for some of God's pilgrims, who had undertaken, "out of devotion, an expedition into the Kingdom of Granada to revenge the sufferings of their Lord and Savior, to destroy the infidels and to exalt the cross." Well, to shorten the story, these crusaders advanced victoriously into Castile. Don Pedro fled into the northwest corner of Spain, and Don Enrique was crowned at Burgos King, in his stead.

# CHAPTER XXII

LET me resume. The Treaty of Bretigny had not brought forth the fruits of peace as abundantly as the framers had hoped. Brittany had been excluded from its operation, and the partizans of Montfort and of the Count of Blois were still fighting. Also the adjustment of the boundary of the ceded provinces, and the cession of towns and castles, as I have said, bred ill will, and the Free Companies were ravaging France worse than ever. The Prince of Wales had kept these rascals out of Aquitaine; and as most of their leaders were Englishmen or Gascons, Charles V, who had succeeded to the crown of France upon his father's death in 1364, believed that under-handedly he encouraged them to stay where they were. Then came the auspicious proposition that Bertrand du Guesclin should lead them into Spain. The Prince, wishing to convince Charles of his good faith, encouraged the English and Gascon leaders to go; but King Edward, who was not much concerned by the misdeeds of the Free Companies, took a different view. It was not to England's advantage to let its ally, Don Pedro, be dethroned, and Don Enrique of Trastamara, a friend to France, be seated in his stead, for in that case Aquitaine would be ringed about by enemies. But, by the time his prohibition reached Bordeaux the English and Gascon condottieri were off and away.

The campaign conducted by Don Enrique and Bertrand du Guesclin was brief and wholly successful. Don Pedro took refuge in Corunna.  There was but one hope left to him, the help of England.  As the Herald Chandos puts it, he called to mind that he had long had alliance and amity, as well as kinship, with the King of England—you remember that death prevented him from marrying King Edward's daughter—and if Edward would help him, *pur amour et pur linage* or *pur dieu et pur vassellage*, for indeed he did not care much as to the motive, "he might still be made whole."  His right-hand man, Fernandez de Castro, confirmed him in this hope.  "Sire, heafken to me," he said, "and send direct to the Prince of Aquitaine, his son, who is a very gallant and brave gentleman, *moult par est preudhom et hardis*, and so puissant in men-at-arms that no man living can worst him.  If you find him of a mind to help you, be sure that you will recover Spain before the year is out."  So Don Pedro wrote a letter in very humble strain, begging the *très noble Prince, puissant, honorable, preu et vaillant*, for God's sake, for love and pity, for their alliance and friendship, for their kinship, and for the righteousness of his cause, to come to his help, and first of all to send ships to fetch him safely to Bayonne.

Don Pedro presented a plausible case.  The contention between the Kings of England and of France, of necessity, made them rivals for the friendship of Castile.  The Spanish navy was good, and if it were to act with France, the English and Gascon coasts would be in danger, whereas, if it acted with England, the two fleets could sweep French shipping from the seas, and King Edward would be able to land troops in France when and where he pleased.  Don Pedro's envoys sailed to Bayonne, rode on to Bordeaux, and found the Prince at the monastery of Saint-André, *où tout respirait l'orgueil*, if one is to believe a French chronicler.  The Prince read the letter, told the envoys that they were most welcome, gave orders that they should be handsomely entertained, and sent for Sir John Chandos and Sir William Felton. "My lords," he said with a smile, "here is great news from Spain. Our Cousin, Don Pedro, complains grievously of his bastard brother Henry, who has driven him from his kingdom, as you may have heard from those who are come here. He entreats us for help, as his letter explains." The Prince then read them the letter, and asked their advice. At first they looked at each other and hesitated. It was a serious matter; and responsibility is sometimes a dangerous thing. The Prince admitted his desire to accept; he said that God and a righteous cause had enabled them to conquer what had been due to them from the great Kingdom of France, and that if the same should happen in Spain, their reputation would grow great. The two knights discussed the passage of the Pyrenees, and the necessity of securing the cooperation of Charles le Mauvais, King of Navarre, as the only feasible pass was that of Roncevaux; they advised the Prince to convoke a council of the barons of Aquitaine, and in the meantime to send ships and an escort to Corunna for Don Pedro. A company of distinguished knights was chosen and went to Bayonne, where they were detained by contrary winds; and, before they could sail, Don Pedro came himself, with his three daughters, Beatrice, Constance and Isabel, and a few followers, and bringing what valuables he had been able to lay hands on.

In the meantime the Prince's council, composed of Englishmen and Gascons, felt doubts about the project, and, according to Froissart, formulated their opinions in some such form as this: "My Lord, you have heard the old proverb, 'He that too muche embraceth, holdeth the weaklier.' You are one of the most illustrious princes of this world, most esteemed and most honored, you possess a great principality here by the sea, and, thank God, you are at peace with every one. It is well known that no King, far or near, at this present time, dares to provoke you; your reputation for valor and good fortune is so great. You should be content with what you have, and make no new enemies. We must add that Don Pedro, who has been driven from his kingdom, is a man of arrogance, very cruel, and of a bad disposition. His kingdom suffered many grievances at his hands . . . that is why he lost it. Besides he is an enemy to the Church, and has been excommunicated by the Pope. He has made war unjustly on his neighbors; he is believed to have murdered his wife. You ought to pause and consider well before you enter into any engagements with him. His sufferings are punishments from God, who has inflicted them as a warning to Kings."

But the dream of new glory, of carrying the banner of England into Spain, wrought upon the Prince's imagination. "My Lords," he answered, "I take it, of course, for granted that you gave me the best advice you have to give. But I may inform you that I am perfectly well acquainted with the life and conduct of Don Pedro. I know that he has committed numberless faults, and is now suffering for them. And I will set forth to you the reasons that induce me to help him. I do not think it decent that a bastard should possess a kingdom as an inheritance, nor drive from the kingdom his own brother, the legitimate lawful heir. Such a deed is greatly prejudicial to royalty; and no king, no king's son, should suffer it. Besides, my father and Don Pedro have been allies for years, and we are bound to assist him if he is in need of us." He had made up his mind and nothing they could say shook his resolution.

So, when Don Pedro arrived at Cap Breton, at the mouth of

the River Adour, the Prince of Wales rode to meet him and do him honor.  According to Cuvelier, whose attitude toward the Prince is critical, at their meeting, after mutual unbonneting, the Prince said: "Put on your hat, which out of courtesy you have taken off, and by Our Lady, I warrant you, be it wisdom or folly, that I will put back upon your head the crown of Spain that has been taken from you, even if it cost me my dukedom, and my life to boot; and I will make the bastard, and all who come in his company, fly in dismay.  A bastard never wrought an act of folly as great as this, without paying for it at the edge of the sword." Don Pedro replied suitably, and the Prince ordered wine, which was fetched by a cavalier with gilded spurs;

*Car li princes estoit de telle auctorité,*
*Que nulz ne le servoit de vin ne de claré,*
*Ne d'espices aussi, ne de biens a plenté*
*S'il n'estoit chevalier à esperon doré.*

For the Prince lived in such state and dread,
That no man served him wine, or white or red,
Nor spice, nor platter plentifully furnished,
Unless he were a Knight, with gold spurs burnished.

Froissart, who was then, or a little later, at Bordeaux, says that no prince knew so well what was required of good breeding. Don Pedro told his story; and the Prince encouraged him to be of good hope, for, though he had lost all, it was within the power of God to restore it and more, and also to grant vengeance upon the wrongdoer.  The King was lodged in an apartment in the monastery of Saint-André, and honored with many banquets and festivities.  Business was not neglected, and Don Pedro did his best to strengthen the Prince in his purpose, and furnish him with arguments to present to his nobles and knights. Both Englishmen and Gascons, Froissart says, are of a covetous nature. Don Pedro promised that he would make the Prince of Wales' eldest son, the two-year-old baby Edward, King of Galicia, a province in northwest Spain, and that he would divide between him, his officers and men, the great riches he had left hidden in Castile. His promises glittered and coruscated. As earnest of what he would give thereafter, he presented the Prince with a ruby ring, now one of the British crown jewels, and with a golden table, garnished with a carbuncle of prodigious size, and so brilliant that at night it emitted as much light as several torches, and ornamented with other rich jewels as well.

At Bayonne the Prince and Don Pedro held a general council, at which Charles of Navarre, slippery as Proteus, was present, also envoys from the King of Aragon, although both those worthies were in alliance with Don Enrique, as well as many Gascon nobles. The issue of such an enterprise was doubtful, and the riddle of the future hard to guess. The Comte d'Armagnac, foremost among the Gascon barons, asked leave for them to deliberate apart. This was agreed to, and in private the Comte addressed his fellow Gascons: "You have heard, my Lords, what the Prince asks of you. It is my opinion that we ought to aid him in this war with all the men we can assemble, for as Duc de Guienne he is our overlord, and, up to now, he has asked for nothing. Nevertheless, I am much surprised that he ignores Pedro's faithlessness, for he knows that Pedro murdered his wife Blanche, sister to the Queen of France. . . . And he well knows that the Spanish crown belongs to Don Enrique. I know it for a fact. Enrique is the oldest son to King Alphonso, for he was born first. His mother, a noble lady, had been betrothed to the King. But it does not belong to a vassal to discuss rights or reasons when his seigneur wishes to go to war. It is his duty to serve when called upon, and to think that his lord has decided right. So my advice is to march with the Prince. On the campaign we can find out whether the Prince finds our service acceptable to him. I say this because he has so far shown little love for us, and makes more account of an English varlet than of the greatest lord in Guienne." The others agreed with him and pledged themselves, one to bring five hundred men-at-arms, another three, others one and so on.

But they were all still reckoning without knowledge of King Edward's wishes. So messengers were dispatched to England, who came back with the King's answer of approval. Another assemblage of the barons was held, at which the King's letters were read. The King said that in his opinion his son, the Prince of Wales, ought to undertake to restore Don Pedro to his throne, from which he had been deposed unjustly, and that he held himself obliged by the treaties between himself and Don Pedro to grant him help and succor. He ordered his vassals, and besought his friends, to help the Prince of Wales in every way, in the same manner as if he himself were present. The barons at once accepted the King's will, declared that they would heartily obey his command, but, they said, they wished to know by whom they were to be paid. The Prince turned to Don Pedro: "You hear what our people say; it is for you to give the answer." Don Pedro answered, "Dear Cousin, the gold and treasure I have brought from Spain, which is not a thirtieth part of what I have there, I am ready to divide among your people." To this the Prince replied: "My Lord, it is well said. As to the surplus of your debt to them, I will take that upon myself. I will order whatever sums you may want to be advanced to you as a loan, until we shall arrive at Castile." "On my soul,"

Don Pedro answered, "you will do me a great kindness." The Prince, as I say, was on fire to have the banner of England cross the Pyrenees, and he went, neck or nothing, into the enterprise. Don Pedro, on his part, solemnly promised to repay everything. That arrangement disposed of the Gascon barons.

A second minor matter was to appease the Pope, and keep him as far as possible neutral. Don Pedro was as ready to take an oath as to make a promise. He swore: To practise and maintain the Catholic Faith for ever with an unfeigning heart; to uphold the Holy Church, and all her ministers, and shield her from harm; to fight against all who might attack her; to increase and multiply her rights and liberties; to restore everything taken from her by him, or his people, and never permit anything to be taken from her in the future; to make every effort to expell all Saracens and other miscreants from his kingdom; to forsake Saracen wife, or concubine, and keep to a Christian wife; never to violate the Seventh Commandment. That difficulty, too, then was out of the way, leaving the more arduous matter of the mutual agreements between Don Pedro, Charles of Navarre and the Prince for further discussion. The main difficulty lay in Navarre's attitude, for Don Pedro was ready to promise almost anything, and the Prince to offer to pay for almost everything. Navarre was embarrassed by his agreements with Don Enrique; but the Pass of Roncevaux, virtually the only way by which the Prince could invade Castile, had never been so valuable before, and it would have been folly not to get as high a toll as he could; besides, England was his friend, and France his enemy, and it would be better to have so great a warrior as the Prince, especially as he was a neighbor, on friendly terms. After a great deal of bargaining, the three contracting parties—Peter, by the grace of God, King of Castile and Leon, Charles by the same grace, King of Navarre, and Edward, Eldest Son of the King of England, Prince of Aquitaine and Prince of Wales—executed a solemn covenant: First, they shall be good, loyal and true friends, and shall aid one another well and faithfully, without deceit or color of deceit, against all who are or may be against them, especially Don Enrique and so forth.    Item: Don Pedro should cede to Navarre the province of Guipuscoa, with its seaports, the city of Vitoria and all Alava, Logroño, Calahorra together with certain territories contiguous, etc.; he should also pay Navarre two hundred thousand gold florins, of which he was to receive twenty thousand down, to be paid by the Prince.    On his part Navarre was to open the Pass of Roncevaux and to provide one thousand men on horse, and one thousand on foot, at wages of thirty-six thousand florins a month; the wages for the first month to be paid by the Prince and after that by Don Pedro. And Don Pedro was to bind himself by legal documents, and under the strongest penalties possible, to fulfill all his covenants loyally, without trick or deceit, and never to contravene them, in whole or in part, of himself or by another, or in any other way.    The two rascals distrusted each other, quite as much as each deserved; but both trusted the Prince of Wales, and it was provided that, if either acted disloyally, the Prince was to side with the wronged party against the other.    Don Pedro was to give to the Prince of Wales, in return for his aid, certain towns on the seacoast of Biscay, Bermeo, Bilbao, Lequeitio and Castro Urdiales, virtually the province of Viscaya—you remember that this is the province from which the truculent squire came, whom Don Quixote overthrew in his First Adventure. For security Don Pedro left with the Prince as hostages his three daughters by Maria de Padilla, whom he affirmed in the teeth of all evidence to be legitimate, Beatrice, Constance and Isabel, as well as the wives and children of the Master of the Order of Alcantara, and of his Chancellor. It was further stipulated that prisoners should belong to those who captured them, with the exception of Don Tello and Don Sancho, Pedro's illegitimate brothers, their wives and children, and also those who had been adjudged traitors, who were, if captured by the Prince's men, to be surrendered to Don Pedro. As for the moneys advanced, Don Pedro pledged himself to repay them *Serenissimo Edwardo, regis Angliae primogenito, principi Aquitainae et Walliae, consanguineo nostro* at Bordeaux before the twelfth of June.

# CHAPTER XXIII

THE impatient Prince, thinking it "an easy leap to pluck bright honor from the pale-faced moon," little heeded the net in which he was enmeshing himself. He paid money for Don Pedro, he promised money for Don Pedro, underwrote all his obligations. He was sowing dragon's teeth. A prophet with any knowledge of political economy might have read the future and foretold the harvests that would spring from these seeds. The Princess of Wales was clearer-sighted than her husband. She heard of his undertaking with great dismay. Even the jeweled table that the Prince passed on to her did not mollify her. She said that evil would come of it all. The Prince shrugged his shoulders, he said that she always wanted him to stay by her side in her apartments, which would not be suitable for a man. And, indeed, she was great with child, and perhaps nervous after the manner of women and wished to keep her husband with her until the child was born. As she was extravagant, the consequences of the debts perhaps did not occur to her, rather the dangers from battle and disease in a foreign land, and in what seemed to her a bad cause. But the die was cast, and the money must be raised. The Prince took all the gold and silver vessels and ornaments that he had, melted them and coined them. He also wrote to his father asking if he might not have a slice of the money to be paid by France; and Froissart says that he received one hundred thousand francs.

In the end the Prince's energy triumphed. Sir John Chandos and Sir William Felton advised him not to tax Aquitaine, and he forbore; but, in one way or another, the initial expenses were met. Collecting an army was easier. An order had been dispatched to Sir Hugh Calverley, Sir Eustace d'Aubréchicourt, Devereux, Cresswell, Briquet and other English or Gascon condottieri, who had gone with du Guesclin and Don Enrique, to return at once and join their Prince's standard. These leaders obeyed promptly and took leave of Don Enrique, who, having attained his object, was glad to be rid of them. The French chroniclers say that as soon as they came near the frontier, although they had pledged themselves to good behavior, "they pillaged, robbed, ransomed, and burned; they violated women and cruelly maltreated the people," that is, they resumed their normal way of living. Don Enrique remarked to Bertrand du Guesclin: "Ha! *Bel Ami*, Calverley and his companions have been up to their English tricks; no Englishman ever keeps his word." And he did his best to bar their way back to Aquitaine, but without success. Calverley raided two towns in Navarre. Some historians seemed to think that he wished to bring pressure upon Charles le Mauvais to espouse the Prince's cause; but plunder was quite sufficient motive. Altogether, according to Froissart, the Prince hired about twelve thousand of these brigands.

In addition he called upon the lords in Aquitaine to come as they had agreed. He asked the Sire d'Albret, head of a great family, and nephew to the comte d'Armagnac (whose territory the Prince ravaged in his foray of 1355) how many men he could bring. D'Albret was proud, and perhaps irritated; you remember that his uncle, the Comte d'Armagnac, had said that the Prince rated his varlets higher than the barons of Gascony.

He said, "My Lord, if I ask all my vassals, I can bring a thousand lances, and leave enough at home to guard the country." "By my head, that is a handsome offer, Lord d'Albret," the Prince rejoined, then turning to his English knights he said in English, "By my faith, that land should be highly prized, which can attend its lord with a thousand lances." He then turned again to d'Albret, and said, "I am very glad to engage them all." "So be it, in God's name," the nobleman replied. The engagement was both public and definite. But the Prince changed his mind; possibly he had asked for more men than, in the end, he found necessary, perhaps he was a little suspicious of d'Albret's loyalty and did not care to have him attended by so large a company. At any rate, by advice of his council he wrote him in these terms:

"Bordeaux, December 8, 1366.

"My Lord d'Albret, whereas out of our liberal bounty we have retained you to serve under us with a thousand lances on this expedition, which, by God's grace, we mean speedily to undertake, and speedily to finish, having duly considered the matter, and the costs we are put to, both for those in our military service, and for the Free Companies, whose number is so great that we do not wish to leave them behind, for fear of what might happen, we have decided that some of our vassals should remain at home in order to protect the country. For these reasons it has been determined in our council that you shall bring on this expedition two hundred lances only. You will choose these, and the remainder will be left to their usual occupations. May God keep you under his holy protection!"

The Lord d'Albret was then in his own country, getting together his thousand lances, and making ready for the campaign. The letter made him very indignant: "How is this?" he cried. "My Lord, the Prince of Wales, is making fun of me, when he orders me to disband eight hundred knights and squires, whom by his command I have engaged and diverted from other means of attaining honor and profit." Still angry, he called for his secretary and dictated his answer:

Dated etc.

"My dear Lord,

"I am marvelously surprised by the contents of the letter you have sent me. I do not know, nor can I imagine, what answer to make. This order will be of the greatest prejudice to me, and bring much blame on me. All the men-at-arms, whom I have engaged by your command, are ready and prepared for the campaign, and I have prevented them from seeking honor and profit elsewhere. Some of these knights had thrown up engagements to go oversea, to Jerusalem or Constantinople, some to Prussia. They will take it very ill to be left behind now. I, also, take it ill; and I can not conceive for what reason I have deserved this treatment. My dear Lord, be so good as to understand that I can not separate myself from them in this matter. I am the least worthy among them. If any are dismissed, I am convinced that they will all go their own way. May God keep you in His holy protection."

This answer did not please the Prince. He brooked no opposition. Cuvelier, the French poet, harps upon his pride:

*Tant estoit orgueilleux et de grande fierté*
*Qu'il ne doubtait homme tant y ot de fierté*
*Tant par l'avoit orgueil espris et alumé.*

So proud was he and of such great arrogance
That he feared no man, so much arrogance had he,
So much solid and fiery pride had he.

However that may be, the Englishmen on his council also thought d'Albret's letter very presumptuous. The Prince, speaking in English, said: "This Lord d'Albret, if he disobeys the orders of my council, is too great a man for this country. But, by God, it shall not be as he proposes. Let him stay at home, if he wishes; we will perform this enterprise, please God, without his thousand lances." The Englishmen present fanned his anger: "My Lord," they said, "are you so little acquainted with these Gascons and their thoughts, do you not know how vainglorious they are? Little is the love they have for us; and so it has been for some time past. You remember their arrogance, when King John was brought to Bordeaux, how they pretended that by their means alone you had won the battle of Poitiers, and taken him prisoner. They had long plans in their heads; and there were four months of negotiations with them before they would consent that King John should go to England, and you were compelled to comply with their demands in order to keep their allegiance."

Such a beginning was of bad augury for the Spanish expedition. Froissart, who is very well informed concerning these events, said that for a time d'Albret was in great danger, as the Prince was of an overbearing spirit, and cruel when his anger was up. He wished, right or wrong, to have his vassals come to heel when he whistled. However, Albret's uncle, Comte d'Armagnac, on hearing of the quarrel, came hurriedly to Bordeaux and, Sir John Chandos and Sir William Felton aiding, smoothed down the angry feathers. The Lord d'Albret was the one that gave way; he had to content himself with two hundred lances. Altogether, counting the levies in Aquitaine, the Free Companies, the Prince's own English army, and a detachment brought from England by his brother, John of Gaunt, now Duke of Lancaster, the total forces amounted to thirty or forty thousand men. The rendezvous was at Dax, a little to the northeast of Bayonne, and very close to the boundary of Navarre, where that little kingdom jutted up across the Pyrenees. There, the army gradually assembled, camping roundabout in the foot-hills, while winter advanced, and the Pyrenees began to look black and fierce, as they had done when Charlemagne traversed the Pass of Roncevaux, with Roland, Count of the Breton March, in command of the rearguard.

> *Halt sont li pui, et li val tenebros,*
> *Les roches bises, li destreit merveillos,*

> High are the hills, the valleys tenebrous
> The rocks are dark, the defiles sinister.

The Duke of Lancaster had not yet arrived with the reenforcements from England, and, what was more, there was considerable uncertainty about the intentions of Charles le Mauvais, who, according to rumor, was trying to run with the hare and hunt with the hounds. However, the Prince had still a great deal to do, collecting stores. Christmas came and went, and no start had been made.

Long years afterward Froissart wrote: "I was in the city of Bordeaux when King Richard was born; he came into the world on a Wednesday, on the point of ten o'clock. At that hour Richard de Pontchardon, at that time Marshal of Aquitaine, came and said to me, 'Froissart, write down and make a record that the Princess is brought to bed of a fine boy, who has come into the world this day of the Magi (Twelfth Night, January 6). He is the son of a King, for his father is King of Galicia. Don Pedro has given him this kingdom and he is going to conquer it. The baby comes of royal line, and of right shall be a King.' " And on the following Friday the baby was baptized in the Cathedral of Saint-André by the Archbishop of Bordeaux. The Prince, having waited for the birth and baptism, was then obliged to join the army. The Herald Chandos may exaggerate, but he can hardly have invented, the mutual affection of the Prince and Princess, and their sorrow at parting:

> *E lor très ameres dolours*
> *Eut a coer la noble Princesse;*
> *E lor regretoit la dieuesse*
> *D'amour qui l'avoit assene*
> *A si tres haute majeste,*
> *Car elle avait le plus puissant*
> *Prince de ce siècle vivant.*

> And then very bitter grief
> The noble Princess had at heart;
> And then regretted the goddess
> Of love who had mated
> Her with such high majesty,
> For she had the most puissant
> Prince in the world of men.

She was often heard to say: "Alas, what should I do, O God of Love, if I should lose the very flower of chivalry, the flower and top of all that's noble, who truth to tell has no peer for valiancy throughout the world? Death then shouldst be my neighbor. Heart, blood, veins, all fail me, when I think of his going away; for everybody says that never a man has embarked on so perilous an enterprise." And she prayed God to have pity on her. The Prince bade her dry her tears, and tried to comfort her; for, he asserted, all lies in the hands of God; "Lady," he said, "we shall surely see one another again, I feel it in my heart, and we shall have great joy, and so will our friends." They embraced tenderly and, kissing, bade good-by:

> *"Moult doulcement s'entrecolerent*
> *Et en baisant congie donerent,"*

and on Sunday, the Prince, with his English soldiers, went to Dax, where he was afterward joined by his brother John, Duke of Lancaster, with his archers and men-at-arms.

Still the question of the passes over the Pyrenees had not been finally settled. There was deep distrust on both sides; the Black Prince heard rumors that King Charles was really in alliance with Don Enrique, and Charles was fearful to let the Free Companies into Navarre. Envoys went to and fro, and finally another meeting was arranged between the Prince, Don Pedro and King Charles at Peyhehorade, a few miles south of Dax, across the Navarrese border. Even then there was great uncertainty whether they would come to an agreement; in France it was believed they would not, and many of the barons from Poitou and Gascony were so doubtful that they had not yet set out for the rendezvous. Mutual assurances were, however, at last successful, oaths were reiterated on the sacred wafer and all the laggards came in, the Sire d'Albret the last, with his two hundred lances.

# CHAPTER XXIV

It was well into February, 1367, before the invading force set out from Saint-Jean-Pied-de-Port to cross the Pass of Roncevaux. The army was divided into three divisions. The vanguard was under the Duke of Lancaster, John of Gaunt, now twenty-seven years old. With him went Thomas d'Ufford, son to the Earl of Suffolk, William Beauchamp, son to the Earl of Warwick, John Neville, Lord of Raby, Sir John Chandos, the most experienced of them all, Creswell, "true-hearted" Robert Briket, Willecock *le Boteller,* Peverell "of the proud heart," John Sandes, "a man of renown," John Shakell, Robert Hauley and so on, all freebooting adventurers. Their number might amount, Froissart says, to ten thousand horses. They set out on Monday, February fifteenth. The road from Saint-Jean-Pied-de-Port crosses the little River Nive, and winds up slowly through a gorge, under great rocks and cliffs, three thousand feet above the level of the sea. There was frost, and snow, and bitter cold; and as the long line straggled up through the defiles, horse and man slipped, and tripped, and tumbled. No man lent a hand *la n'y avoit point de compaigne,* no father stopped to help his son, for every man had all he could do to look out for himself. And as they passed in narrow file through the Val Carlos, where in a dozen places a little band of enemies could have stopped the whole army, the leaders, at least such as were clerkly enough to remember the fate of Charlemagne's rear-guard, five hundred years before, must have coupled

229

Ganelon and Charles le Mauvais in their thoughts, and blessed their stars as they emerged into the gracious slopes upon the southern side. The line was so long that only one division crossed in a day.

On Tuesday, the sixteenth, the main body under the Prince of Wales and Don Pedro followed, the King of Navarre with them, and a long line of famous soldiers from Normandy, Hainaut, Brittany and Gascony, as well as from England. The Herald Chandos, who was there, says that twenty thousand horses were in this division, Froissart says twelve thousand. They, too, suffered much; it was bitter cold, the wind blew shrewdly and there was a fall of snow. The next day, Wednesday, the rear-guard crossed under Don Jayme, the dispossessed King of Majorca, and the Comte d'Armagnac, and with them sundry gentlemen adventurers, Bour de Breteuil, Bour Camus, Naudon de Bageran, Bernard de la Salle and others. Froissart says that there were ten thousand horses in the rear-guard. Finally, all passed safely through and descended into the rolling land beyond and on to the neighborhood of Pamplona, where they tarried for a few days. Here, as usual, the Free Companies robbed and pillaged, in spite of the solemn assurances given to the King of Navarre. It was too late now, he could only complain and protest.

In the meantime, Don Enrique had been King of Castile for nearly a year, nursing the hope that Don Pedro would not be able to come back. He had made a treaty with Charles le Mauvais very similar to that made by Don Pedro, with the difference that Charles covenanted with Enrique to keep the Pass of Roncevaux shut and with Pedro to keep it open. Enrique probably understood the value of Charles's covenants. When it became certain that the Prince of Wales was coming

with a great army, Don Enrique gathered together his friends
and their vassals, and sent word to Bertrand du Guesclin to
come back with all the French troops he could. In due course
news came that the Black Prince had crossed the Pass and was
marching through Navarre. At this Don Enrique wrote him
the following letter:

"Santo Domingo February (?,) 1367

"Most Puissant, Honored and Noble Prince of Aquitaine
   "Dear Sir
            "I have heard for certain that you mean to enter my
Kingdom of Castile with a great army in company with my
enemy and adversary, at which I am greatly astonished, for I
did not imagine that I had any controversy with you, who have
performed such great and honorable deeds. I do not know
who advised you, for I have never done you any wrong or
harm, for which you should hate me or take from me what
God of His will has given me. But as I know that there is no
lord of any realm in the world, nor any man, to whom God
has given such good fortune in war as to you, and as I know
that you and your men are desirous to do battle, I send to learn
in what place you propose to enter my Kingdom of Castile,
for with the help of God and of my loyal subjects and friends,
we shall go to meet you, and it will not be long before you
have battle, for it has been reported to me that you and your
people desire it very much. I wish God, and you, and all the
world to know that I am sorry for it, but of necessity I am
obliged to defend my Kingdom and my subjects.

"Yours etc."

At the time of receiving this letter the Prince was still near Pamplona.  His purpose was to march on Burgos, the capital of Castile.  There were two roads, the more direct, via Salvatierra and Vitoria, that led through hilly country, and a longer way, but by more level ground, that went via Logroño on the River Ebro.  In order to discover where Don Enrique's army might be, the Prince sent out a scouting party, of eight score lances and three hundred mounted archers, under Sir Thomas Felton.  This party rode to the south, crossed the Ebro at Logroño, a city that had remained loyal to Don Pedro, and approached near enough to the Spanish army to make observations.  While they were gone, a strange thing happened.  The King of Navarre, while on his way from one of his towns to another, was kidnaped.  His Queen sent his *alferez,* Martin Enriquez de la Carra, to the Prince with the news, and begged him to act as viceroy of Navarre and offered to furnish guides to conduct the English army out of Navarre into Castile.  It also transpired that the kidnaper was Olivier de Mauny, a cousin and officer of Bertrand du Guesclin.  As it was well known that Charles le Mauvais had been bargaining with both sides, the English jumped to the conclusion that it was a put-up job to keep him in safety until the issue between the contending parties had been decided.  The Prince answered diplomatically: "I am very sorry for his capture.  I can not rescue him now.  And you know, in good sooth, that the best I can do is to depart from his territory.  If good befalls me, it shall be as much for him, please God, as for me.  I have no other suggestions to make."  And accordingly, off he went, by the direct road to Burgos, and advanced as far as Salvatierra.

The little city opened its gates at once to Don Pedro.  That amiable monarch wished to punish the town severely, and

the Free Companies were eager to sack it, but the Prince inter-
posed. Here they waited several days for the result of Felton's
reconnaissance; which was that the Spanish army had crossed
the Ebro and was coming on. "By my faith," the Prince said,
"this bastard is a bold and gallant knight and shows great valor
and enterprise in coming to seek us. Since he is as eager to
find us as we are to find him, it is most likely that that will
happen and we shall have a battle. Our best plan will be to
decamp at once in order to reach Vitoria before they do." So
they proceeded, and there the Prince saw Sir Thomas Felton
himself. He had pleasant ways with his English friends, and
riding up to the scouting party, he called out: *"Biaux seigniours
dous, plus de cent fois bien veigniez vous* [Good Gentlemen,
you are a hundred times welcome and more]." While they were
talking, word came in that the Spanish army must be near at
hand. There was great stir, alarums, cries of "To Arms!"
and every man ordered to his post. The Prince was very
anxious, for the rear-guard was miles behind; but he drew up
the army in battle array. The Herald Chandos, who was there,
says it was a beautiful sight: thousands of men, in gleaming
armor, drawn up in rank upon rank, with their banners and
pennons, gold, azure, silver, gules, sable and so on, all fluttering
and flapping in the March wind. Sir John Chandos' showed a
pile gules on a field argent, while Sir Hugh Calverley displayed
in the center of his a small white shield surrounded by a series
of eight owls, gray on a field sable. While waiting, the Prince
knighted Don Pedro and his own stepson, and John of Gaunt
knighted several of his followers. The army remained in
formation of battle all day, but no enemy appeared, and at
vespers the soldiers went to their quarters, with orders for
every man to be ready to fall in line at daybreak.

The alarm turned out to be false. The main body of the
Spanish army had not come near; it was merely a detachment
sent out to cut off English foraging parties. But two minor
engagements did take place. Once the Spaniards made a night
attack and took the company under Sir Hugh Calverley by surprise, and did some damage to the pack-train, but the English
army hastily fell into position and the raiders made off. On
the second occasion, a large body of Spanish soldiers surrounded
Sir Thomas Felton and his scouting party, and killed or captured
them all, in spite of heroic resistance. Sir Thomas's brother,
William, dashed alone into the Spanish ranks "like a man
devoid of sense and discretion," and Ralph de Hastings showed
he did "not care two cherries for death," and all gave the conquerors their bellyful of fighting. But Don Enrique held a
strong position in a hill country, and would not come down
into the plain. The Prince saw that it would be foolhardy to
attack him under such a disadvantage. The weather was
odious; March did its worst, there were wind, rain and snow,
and provisions were scarce. The Prince, therefore, broke up
his camp, abandoned the direct road to Burgos and, turning
southward, marched to Logroño, a city that, as I have said,
held for Don Pedro. Here the English army crossed the Ebro.
From Logroño, the road to Burgos passed through the towns
Najera and Santo Domingo, and a country that though high in
places presented no natural obstacles. This maneuver obliged
Don Enrique to abandon his position in the hills, recross the
Ebro and hurry to Najera, to interpose his army between the
Prince and Burgos. Here he encamped in vineyards close to
the town. Najera lies on a little river, the Najerilla, a tributary
to the Ebro, which at that time was swollen by melting snows
and spring rains and made an impassable barrier.

The two armies were separated by only a few miles, and the Prince sent to Don Enrique the following letter:

"Edward, eldest son to the King of England, Prince of Wales and of Guienne, Duke of Cornwall and Count of Chester, to the noble and puissant Prince, Don Enrique, Count of Trastamara. Let me inform you that in these days past the very puissant and high Prince Don Pedro, King of Castile and Leon, my very dear and beloved kinsman, came to that part of Guienne where I was and told me that when his father, King Alphonso, died, all the inhabitants of Castile and Leon accepted him in peaceable possession and acknowledged him their Lord and King. Among these you were one of those who did him obeisance, and for a long time remained a loyal subject. But since then, about a year ago, or a little more, you with bands of men of various sorts invaded his kingdoms and took possession of them and called yourself King of Castile and Leon, took his treasure and his revenues, and now hold them and his kingdoms by force, and allege that you will defend them from him and from those who may wish to aid him. At all of which I am much amazed that a nobleman like you, a king's son, should do things that are shameless to do against your Lord and King. And King Don Pedro sent to tell my Lord and father, the King of England, of these things, and has requested him, first because of the relationship that the Houses of Castile and England have to each other and because of the treaties which King Don Pedro made with my Lord and father, the King of England, and with me, that we should aid him to recover his kingdoms. And my Lord and father, the King of England, seeing that his kinsman, King Don Pedro, had sent to ask of him right and justice, a reasonable thing, in which every King should help, was pleased to do so; and sent to bid me go, with all his vassals, subjects and friends that he has, to give him aid and comfort, as was in conformity with his honor, since you have treated him ill. For these reasons we have come here and are now in the town of Navarette, in the confines of Castile, and, if it be God's will that so great shedding of Christian blood can be avoided, as will happen if there must be a battle, which God knows would displease us greatly, therefore we ask and request you, for the sake of God and Saint George the Martyr, please to let us be just mediators between King Don Pedro and you, and to let us know of it; and we will labor that you shall have so great a portion in his kingdom and in his favor, that you can honorably maintain your state. And if there are some things between you and him that need discussion, by God's help we mean to put those matters in such a position that you will be content. And if this does not please you, and you desire the arbitrament of battle, God knows that I shall be sorry, nevertheless I can not avoid going with King Don Pedro, my cousin, to gain his Kingdom; and, if any shall seek to bar his way, we will go with him, and by God's help we shall do much to help him.

"Dated Navarette in Castile, April 1, 1367."

Don Enrique was advised by some of his nobles not to answer as he had not been addressed as King, but the opinion prevailed that it is well to be courteous even to enemies, so he answered as follows:

"Don Enrique by the grace of God King of Castile and Leon, to the very high and puissant Prince Don Edward eldest son to the King of England, Prince of Wales, Duke of Cornwall, Count of Chester. We have received your letter by your herald, in which various things are said on behalf of my adversary who is with you. It does not seem to us that you have been well informed how our adversary behaved during the time that he held these kingdoms, for he ruled them in such manner that all who know may well wonder that he was endured so long. For everybody in Castile and Leon bore with his misdeeds, with trouble, hurt, danger, death, disgrace, until they could no longer endure them. The list of his misdeeds would be too long to tell. God in His mercy had pity on these kingdoms so that this wrong should not be done every day. No man deprived him of his dominion, none was disloyal, all were ready to aid him and maintain these kingdoms, and Burgos the capital city, but God gave judgment against him. Of his own free will he abdicated and went away. And all the inhabitants of the Kingdoms of Castile and Leon were delighted and felt that God had had compassion upon them to free them from a tyranny so cruel, so harsh, so dangerous, as he had maintained. And all the inhabitants of those Kingdoms came to me of their own accord to take me for their Lord and King, prelates, knights and gentlemen, cities and towns. I am induced by these circumstances to believe that this was the handiwork of God. I was made King by all the inhabitants of those kingdoms, so you have no right to disturb me. And if there must be a battle, God knows that I shall be very sorry for it, but I can not avoid putting my person in defense of these kingdoms, as I am bound to do against anybody, whoever he may be. Therefore, I ask and require you, for the sake of God and His Apostle Saint James, that you do not enter these kingdoms in warlike guise, or do any damage therein—if you came peaceably I could excuse any incidental harm—for otherwise I can not avoid defending them.

"Dated at my camp by Najera, April 2, 1367."

The Prince of Wales read the letter, turned to Don Pedro, remarked that the reasons averred were not sufficient, and that the arbitrament must be left to battle and to God.  So, on the next day, the Saturday before Easter, April third, both sides prepared for the fray.

# CHAPTER XXV

KING CHARLES, though he had run away from the field of Poitiers, had learned as much concerning the military abilities of the Black Prince and the fighting capacity of the English soldiers, as if he had stayed to the end. He laid it down as a primary rule of strategy not to face them in a pitched battle. Du Guesclin cordially agreed with him. Both desired to inculcate this rule upon Don Enrique. King Charles wrote him a letter strongly advising him not to risk a battle, but rather to fight a guerrilla war, harass the English, attack their foraging parties, cut off their supplies and starve them into a retreat. Du Guesclin and Marshal d'Audrehem, who had come with such of the French Free Companies as they could secure, insistently advocated the same policy; they were well aware that the Prince commanded a better fighting force than any that they could oppose to it. Don Enrique was no fool, and he knew the value of du Guesclin's opinion; he said that they were right, but that it was impossible to follow their advice. He had consulted his chief officers and they were all agreed; if he were to show any fear of a battle, all the principal nobles of the Kingdom would forsake him and go over to Don Pedro and the towns and villages would do the same, for all were mortally afraid of Don Pedro, and if they saw that no one dared take the field against him, they would all desert. To make them remain true to him, he must show them that he wished to fight, and that he trusted in God and expected to win the victory, that he wished them, also, to have confidence in the issue. In short he had set his crown "upon the cast and would stand the hazard of the die." Don Enrique was probably right; the nobles and commons of Castile had hesitated and balanced chances as to which side to take, Don Pedro was a tyrant, Don Enrique a usurper, all they wished was to be on the winning side, and if one claimant showed the white feather they would all flock to the other. Don Enrique's wisest policy must be to show complete confidence.

Navarette, where the English were encamped, and Najera are scarce a dozen miles apart. The land is flat, covered by grain or grass, nearly level, except for uplands near Navarette. Don Enrique might have stayed in Najera behind the swift swollen river, and some of his officers strongly advised it; but he would not, he crossed the river and advanced to meet the invaders. Pero Lopez de Ayala, the historian, who was there and carried the banner of *Los Caballeros de la Vanda,* says that this was due to his pride and courage; but it is more likely that the fear of his troops deserting haunted him, and, indeed, some had deserted a week ago, and others deserted just before the battle. To stay on the far side of the river, which was a hundred yards wide, was avoidance of battle, and, besides, his army consisted in great part of light-armed horsemen, who could only operate to advantage in a large plain. So the two armies advanced upon each other. It was the third day of April, "the time of the year," as the Herald Chandos says, "when sweet and gentle birds renew their songs in meadows, woods and fields."

The Prince's army passed over the high land beyond the town of Navarette and descended into the plain, in compact columns, with pennons flying, and shields gay with red crosses on a white ground, the emblems of Saint George. The enemy was now in sight. Sir John Chandos came to the Prince, carrying a silken banner, and said: "Sire, by God's grace I have served you in the past, and everything, whatsoever God has given me, comes from you, and you know well that I am all yours and always shall be. Now, if it seems to you that this is the time and place for me to display a banner, I have means enough, which God has given me, to maintain it. Do your pleasure with it. Behold it, I hand it to you." The right to carry a banner belonged to a banneret, and was of greater honor and rank than to carry a pennon. The Prince, Don Pedro and the Duke of Lancaster, all three, unfurled the banner and gave it back to Sir John saying: "God grant that you gain honor with it." The new Banneret then turned to his officers: "Gentlemen, see my banner. Guard it as if it were yours, for indeed it is as much yours as mine"; and handed it to his standard-bearer, William Alby. Order was then given to dismount, and the Prince addressed the soldiers in a tone of gay confidence: "Sirs, there was no other way. You know well that famine is at our heels, and you see that our enemies yonder have plenty of provisions, bread and wine, salt fish and fresh, both from river and sea. We must obtain those things with sword and spear and now let us so act this day that we may depart in honor." He then clasped his hands and looked upward and said: "Sovereign Father, who has created us, as Thou knowest that, in truth, I have not come here save for the maintenance of right, for all that befits a gentleman, for all that urges men to lead a life of honor, I beseech Thee this day to guard me and my men." He was fair to look upon, (the Herald says) while he was praying. Then he gave the order: "Advance, Banner! And may God help us in our right." And, stepping up to Don Pedro, he took him by the hand, and said, "You shall know to-day whether you will have Castile again. Trust in God."

The army moved forward. The first division, all on foot, was under the command of John of Gaunt. With him were Sir John Chandos, Hugh de Calverley, William Beauchamp, son to the Earl of Warwick, Robert Briquet, Aimery de Rochechouart, Gaillard de la Motte of the Château de Rochetaillée, William de Ferinton, and others, all "full of valor and of noble and puissant lineage." The Duke remarked to Beauchamp: "These are our enemies; and, so help me Jesus Christ, if death does not hinder me, you shall see me a good knight this day." He knighted a number of his followers, including a Fleming, Jean d'Ypres "of the proud heart," and walked out in front of the battalion. "Let us," he said, "take the Lord God for our protector, and let each man do his duty. Banners! Advance!" The second division was led by the Prince of Wales; with him was Don Pedro. To the right of the Prince's division the Captal de Buch commanded a battalion, and to the left Sir Thomas Percy, Earl of Worcester, a similar battalion. The third division was under the command of the King of Majorca, the Comte d'Armagnac, the Sire d'Albret and other Gascon nobles. The numbers, as usual, are uncertain; I should suppose that the Prince's army consisted of about ten thousand men-at-arms, and perhaps another ten thousand archers and spearmen. Pero Lopez de Ayala says they included *"la flor de la cavalleria de la christianidad* [the flower of chivalry of all Christendom]."

Across the plain the Spanish army came on, their banners fluttering, and on their surcoats a red scarf, to distinguish them from the enemy. It also consisted of three divisions. The first comprised the French contingent under Bertrand du Guesclin and Maréchal d'Audrehem, together with picked Spanish men-at-arms, Knights of the Order of the Scarf, under Don Sancho, the Bastard's brother, among whom were the noblest names in Castile, Pero Manrique, Pero Fernandez de Velasco, Gomez Gonzales de Castaneda, Garcilasso de la Vega, and many other caballeros and hidalgos; in all, Ayala says, one thousand men-at-arms. They were on foot. The second division was divided, like that of the Prince of Wales, into a center of fifteen hundred knights under Don Enrique, and two wings of a thousand men-at-arms each, all mounted, the left under the command of Don Tello, and the right under the Conde de Denia, a nobleman from Aragon. There were also slingers, crossbowmen, a great number of *genators*, light armed horse such as those in the Moorish armies, as well as a rear division of infantry, nobody knows how large, composed of levies of yeomen and burghers from Guipuscoa, Viscaya and Asturias, but these as Ayala records *"no aprouecharon mucho en la batalla, ca toda la pelea fue en los hombres de armas* [were not of much use in the battle for all the fighting was done by the men-at-arms]." Don Enrique's distrust in the loyalty or courage of his subjects was justified at the very outset, for shortly before joining battle, as I have said, several companies deserted and went over to Don Pedro, and their conduct seems to have greatly affected the Spanish right and left wings and rear.

Don Enrique sought to profit by the battles of Crécy and Poitiers; in the first the attack by crossbowmen had failed, in the second the attack by cavalry. Accordingly, his first division, under du Guesclin, advanced on foot and met Lancaster's division hand-to-hand. The English archers stationed on the wings, rained arrows on the Spanish horse; Don Enrique's slingers and crossbowmen answered. After the first clash the men-at-arms threw down their spears, took sword and battle-ax and then "of a surety, there was no heart in the world so bold as not to be amazed at the mighty blows they dealt with the great axes they bore, and with sword and dagger." The din and dust were great. Not a pennon or banner but was cast to earth. "Saint George!" "Guienne!" "Santiago!" "Castile!" At one time Sir John Chandos and a gigantic Spaniard met. The Spaniard struck Chandos to the ground, fell upon him, and tried to drive his sword through the other's vizor, but Chandos managed to draw his dagger and thrust it into the Spaniard's body, and he rolled over dead. Chandos leapt to his feet, and wielding his two-handed sword, dealt death right and left. The Duke of Lancaster, too, was most valiant, and in jeopardy every minute. Nevertheless the English were forced to give ground, and the Spaniards thought they had won. But soon the aspect of battle changed. The Captal de Buch with his battalion advanced against the Spanish left. Don Tello, its commander, lies under suspicion of treachery; but it seems more likely that his men, already inclined to desert, needed only the argument of English archery to reach a definite conclusion. When the Captal and his Gascon corps charged, they turned and fled without a blow. The Captal swung his corps round and attacked du Guesclin's battalion in the left flank and rear. Simultaneously, the Prince's left wing, under Lord Percy, had the same experience; the Spanish right opposite them did not abide their onset. It too swung round and closed in on du Guesclin's right flank and rear. At the same time the Prince's division came up into action, *et furent avironnez de toutes pars comme les oiseaulx entre les raseurs,* so that du Guesclin's division "was surrounded on every side like birds encompassed by beaters."

Three times Don Enrique charged gallantly to break the circle encompassing du Guesclin, but fewer and fewer followed him, and he was driven back. He shouted out, "Help me for God's sake! You have made me King, you have sworn to help me loyally. Help me!" All in vain the attack waxed stronger, the English archers twanged their bows, all the Spanish horse fled and Don Enrique was obliged to turn and fly too. The French corps and the Spanish knights of the vanguard held fast, surrounded though they were, and fought desperately. But the rest of the army was in headlong rout toward the river and the English, Gascons, Bretons, having mounted, followed hard, striking the fugitives down with sword and lance. The vanguard could hold out no longer; many had been killed, the rest surrendered, among them du Guesclin, Don Sancho, the Maréchal d'Audrehem, Pero Lopez de Ayala and such. The field was now a terrible sight; the Spanish army was one mad rabble, slingers, bowmen, city train-bands, country levies, *genators* and knights, flying for their lives, all making for the only bridge that led to safety. Multitudes flung themselves into the river, tumbling over one another. "So great was the discomfiture," the Herald Chandos says, "that methinks no man ever saw the like." Don Pedro rode fiercely over the field among the fugitives, crying out: "Where is that whoreson that calls himself King of Castile?" and on his way met a Gascon knight bringing in a prisoner, Iñigo Lopez Orozco, one of his old courtiers who had abandoned him. His wicked temper flared up, and forgetting his pledges to the Prince of Wales, he killed Orozco with his own hand, in spite of the Gascon's intervention. The Gascon was angry to lose his ransom; and the Prince, on being told, was angry at the violation of the covenant, and hot words passed between him and Don Pedro. It was the first rift between the allies.

The Prince's men, in the rush of pursuit, pressed on, across the bridge, into the town, where, it is said, a thousand more Spaniards were slain. The Prince himself remained out in the fields this side of the river, and raised his banner as a signal for the soldiers to return. It was the very spot where Don Enrique had lodged the night before. There he pitched his tent and held high revel, for they found an abundance of food and wine; but first he rendered thanks to God the Father, God the Son, and His Blessed Mother, for the grace they had done unto him. After supper the officers who had been sent to number the dead, made their report. They said that of the enemy five hundred and sixty men-at-arms lay dead and seventy-five hundred common soldiers, not counting those who were drowned, and that of the Prince's army, only four knights had fallen, two Gascons, one Englishman and one German. The Prince asked, in the Gascon dialect that he usually spoke: *"Et lo bort, es mort ó pres?* [Is the Bastard dead or taken?]" The officers reported that there was no news of him. The Prince exclaimed: *"Non ay res fait.* [Nothing is accomplished.]" On the next day, Easter Sunday, Don Pedro came to pay his respects: "Dear Cousin, indeed I must thank you. You have done so much for me that all my life long I shall never be able to repay you." "Sire," the Prince answered, "if it please you, render thanks unto God and not to me; for, by my faith, God has done this, not I. Therefore, we should all be minded to pray Him for mercy and to render Him thanks." Don Pedro said that was so and he should do so gladly. "But, Fair Cousin, I beseech and entreat you as a mark of friendship that you will have the kindness to deliver up to me the traitors to my country, especially the bastard Don Sancho and others, that I may chop off their heads, for they have done me much harm." The Prince answered quickly: "Sir King, grant me a boon, I pray, if it so please you." Don Pedro replied: "Why do you ask? All that I have is yours." The Prince continued quickly: "Sire, I want nothing of what is yours. But I counsel you for your good, if you wish to be King of Castile, that you publish a proclamation saying that you will grant full pardon to all who have been against you, that if, through ill-will, or by evil counsel, they have sided with King Henry, you will pardon them, provided that they come in and ask to be forgiven." Don Pedro assented but sorely against his will. "Dear Cousin," he said, "I grant your request, except for one man. Not for all the gold in Seville would I spare Gomez Carillo, for he is the traitor that has wronged me most." The Prince replied, "Do as you will with him, but pardon all the rest." So Don Pedro pardoned his half-brother, Don Sancho, and a number of others for the Prince's sake. But Gomez Carillo was in a separate category; he had been proclaimed a traitor prior to Don Enrique's rebellion, so he was made ready, dragged out before the army and "his throat cut under his chin."

Later, all the prisoners of rank were brought up before the Prince, and when he saw Marshal d'Audrehem, he cried out "Disloyal traitor, you deserve to die." "Sir," the Marshal replied, "you are the son of a king, and so I am unable to give the answer I should, but I say that I am not a traitor, nor disloyal." The Prince asked if he were willing to leave the decision to a court martial to prove his justification. The Marshal said that he was. So the Prince appointed twelve knights, four English, four Gascons and four Bretons, to make the court. The Marshal was brought before them. The Prince said, "Marshal, you know that at the battle of Poitiers, where the King of France was captured, you, too, were my prisoner, and I had you in my power. I let you be ransomed, and you did me homage under pain of treason and disloyalty, except as against the King of France, your lord, or some one of the lineage of the Fleur-de-lys, and pledged your word that you would not fight against my father, or me, until your ransom had been paid, and as yet that has not been paid.  And to-day the King of France, your lord, had no part in this battle, nor any one of the lineage of the Fleur-de-lys, and I see you in arms against me, although you have not paid your ransom, as you agreed with me.  So I say that you have been false to the homage you did me.  You lie in a bad plight.  You have broken faith, you have lied, you have not kept your promise in this matter, as I say."

Many of those present judged that the Marshal had a bad case, and that he could not escape death, though all liked him very much as he was a brave knight.  Then the Marshal spoke in his defense.  "My Lord," he said to the Prince, "with deep respect I beg, if you have anything more to say against me before these gentlemen in this case, that you will say it now." The Prince said that he had not.  The Marshal then went on, "My Lord, I beg you not to be angry with me, if I say my say, because this matter touches my reputation and my honor."  The Prince replied that of course he should say what he wanted to, because this was a court martial, and that it was only right that every man should defend his reputation and his honor.  Thereupon the Marshal said to the Prince, "It is true that I was your prisoner at the battle of Poitiers, when my Lord, the King of France, was captured, and it is true, my Lord, that I did homage to you and pledged my faith that I would not take up arms against the King of England, or against you, until my ransom was paid, save the case that I fought under the King of France, or of some one of the lineage of the Fleur-de-lys.  Nevertheless, my Lord, I am not in an ill plight, nor disloyal, and I did not bear arms against you to-day, for you are not the commander-in-chief of your army. King Pedro is commander-in-chief, and you are in his pay, and as a mercenary soldier you have come here to-day, and not as captain of the host. And so, my Lord, you see that since you are not, as I have said, commander-in-chief of the army, but merely a hired soldier, I did no wrong. I did not bear arms to-day against you but against King Don Pedro, who is commander-in-chief on your side."

The court martial announced to the Prince that the Marshal had answered well, according to right and to reason, and that they held him acquitted of the accusation. And the Prince accepted their verdict. And not only that, but the chronicler says, that he, as well as the others, was much pleased that the Marshal had been able to produce a good defense, for he was a very good knight. The decision was accepted as a rule of martial law, and all other accusations of the same tenor against others in the same situation were quashed. That day the army remained in camp, and next day marched on to Burgos.

The news of the victory was received in England with great jubilation,

*Gloria cunctorum detur Domino dominorum!*

a jubilation scarcely marred by orthographic difficulties in telling what Spaniards had been killed; Shenco Donesveske, Schenco Senchus de Roger, Garsy Bisies, Ganselivus Gomus de Civeris, Albaris Ferandus de Bosco, and so on, poor names, worse mutilated still than their poor bodies, pitched hugger-mugger into unepitaphed graves.

# CHAPTER XXVI

DON ENRIQUE of Trastamara had escaped, and, as the Prince had said, nothing was accomplished by the great victory. He fled, a wanderer, into France, where, at first without resources, he lived meanly. Tradition says that he lodged at one time in Toulouse, at the Hôtel des Balances, at another time, in Montgiscard at the Pomme d'Or. But before long he got together enough soldiers to harry the borders of Aquitaine. In this, the Prince suspected that, in spite of the peace with France, Louis Duc d'Anjou, the King's brother, had helped him. But let us leave Don Enrique in exile, and return to the victors. They fell out, not over dividing the spoil, but in adjusting the costs of victory.

Don Pedro went on the Monday to Burgos, the capital of Old Castile, whither lords and commons flocked in haste to make their peace and renew their allegiance; and the Prince of Wales followed him with his army a few days later. The dissension that had started over Don Pedro's murder of a prisoner of war, grew and expanded. War, apart from tactics and strategy, is a matter of very elaborate business; it requires, not merely intelligence and imagination, but also an immense patience in the study of details, and of all details, those of finance need the most careful consideration. The Prince, whose fame had winged its way all over Europe, in France, England, the Low Countries, Germany, Italy and Spain, now found himself confronted with a mess of documents and figures that needed lawyers, accountants and what-not to straighten out. He had acted impetuously, believing, or pretending to believe, that Don Pedro and Charles le Mauvais were men of honor; in fact, they were a couple of precious rascals. Don Pedro at once violated his pledge of amnesty; the Prince remonstrated. Don Pedro suggested that the Prince should return to Guienne. The Prince, doubtless, wished that he were back in Bordeaux; he did not feel well, and reports were coming in of French raids in Aquitaine, but matters with Don Pedro had to be settled first. According to Froissart, he expressed himself politely but plainly: "Sir King, you are now, thanks to God, king over your country. All rebellion and opposition to you are at an end. We are remaining here at very great expense. I suggest that you should provide yourself with enough money to pay those who have placed you back in your kingdom, and that you now fulfill all the articles of the treaties which you have covenanted and sworn to perform. That will be very satisfactory to me. And the more speedily you do so, the more it will be to your advantage; for you know that soldiers will live, and if they are not paid their wages, they will help themselves." The King replied: "Sir Cousin, I will punctually perform, as far as shall be in my power, whatever I have promised and sworn to, but just now I have no money. I will therefore journey to Seville, and there collect enough for every one. You may stay here or go to Valladolid, where there are more provisions, and I will come back as soon as I can, by Pentecost, at the very latest."

So saying, Don Pedro set off for Seville, and the Prince conducted his army to Valladolid. I am not sure of the chronology, but it seems that after Don Pedro was safely out of the Prince's way, he or his counselors abandoned and renounced the acquiescent attitude that he had adopted while with the Prince. They higgled, and haggled, and pettifogged, at least so the English thought, and enmeshed the whole matter of the dealing between the Princes in a net of chicanery. To straighten matters out, both sides appointed commissioners. The English formulated their demands: repayment of subsidies and loans, delivery of seaports and so on. The Spaniards answered with complaints on their side: the Prince's troops had done great damages, which the English must pay for; the Prince had exacted a usurious charge on the Spanish moneys paid by Don Pedro at Bordeaux; the jewels Don Pedro had given had been reckoned at half their value; and they demanded that all the pecuniary matters should be reexamined from the beginning. The English protested that, in their haste to raise moneys for the expedition, they had been obliged to sell the jewels for less than they had allowed for them, and, at any rate, it was too late to raise such questions now, and they demanded that twenty castles be handed over as security for the indebtedness until Don Pedro was able to discharge it. The Castilians said that such a demand outraged their national pride. So things went; tempers became chafed and the commissioners grew hotter and hotter over facts and figures. The English right to the seaports of Viscaya under the treaty was too plain for argument. To this the commissioners said that Don Pedro agreed, and had sent instructions of cession to the Basque ports. The English, however, suspected that privy instructions to the contrary had also been sent, or, at least, that Don Pedro had known from the beginning that the Basques hated them, and would never consent to the cession.

Finally, however, an ostensible agreement was reached. The cost of the expedition was settled, and some sort of account stated, and Don Pedro promised to pay half at the end of four months, during which time the English army, at his expense, should stay in the province of Valladolid, and his daughters should remain hostages at Bordeaux. Officers were appointed to deliver the seaports; Sir John Chandos was to receive the city and seigniory of Soria, a town fifty miles south of Logroño; and Sir Hugh de Calverley was to receive the country of Carrion, a place famous in the epic of the Cid, and the Prince and Don Pedro once more solemnly swore by all religious sanctions to observe their covenants.

Weeks went by, and no remittance; the army lacked bread and wine, and "suffered sore distress of thirst and of hunger." The Herald Chandos remarked apropos of it: "A proverb says that a man should contend for his wife and fight for his victuals." He also says that many soldiers went hungry for lack of food, and that out of obedience to the Prince's orders they did not attack towns or castles until that was the only alternative to starvation. The Prince was ill. The situation was bad enough; and then came a letter from Don Pedro of this tenor: He gave the Prince great thanks for the service he had rendered him, for he was now King of Castile, but said that, on his demands for money, his people both great and small had answered him that the Prince could not have the money if he did not withdraw his men, and accordingly he prayed the Prince, as courteously as he could, that it should please him to go back to Aquitaine, as he had no further need of him, and would he be pleased to appoint delegates to receive payments. The Prince "marveled greatly," as indeed he might, as the recesses of Don Pedro's character revealed themselves, and for answer sent three knights to say that the King of Castile had broken his pledges and his word. Accordingly Sir Nigel Loryng, Sir Richard Pontchardon and Sir Thomas Banister rode off to Seville, where Don Pedro, to all outward appearance, received them with great joy. The knights delivered their message punctiliously. Don Pedro replied: "My Lords, it is certainly very displeasing to me, that I have been unable to perform what I had covenanted to do with my cousin, the Prince. I have remonstrated myself, and others, too, with my subjects frequently in this business; but my people excuse themselves by saying that they can not collect any money as long as your Free Companies remain in the country. They have already killed three or four of my treasurers who were carrying money to my cousin, the Prince. You will therefore tell him from us that we entreat him to have the goodness to send those wicked Companies out of my Kingdom, and to leave with us some of his knights, to whom, in his name, I will pay the moneys that he demands, which I hold myself obliged and bound to pay him." Sir John Chandos had a somewhat similar experience. When he went to claim his patent of investiture for the seigniory of Soria, the Castilian chancery demanded fees that equaled the value of the seigniory.

However, there was one thing that was very clear, Don Pedro could not pay, even if he wanted to. The Prince called a council to consider what should be done. There was really no choice; the army from insufficient food, or poor food, or the great heat of the Castilian plateau, or the water, or the wine, suffered from dysentery, and was dwindling away (it is said that but one man in five reached home), and Don Enrique, with moneys or men furnished by France, was harrying the borders of Aquitaine. The King of Majorca was ill in bed, the Prince himself was ailing and in low spirits. It was unanimously agreed that they should return to Aquitaine. Sir John Chandos negotiated with the Kings of Aragon and Navarre for permission to pass through their respective territories;

both were glad to have these terrible freebooters across the Pyrenees. Charles le Mauvais, by one of his dextrous devices, had got out of prison and put Olivier de Mauny in; he came to meet the Prince, and showed him the greatest respect, only he hoped that the army would choose Aragon and not Navarre for their road home. The Prince, however, was firm with him, and plighted his word that his men should do no damage and would pay for all they took. So it was done, and the King of Navarre accompanied them as far as Roncevaux. It was now the end of August.

I will interpose here an account of the issue of the struggle between Don Pedro and Don Enrique. History does not always deal poetic justice, but on this occasion she proved her power to do so if she will. Don Enrique, I think, was at Bagnères de Bigorre, that charming watering place in the Pyrenees, which literary people associate with memories of Marguerite of Angoulême, when he heard that the Prince of Wales and his invincible army were back in Aquitaine. There were plenty of freebooters out of employment, and by dint of hiring, ransoming and promising Don Enrique gathered together some four hundred lances, and when the Prince was safely out of the way and obviously of no mind to help Don Pedro, he crossed the border from the great fortress of Pierrepertuse about September twentieth, and set out on his adventurous enterprise. On passing over the Ebro and coming upon Castilian soil he knelt down and drew a cross: "By this cross," he said, "a picture of the instrument of our redemption, I swear, come what dangers or misfortunes come may, I will never go out of the Kingdom of Castile alive." Partizans rallied to his banner as he advanced. Burgos opened its gates, and there he captured the unfortunate King of Majorca, whom the Prince of Wales had been obliged

to leave behind, ill in bed. As he progressed through Leon and
Castile his party swelled. Don Pedro was in Andalusia trying to
raise an army. The north was in the main for Enrique, the
south for Pedro. Enrique marched to Toledo and laid siege.
You know the city, perhaps, in El Greco's pictures. The tawny
muddy Tagus, circling three-quarters around, holds the city in
its lap; and the bare gaunt heights roundabout cast over it a
wild, half-crazed look as of a town bewitched upon a blasted,
barren island. The towered bridges to east and west, Puente
de Alcántara and Puente de San Martín, high above the river,
stand like giants turned to stone. But during the siege Don
Enrique heard that Don Pedro had left Seville and was coming
up to relieve the beleaguered city. By good luck he had been
greatly reenforced.

Bertrand du Guesclin, you remember, had been captured at
Navarette. His reputation as the first soldier in France made
him a great prize, and the Prince of Wales was well content to
carry him to Bordeaux, especially as trouble with France was
brewing. But one day, at Bordeaux, the Prince was surrounded by his chief nobles, English and Gascon, and they fell
to talking "of love, of arms, of battles, of taking fortresses, of
marches, of encounters and ransoms," and the Prince said:
"Gentlemen, when a brave knight is taken in battle, he ought to
be treated with great consideration, and no ransoms should be
asked so large that he would be unable to free himself." The
Lord d'Albret spoke up: "Sire, you say well; but if you will
permit me, I will remind you that the very opposite of what you
have spoken is being said of you." The Prince flushed and said:
"That knight is a poor friend to me who hears said of me something that reflects on my honor without telling me. I insist
that you tell me what is said of me." "Sire," Lord d'Albret

replied, "everybody knows that you keep captive in your prison Bertrand du Guesclin, and that you are not willing to accept a ransom, because you are apprehensive of his capacities." The Prince was angry and answered indignantly: " I wish you to know, my Lords, that if every knight living were in my prison, I should not be too apprehensive to ransom them. You speak of ransoming Bertrand? I am willing. Send for him; and his deliverance shall not depend on me." All of them, English and Gascons, liked and admired du Guesclin, but some of them thought it politic to keep him in captivity. However, du Guesclin was brought. The Prince asked him how he was. "Monseigneur," du Guesclin answered, "I shall be better whenever you please. You have made me listen to the song of the rats for a long time. *O gai!* When you please to humor me, you will unlock the meadows so that I may hear the song of the birds." The Prince asked him if he would be willing to give his word not to take arms against King Edward, or himself, nor give aid to Don Enrique. Du Guesclin replied that he was astonished that the most redoubtable prince in Christendom should impose such a stipulation, for it would seem that the Prince were afraid of a simple knight. The Prince said: "Since you refuse the oath I ask and charge me with being afraid, I will ransom you so than no man shall have an excuse for any such reproach. But you shall not go without ransom." So ransom was fixed, some say at du Guesclin's suggestion, of one hundred thousand gold *doubles,* a Castilian coin. Legend says that when the Prince asked him where he would get the money, he answered that every woman with a spindle in France would spin till they had raised that sum; but in fact, the King of France, various nobles and merchants, even some of the English, it seems, went security for him. He was set at liberty, and after some delays crossed the Pyrenees with six hundred lances and joined Don Enrique at the siege of Toledo, in February of 1369.

Soon after this Don Pedro left Seville and marched northward to relieve the city, and Don Enrique went to meet him. The route that Don Enrique followed, as he took the most direct way, must have passed close to the famous inn where Don Quixote was to receive the order of knight errantry. They met on the plains of La Mancha, near the Castle of Montiel. Don Pedro was taken wholly by surprise, and his forces were completely routed; he fled to the castle. Don Enrique sat down before it. Don Pedro, seeing no other possible means of escape, tried to bribe du Guesclin. Prosper Mérimée was troubled in spirit by du Guesclin's action. I submit the facts. Du Guesclin pretended to acquiesce, and revealed all to Don Enrique. Don Pedro, relying on du Guesclin, slipped out of the castle with a few friends by night; their horses' feet were muffled. They were allowed to enter the lines and met du Guesclin. "To horse, Sir Bertrand," the King whispered, "it is time to go." No answer. Somebody grasped the King's bridle and he was told to dismount and enter a tent. He and his companions went in and walked into a space surrounded by armed men. There was a great silence. As he stood there, a man entered the tent, armed from head to foot; it was Don Enrique. The two had not met for fifteen years. Don Enrique looked at the group of fugitives: "Where is this son of a Jewish b—ch," he cried, "who calls himself King of Castile?" Don Pedro was no coward; he stepped forward and said: "It is you who are the son of a b—ch, and I am the son of Alphonso." At this Enrique struck him in the face with his poignard. Don Pedro seized Enrique, and the two wrestled in fury. The bystanders drew back. In their struggle, the two stumbled against a camp bed, and Pedro, by luck or being the stronger, came down uppermost. He felt for his dagger, and would have killed Enrique, but a knight from Aragon, Viscount Rocaberti, caught Pedro by the legs and turned the two over, so that Enrique came on top. Enrique then drove his poignard under the coat of mail into Pedro's body.

A man's real character is not well known to himself, and but little better to others. A Spanish historian apostrophizes Don Pedro thus: *"Hombre altivo y desgraciado, rey valiente y justiciero, duerme en paz!* [Noble and unfortunate man, valiant and upright King, rest in peace.]" And Dan Chaucer says:

> O noble, o worthy Petro, glorie of Spayne,
> Whom fortune heeld so by in magestee,
> Wel oughten men thy pitous death complayn!
> Out of thy lond thy brother made thee flee,
> And after at a sege, by subtiltee,
> Thou were bitrayed, and lud un-to his tente
> Wher-as he with his owene hond slow thee,
> Succeeding in thy regne and in thy rente.

But then, Don Pedro's daughter Constance married John of Gaunt, Chaucer's friend and patron.

# CHAPTER XXVII

LET us now go back to the Black Prince on his return to Bordeaux in August, 1367. The King of Navarre accompanied him through the Pass of Roncevaux to Saint-Jean-Pied-de-Port, where they had a jolly good time,

*"ffestierent par granz deporz."*

Navarre went back and the Prince continued to Bayonne, where he disbanded his men, and bade them come to Bordeaux for the moneys due them. It was good to be at home again, and they celebrated their return with five days of junketing,

*"La fut V jours en granz reviaux."*

At least, so Chandos the Herald says. From there the Prince went to Bordeaux, where there were great joy and great celebration. Long processions came to meet him; cheers, hurrahs and chaunts and hymns. But the Prince rode direct to Saint Andrew's where his wife was; she came out to meet him, bringing their oldest son Edward.

*"Moult doulcement s'entrecolerent*
*Ensamble quant ils s'encontrerent."*

Very sweetly they put their arms round each other's neck when they met together. At first it was roses, roses, all the way, but soon the silver lining passed, and the clouds became black.

Some six thousand men followed to Bordeaux demanding their pay. There were Robert Briquet, John Tresnelle, Robert Cheney, Gaillard Viguier, le Bour de Breteuil, le Bour Camus, le Bour l'Esparre, Naudon de Bageran, La Nuit and others, all professional freebooters. The Prince had no money; and as the soldiers had had little to eat, and many were barefoot, they helped themselves. The Prince begged them to leave Aquitaine; and that meant they went into France "where they did much damage and such wicked acts as caused great tribulation." The French said that the Prince encouraged the freebooters under-hand. Duns, freebooters, the French, and illness, nothing was going well; and the Plantagenet temper was never under very good control in times of illness. Moreover, it is hard for a hero, coming home in a blaze of glory, to be surrounded by creditors and to meet criticism and complaint at every turn. A minor incident pointed to trouble ahead. You remember that the Seigneur d'Albret had been much put about by the Prince's refusal to accept more than two hundred lances for the expedition into Spain, and that it was he who insinuated that the Prince was not behaving chivalrously to Bertrand du Guesclin. There was, also, a more ancient cause of ill-will, which perhaps had predisposed d'Albret against the Prince; another d'Albret, an uncle I think, had been betrothed to the Prince's sister Isabella, and almost at the last minute she had jilted him. At any rate the Seigneur d'Albret had evidently made up his mind to abandon the English cause. He now betrothed himself to a lady of the royal family of France, Marguerite de Bourbon, sister to the Queen. This marriage, of course, was big with political significance. The Prince was very angry; he spoke, so Froissart says, very rudely and coarsely both of Albret and his wife. The members of his council, recognizing that he was ill and troubled, attempted to make excuses for Albret, and represented to the Prince that so long as a man was loyal to his allegiance, it was quite proper for him to better his fortunes in any way agreeable to himself. They made the most plausible case they could, but the Prince was right; the marriage showed which way the wind blew. But the real matter that troubled him most was his indebtedness. Economy does not seem to have presented itself to his mind. The Plantagenets had a right to luxurious splendor. Froissart, who had seen a great deal of royal ways, says, "the establishments of the Prince and Princess were so grand, that no prince in Christendom maintained greater magnificence." The council debated how they should raise money; a hearth tax was proposed, contrary to the opinion of Sir John Chandos.

The *États-Généraux* of the Duchy of Guienne were summoned to meet at Saint Émilion in November, 1367, and again in January, 1368, at Angoulême. Something radical had to be done; and a tax of ten pence for five years was imposed on every hearth, big or small. The provinces that had long been under English rule, Poitiers, Saintonge, the Limousin and others, accepted the tax, but the Gascon lords strictly objected. The Comte d'Armagnac, to whom the Prince owed two hundred thousand florins, did not attend the meeting, and when the Prince asked him to let the tax be collected in his lands, he answered no. He said he was too poor, that he and his had nothing to eat, that he had a daughter to marry and that he had consulted the most learned men in law and in divinity and they had all approved his refusal to pay the tax. The Seigneur d'Albret, the Comte de Comminges and many others followed this example. They remonstrated; they said that while they had been under French allegiance they were not subjected to any tax, and that they would never submit to such oppression as long as they could defend themselves, that their lands were free from all imposts, and that the Prince had sworn to respect their rights. The bond of allegiance was stretched to the straining point. The Gascon lords addressed a further remonstrance to the Prince and to Edward III, and continued steadfast *"en leur dur propos."* These complaints caused considerable anxiety in England, when, from jealousy perhaps, there was a party unfriendly to the Prince. Thanks to them, or to the Gascon allegations, it was said that the Prince showed himself arrogant and overbearing, that he would brook no interference, that he made the lords of Gascony who wished to speak to him wait three or four days before he would deign to receive them, and when admitted they were obliged to wait upon their knees until he bade them rise. These stories were probably false, but if true they show that he was ill; so Richard Plantagenet or Henry II might have acted.

The next step of the Gascon malcontents was to go to Paris, under the excuse of attending Lord d'Albret's marriage. They were received very cordially by the King of France, and gaily fêted in Paris. They laid their grievances before the King and his counselors. The King replied that he was anxious to preserve and augment the jurisdiction of the crown, but that he had entered into covenants with England, and must examine them carefully, and that he would endeavor to patch up the differences between them and his dear cousin, the Prince of Wales, and suggested that the Prince's encroachment upon their rights might be due to evil advisers. It turned out that, among the voluminous provisions of the Treaty of Bretigny, there was this clause: "Saving and reserving to the crown of France the right of sovereignty and jurisdiction in the last resort until all the renunciations have been made." Now, admittedly, "all the renunciations" had not been carried into effect. The English cried out that Charles was *un homme false, failles, et perieurs* (false, faithless and perjured) and was acting *denaturellement et tortuosement*. But the King of France went ahead. Albret married the Bourbon princess, and promised to fight against the French King's enemies, and received ten thousand francs as well as an annuity. And a secret treaty was made, by which the Gascons returned to their French allegiance, and the King promised to protect them. But outwardly matters moved more slowly. The petition of the Gascon lords to the King of France to entertain their appeal had been made in April, 1368, but he did not take them under his protection until November. On December twenty-eighth an Assembly of Notables was held, and they decided that, if the King should refuse to entertain the appeal, he would be guilty of a deadly sin. A summons was therefore issued to the Prince of Wales to come into the court of his suzerain to answer the complaints made against him. Two commissioners were dispatched to Bordeaux to deliver the mandate. They were received by the Prince, who read their credentials and said: "You are welcome. What is your message?" The commissioners then submitted this letter:

"Charles, by the grace of God, King of France, to our cousin, Prince of Wales and Aquitaine, greeting. Whereas several prelates, barons, knights, corporations and societies of the district of Gascony, residing on the borders of our realm, together with many others of the Duchy of Aquitaine have come before us in our court to claim justice for certain grievances and unjust oppressions which you, through weak counsel and foolish advice, have been induced to do them, and at which we are much astonished. Therefore, in order to remedy such things, we take cognizance of their cause, insomuch that we, of our royal majesty and sovereignty, order and command you to appear in our city of Paris in person, and that you present yourself before us, in our Chamber of Peers, to hear judgments pronounced upon the aforesaid complaints and grievances done by you to your subjects, who claim to be heard and to have the jurisdiction of our court. Let there be no delay in obeying this summons, but set out as speedily as possible after hearing this order read. In witness whereof we have affixed our seal to these presents. Given at Paris the 25th day of January, 1369."

The Prince spoke with deliberation: "I will attend willingly on the appointed day, since the King of France sends for me, but it will be with my helmet on my head and I shall be accompanied by sixty thousand men."

# CHAPTER XXVIII

THE Prince lay like a sick lion at Angoulême. Dropsy, some say, had set in; he could not take the field himself, but called his old generals to him. Sir John Chandos, finding his advice about taxation unheeded, had gone off to his estates in Normandy; but came back at the Prince's call. Sir Hugh Calverley, came up from Aragon, and the Captal de Buch, from his Gascon vineyards. In May (1369) King Charles *"fit deffier Edouard le roi d'Angleterre"* and King Edward resumed the title, King of France. Hostilities began, or rather continued, in good earnest. Both sides had foreseen that the breach was coming, and had been preparing. The main operations were likely to be in Aquitaine, so English reenforcements were sent there, and the Prince collected what Free Companies he could. The French did the same. To the English went Naudon de Bageran, le Bour d'Esparre, le Bour Camus, Sir Robert Briket, Gaillard de Motte, Aimery de Rochechouart; to the French le petit Méchin, le Bour de Breteuil, Aimemon d'Ortige, Perrot de Savoye and so on. It is not necessary to follow the endless story of assaults upon castles and towns, victories here, defeats there, forays and counter-forays. These operations strike one, very much as our individualistic system of business does the communist, by the lack of plan. Sir John Chandos had his headquarters at Montauban, and Sir Simon Burley, the kinsman of the Prince's old tutor Doctor Burley, in Poitou. On the French side the Duc d'Anjou confronted Chandos, and in the north the Duc de Berry attacked Poitou. One's sympathies are not all with the English. Chandos, the Captal de Buch, Sir Hugh Calverley, were dogs of war, born and bred in a patch of trumpets and spears, but the Duc de Berry almost makes one think of Fritz Kreisler or Rupert Brooke. Jean Duc de Berry was by nature a dilettante, a connoisseur of *objets d'art*, who happily lived to indulge his tastes. The tourist finds traces of him at the Cathedral of Bourges; his architect Guy de Dammartin constructed the central part of the western façade, where the great windows are; at Chantilly, where you may see his book, *Très riches heures*, with lovely miniatures by Pol de Limbourg; at Riom, where you will find his likeness in the pictured windows of the *Sainte Chapelle*. He survived that lingering medieval epoch of the first half of the Hundred Years' War, and lived to enjoy the early blossoming of the French Renaissance. Probably the arts were rendered sweeter by memories of war. There is a martial memory of him at the assault upon Saint-Severe, a town between Cognac and Saintes. He was there with Bertrand du Guesclin, who had come back from Spain and was soon to be made Connétable de France, and various Freebooters, Alain Taillecol, nicknamed l'Abbé de Malepaye, and so on. Fighting at the walls was thirsty work. Du Guesclin ordered up casks of wine—*fine champagne* from Cognac possibly—

*Et quand nos Francois eurent beu de ce vin cler,*
*Lors furent plus hardi que lyon ne sangler,*

And when our Frenchmen drank this wine so bright
They were more bold than lion or wild boar to fight.

But no doubt, in his old age, in his palace at Bourges, seated among his pictures, sculpture, jewels, cameos, medals, ivories, tapestries, embroideries, porcelains and other bibelots, these rude sights of war were pleasant to look back upon, and furnished wonder tales to tell his young wife—at sixty he married a girl of twelve—how he, too, had fought against the troops of the Black Prince, the greatest soldier in the world.

The whole story of the campaign is made up of these petty sieges, assaults and skirmishes. Meanwhile the great Prince lay sick of the dropsy, too ill to mount a horse, at Angoulême. In that quiet pleasant town, possibly in the Tour de Lusignan, or the Tour Polygone, of the castle, his bed may have been drawn near the window, from which he could see the ramparts with their battlements, perhaps the great towers of the Cathedral, or the roof of Saint-André hard by, and could listen to the clank of men at arms walking up and down the narrow streets, the trumpets of the garrison, and on feast-days the ringing bells. It was a sorry time. And to make matters worse, private griefs fell upon him. His sagacious counselor, his valiant comrade in arms, his faithful friend, Sir John Chandos, was killed in one of these idiotic frays. Chandos had been removed to Poitou, as the more threatened place. There the French captured by treachery the famous Abbey of Saint-Savin, founded by Charlemagne. The noble eleventh-century church, solemnly gay with its radiating chapels, and its old apocalyptic mural paintings, still bears witness to what the other buildings must have been. Sir John made an attempt by night to recover the place; he was unsuccessful. He rode back to Chauvigny, about ten miles away, and put up at the inn. It was the last day of December, and cold. He bade the Herald Chandos light a fire. His lieutenant Lord Thomas Percy asked leave to go off and seek some adventure. Sir John bade him go in God's name, but he himself stayed behind, in low spirits because of his failure at Saint-Savin.  He stood in the kitchen warming himself at the fire of thatch which the Herald was making, talking to those about, who joked and tried to cheer him up and dispel his melancholy.  After a little while, he thought of going to bed, and just as he was asking if it were yet day, a man came in and reported that a band of French soldiers were on their way from Saint-Savin, going, he thought, toward Poitiers.  Sir John asked who they were.  The man told him, Louis de Saint-Julien and Kerlouet le Breton, the two captains who had taken Saint-Savin by treachery.  "Well!" Sir John said, "it is a matter of indifference to me.  I have no inclination to exert myself to-day; they may be encountered without my interfering."  He then remained very thoughtful.  "No," said he, "in spite of what I have just said, I think I will mount my horse; for, at all events, I must return to Poitiers and it will soon be day."  So he mounted with a handful of knights and rode off southerly by a road that followed the course of the River Vienne to Lussac, and near to the bridge there he saw the enemy.  The French had dismounted and were about to march to attack the bridge, when Chandos came upon them, his banner flying, with its pile gules on a field argent, carried by a valiant man-at-arms, James Allen.  Sir John shouted out: "Sir Louis! Sir Louis! and you Kerlouet, you act too much like masters here, as if the country were yours, but by God it is not.  I have been trying to meet you for a year and a half, and I have been told that you were looking for me.  You now have that pleasure."  Without waiting for Sir John to finish, one of the Frenchmen drew his sword and struck an English squire, Simkin Dodenhale, so hard that he knocked him from his horse.  Sir John shouted to his men: "Dismount, dismount." So they did and rushed to Dodenhale's rescue.  Sir John, who was always cool, bade his banner advance before him, and, with his vizor up, strode along behind in his long surcoat, blazoned in front and behind with his arms, the pile gules on the field argent. He looked the part, a strong bold knight, engaged in an adventurous enterprise, sword in hand. The ground was slippery with hoar frost, his foot caught in the skirt of his surcoat and he stumbled. He had lost an eye, five years before, on the heaths of Bordeaux, while chasing a stag, so that when a French squire, a strong fellow, James de Saint-Martin by name, let drive at him, from that side, he did not see the stroke coming. The lance struck his face below the eye, between nose and forehead, and penetrated to the brain. He suffered great agony and never spoke again. His soldiers fought over his body like madmen, and by chance an English force of two hundred lances unexpectedly came up and the French, far outnumbered, surrendered. Sir John's servants laid his body upon shields, and slowly carried it to Mortemer, the nearest castle. There, the next day, the first of the year he died. Everybody, men and women, regretted him; even the French, though they feared and hated him, for they said that he was the one man that might have found some way to make peace between France and England, while the English, who loved him, thought that he would have recovered and held Aquitaine for them. Froissart says: "God have mercy on his soul, for there has not been an Englishman, in a hundred years, fuller of every virtue and good quality than he." His body was buried there, and travelers drive out to see his sepulchral monument.

Another personal blow to the Prince was the death of his mother, Queen Philippa. Lord Berners' translation of Froissart records it in this fashion: "There fell in Englande a hevy case and a comon, howbeit it was right pyteouse for the Kyng, his chyldren, and all his realme. For the good Quene of England, that so many good dedes had done in her tyme, and so many knights socoured, and ladyes and damsels comforted, and had so largely departed of her goodes to her people, and naturally loved always the nacyon of Heynaulte, the countrey where she was borne. She fell sicke in the castell of Wyndsore, the which sickenesse contynewed on her so longe, that there was no remedye but dethe. And the good lady, whanne she knew and parceyved that there was with her no remedy but dethe, she desyred to speke with the Kynge, her husbande. And whan he was before her she put out of her bedde her right hande and toke the Kynge by his right hande, who was right sorrowful at his hert. Than she sayd, 'Sir, we have in peace, joye, and great prosperyte used all our tyme toguyer. Sir, nowe, I pray you, at our departyng, that ye will graunt me these desyres.' The Kynge, right sorrowfully wepynge, sayd, 'Madam, desyre what ye wyll, I graunt it.' 'Sir,' sayd she, 'I requyre you, firste of all, that all maner of people, suche as I have dault withall in their marchaundyse, on this syde of the see or beyond, that it may please you to pay every thynge that I owe to theym, or to any other. And, secondly, Sir, all such ordynance and promyses as I have made to the churches as well of this countrey as beyond the see, whereas I have hadde my devocyon, that it maye please you to accumplysshe and to fulfyll the same. Thirdly, Sir, I requyre you that it may please you to take none other sepultur, wharesoever it shall please God to call you out of this transytorie lyfe, but besyde me in Westmyster.' The Kynge, all wepynge, sayde, 'Madame, I graunt all your desyre." Then the good lady and quene made on her the signe of the crosse, and commaunded the Kynge, her husbande, to God, and her youngest son, Thomas, who was there besyde her. And anone, after, she yelded up the spiryte, the whiche I beleve surely the holy angels receyved with great joy up to heven, for in all her lyfe she dyd neyther in thought nor dede thyng whereby to lese her soul, as ferr as any creature coulde knowe. Thus the good Quene of Englande dyed in the yere of our Lord MCCCLXIX, in the vigyell of our lady in the myddes of August."

A still greater loss was to befall the Prince not long afterward. His eldest son, Edward, a boy of five years or so, died. Meanwhile he had gone to Cognac, where he had ordered his scattered troops to concentrate. There, with his dropsy keeping him in bed, the narrow window shutting out all but a bit of battlemented wall and a patch of sky, and news arriving by post after post that towns and castles had returned to their French allegiance, the old Plantagenet temper fretted and fumed. Then he heard that his trusted friend, Jean de Cros, Bishop of Limoges, had surrendered that city, which was in his charge, to the French. If there is any place hotter than Angoulême in August, it is Cognac. The town affects men like fiery brandy; the sun beats down on stone and brick and tile, and the people there lie off from work in the middle of the day, and any communication of any kind irritates the spirit. The Prince fell into a violent passion, and swore by his father's soul, that he would win the city back, and make the inhabitants pay dear for their faithlessness. With twelve hundred lances, a thousand archers and a thousand foot, he set out for Limoges carried in a litter. The whole countryside was a tremble with fear. Limoges was too strong for an assault, and the Prince's sappers fell to digging mines. The townsfolk countermined, but not successfully. In a few days a great bit of the wall gave way, and the besiegers rushed in, *tout appareillés de mal faire* [on tiptoe to destroy]. "It was a melancholy business." The Prince was in a fury, and enough perished to spread the story that every man, woman and child was put to the sword. Froissart says three thousand perished; Delachenal, a French scholar, relying on a French source of information, puts the number at three hundred. The Bishop was captured and brought before the Prince: *"et la plus belle parolle qu'il li dist, ce fu qu'il feroit trencier la tieste* [and the pleasantest words he said to him were, that he would have his head cut off]." The Bishop, however, was spared, and it seems likely that, after the first mad encounter, the rest of the inhabitants were spared, too, but not their possessions, for the town was pillaged, burned and in great part destroyed, *toute la cités de Limoges courue, pillée et robée sans déport, et toute arse et mise à destruction,* but not totally as Froissart says, for the belfry and the choir of the cathedral show that its Gothic is of an earlier date. But one thinks of the early Limoges enamels with their purples, greens and blues, their delicate perfection, and the attendant work of the goldsmith, for which the Duc de Berry must have shed many regrets, that were carried off by the rude soldiers as old junk, or destroyed out of wantonness.

It was the last spring of the wounded lion. King Edward had been greatly concerned about the situation in Aquitaine, reports reached him that the Black Prince's policy and conduct were to blame, and he knew that the Prince was ill. He sent the Duke of Lancaster with men-at-arms and archers, and with the advice to remit the hearth tax and to pardon all rebels who could submit. How far the criticisms upon the Prince were just is not very clear. King Edward had himself commanded the expedition into Spain, and therefore he was responsible for the expenses incurred, and it was for him to say if England should bear part of those expenses. If Aquitaine was to bear them alone, heavy taxes were necessary, and a hearth tax was not much worse than other taxes. The King of France had laid a heavier hearth tax in his kingdom, and, it was not the peasants, but the nobles that instigated the revolt. The pride and vanity of the nobles may have been hurt by the Prince's preference of Englishmen, but he naturally employed men in whom he trusted most, and his arrogance, which was never noticed by his friends, seems to have been caused, or at least uncovered, by his illness. No; there were large forces at work to bring Aquitaine back under the French crown, otherwise men led by Chandos would not have been worsted by men led by the Duc de Berry; the spirit of nationalism was rising and swelling, like sap in spring-time, the people of Gascony, Guienne, Périgord, Poitou, the Limousin, and their neighbors, wished to be Frenchmen and their country France. The illness of the Black Prince and the coming of du Guesclin enabled them to have their way.

The Prince saw that his physical condition rendered him a burden; his physicians ordered him home. He called the barons of the province to a last audience in Bordeaux. He explained how matters were with him, and begged them to serve and obey the Duke of Lancaster, in his stead. Then in the beginning of January, 1371, he went aboard his vessel with the Princess and his little boy Richard, sailed down the great estuary and out into the Bay of Biscay, and arrived safely at Southampton. The Prince was carried in his litter to Windsor, and after some stay there with his father, retired to his manor of Berkhamstead.

# CHAPTER XXIX

## THE LOWERING OF THE CURTAIN

ONCE or twice again the Black Prince raises his head from his sick-bed and steps into the light of history. After his return from Aquitaine, the French had continued to ride on the flood-tide of success, and were gradually recovering, city by city, almost all the Duchy. King Edward attempted in vain to stay their progress. In June, 1372, he sent a fleet, carrying an army and laden with treasure, to La Rochelle, but, near the Ile de Ré, where long years afterward Buckingham's ships were driven off while Richelieu was besieging the city, it encountered the Spanish fleet sent by Don Enrique to the aid of his French allies. The Spaniards won a complete victory. Again, that same summer, the French were laying siege to the city of Thouars in Poitou, and the garrison had agreed to surrender if it was not relieved by Michaelmas. King Edward decided to forsake the delights of Alice Perrer's society, and lead an expedition of relief himself. The Black Prince, in spite of his illness, went, too. So did the Duke of Lancaster. Lionel was already dead. A great fleet was collected at Sandwich. The Prince's son, Richard, a boy of five, was appointed lieutenant of the Kingdom during the King's absence; and, before sailing, the Prince, gathering the nobles together on the royal flag-ship, the *Grace de Dieu*, made them swear to recognize the boy as their king, in case he and his father should die. The fleet weighed anchor on the thirty-first of August. But the winds and the waves ranged themselves against the English,

275

and the fleet spent idle weeks beating vainly against the equinoctial gales. The fatal day arrived, Thouars surrendered; and the fleet put back to English ports. It is a sorry thought to think of the Prince, lying ill on the deck of the *Grace de Dieu,* watching the pennant at the mast head from hour to hour, in hope that the wind might change. His military career was over.

In civil matters, except on one spirited occasion, his part is rather obscure. His brother, John, Duke of Lancaster, had succeeded him as general of the English armies; and, as John was an ambitious unscrupulous man, it has been thought that the Prince feared lest he should dispossess little Richard of the crown. But, unless his asking Lancaster, with the other nobles, to pledge allegiance to Richard be an exception, there is no evidence of any lack of fraternal feeling between the brothers; the Prince had appointed Lancaster his lieutenant in Aquitaine when he left, and in his will he called him my "very dear and well beloved brother," and made him an executor. And after the Prince's death, his widow, Joan, and the Duke continued to be very good friends. The idea of disagreement, or distrust, between the two seems to have come rather as a deduction from their opposing political views; but the Prince died before Lancaster's opinions became definitely reactionary. And they were not the only men that disagreed. There were conservatives who believed in the established order, and there were various groups of reformers who advocated change. One radical opinion condemned the papal claims to interfere in the secular concerns of England, another the wealth and worldliness of the Church, a third incompetence and corruption in the government; and these opinions were beginning to express themselves in Parliament as never before. Classes and groups shaped themselves according to their several interests.  The Prelates were embarrassed because of a divided loyalty, they held to the Roman organization but did not like to pay Roman taxes; they could not deny that the Church possessed a very disproportionate share of the wealth of the Kingdom, but they objected to double taxation, to paying subsidies to the King on the one hand and to the Pope on the other; they believed that the Pope was the Vicar of Christ on earth and held the keys of Heaven, but they were Englishmen and were subject to English anti-papal legislation.  Their situation was awkward.  The barons held stoutly for the maintenance of their ancient rights and privileges, unabated by one jot or tittle.  The Commons, for their part, were beginning to demand political power commensurate with their social importance; they had been encouraged by the King who, when he wished to share the responsibility of his wars, had asked their advice, and now they were ready to give it unasked.  They were specially indignant because the government, which was in the hands of ecclesiastics, had proved itself incompetent and was suspected of being corrupt.  In these matters the two brothers took different positions.

Lancaster, who cherished an ambition to become King of Castile by right of his second wife, Constance, daughter to Don Pedro, deemed it important to be on good terms with the Papacy, and therefore upheld the Papal party, and, being conservative by nature and in full sympathy with his order, sided with the Baronage against the Commons; but, on the other hand, he disapproved of the wealth of the Prelates and disliked to share power with them, and therefore, in later years, when Wyclif preached his reforms, he supported him.  The Black Prince, on the contrary, shared the national feeling against the

Papal party, and gave the support of his immense prestige to the reformers in their attacks upon abuses in Church and State.

The first manifestation of popular feeling was shown in the Parliament of 1371. The taxation had been heavy, and the war unsuccessful. The brilliant William of Wykeham was chancellor. Parliament petitioned that only laymen should be appointed to office in the court, and in the King's household; Wykeham and his associates were forced to resign. The second manifestation of popular feeling was against the papal partizans. Not only had the exactions of the Papacy become greater, but since it had moved to Avignon, with the consequence that scarcely any one but a Frenchman was elected Pope, the English people believed, and so did ·the Prince of Wales with a vengeance, that it used all its influence on behalf of France. Naturally, the patriotic party felt a strong resentment. An opportunity to show that resentment came in this way. The Pope had fallen out with the city of Florence, he denounced its citizens as rebels and demanded a subsidy from England to enable him to levy war against them; and his ground of demand was that King John had constituted himself the Pope's liegeman and had promised to pay an annual tribute to the Pope as his liege lord. In view of the conflicting opinions on this subject in the Kingdom, the government deemed it prudent to share the responsibility of a decision. I will transcribe a passage from a contemporary chronicle, compiled by some monk, perhaps of Malmesbury, which recounts the doings in this matter:

"After Pentecost [1374] the King gathered together a great council of prelates and lords at Westminster, and asked a certain master in theology, a Franciscan friar, John Mardisle, who had preached before him on Pentecost, to take part. In the middle of the consistory sat the Prince of Wales and the

Archbishop of Canterbury, William Witlesey, a master in
theology. All the prelates sat beside the Archbishop, and all
temporal lords beside the Prince. In front of the Prince and
the Archbishop four masters in theology sat on a bench, to
wit, the Provincial of the Dominicans, John Owtred, a monk of
Durham, who procured a place in the council, John Mardisle,
and Thomas Asshburne an Austin friar. Men learned in civil
and common law sat on a rug in the open space.

"Then the Chancellor announced that the cause of the con-
vocation was this: 'The Pope has sent to our Lord the King
a bull in which he writes that, as he is the lord of all temporali-
ties through the vicarate of Christ, and also the spiritual and
paramount lord of the Kingdom of England through the gift
of King John, he commands the King to levy a tax to aid him
against Florentine rebels and others, and not to delay sending
it to him. Therefore, my Lords Spiritual, say now whether
he is our lord through the vicarate of Christ. And, to-morrow,
my Lords Temporal, you will give your say concerning the
grant of King John. My lord Archbishop, why do you say?'
The Archbishop answered: 'The Pope is the universal lord;
we can not deny that.' And all the prelates in turn said the
same. The Provincial of the Dominican Friars asked to be
excused from so difficult a question, and advised that according
to the custom of his Order in difficult matters the hymn *Veni
Creator Spiritus* be sung, or the Mass of the Holy Spirit, so
that the Spirit should teach them the truth. The Monk of
Durham answered in way of analogy, by taking for his ex-
ordium: 'Lo, here are two swords,' meaning to show by that,
that Peter had power over both temporal and spiritual things.
Mardisle immediately took him up. He quoted: 'Put up thy
sword unto the sheath,' and showed that the swords did not

signify such powers; for Christ did not possess temporal lord-ship, and did not pass it on to His disciples, but taught them to turn from it. This he proved by Holy Writ, by the Gospels, by the opinion of learned men, by the example of religious men who abandoned their possessions; and by the decretals them-selves he showed that the Pope admitted that he did not have universal lordship; and he told how Boniface VIII decreed himself lord over all kingdoms, and how he was rejected by France and England. And that Christ had handed on to Peter the vicarate of spiritual rule and not of earthly domination. For he said that as to earthly domination, according to St. Thomas, the Pope was not the successor of Peter, but of Constantine.

"The Austin Friar said that in the Church, Peter was known by the keys, Paul by the sword. In the forum of faith the Pope is Peter and bears the keys too of the Church. 'You, my Lord Prince, you used to be Paul bearing the sword. But be-cause you have laid down the sword of the Lord, Peter does not recognize Paul. Therefore lift up the sword, and Peter will recognize Paul.' With that the conference broke up that day. The Archbishop remarked: 'There has been good counsel in England without Friars.' But the Prince said: 'Because of your foolishness we were obliged to call them. Had we followed your counsel, we should have lost the Kingdom.'

"On the next day the Archbishop said that he did not know what to say. The Prince said to him (when he was ill, the wild Plantagent blood unloosed the customary restraint of his gentle manners) 'Answer, you Jackass! It is your business to instruct all of us.' The Archbishop answered: 'My voice is that the Pope is not lord here,' and all the prelates accordingly said the same. The Monk of Durham also said that the Pope was not lord. 'What has become of the two swords?' the

Prince asked. 'My Lord,' the Monk replied, 'I am better instructed now than I was.'

"Then the temporal lords gave their answer saying that King John had granted the Kingdom to the Roman Curia without the consent of the barons of the realm, which he could not lawfully do; so they said that his conveyance or grant had no validity. Envoys, therefore, were sent to the Pope to carry to him this answer."

A little later a conference was appointed to be held at Bruges to settle the contentions between England and the Papacy, and also those between England and France. The Black Prince was too ill to go. The Duke of Lancaster went, and among others "Master John de Wicliff, professor of theology," but nothing of any consequence was accomplished. That the Prince was in hearty accord with the national desire to curtail Papal pretensions, there can be no doubt; and, also, that he was gravely concerned about the public weal. The old King was but the shadow of his former self, and John of Gaunt, intent upon his own ambitions, had wilfully, or negligently, let great corruption into the government. Parliament met again, after three years, in April, 1376. The Prince was carried on a litter from Berkhamstead to Westminster in order that he might be near. Matters had so taken shape, that two parties confronted each other, a conservative court party, headed by the Duke of Lancaster and supported by the name of the King, and a patriotic party, eager for reforms, *ut creditur divinitus inspirati* [inspired from on high, as we believe], and supported by the prestige of the Prince of Wales, though he could take no active part, and by William of Wykeham and other prelates, who wished to get back into power in order to defend their order and themselves. It has been suggested, as I have said, that the Prince, quite apart from his concern for the purification and improvement of the government, felt some apprehensions lest Richard be set aside, and indeed, in those days the legal right of an infant son to succeed to the crown, in preference to an adult uncle, was by no means so well settled as it is now.

As soon as Parliament met, the Commons, full of righteous indignation, began at once, under the lead of the Speaker, Sir Peter de la Mare, the work of setting matters to rights. They submitted a hundred and forty petitions, alleging grievances and demanding reforms; they denounced oppressive taxation and the mismanagement of the war; they demanded an account of the public expenditures; they charged Lord Latimer, Lord John Neville, Richard Lyons, Sir Richard Sturry, William Ellis, John Peachy and others with dishonesty and misdeeds of various kinds, and even brought accusations against a "certain proude woman called Allice Perrers, who by overmuch familiarite that she had with the King, was the cause of much mischief in the realme." Richard Lyons, "fearing for his skin," sent to the Prince of Wales a barrel labeled "sturgeons" which contained one thousand pounds; the Prince sent it back and bade Lyons "reap the fruits of hys wages and drink as he had brued." All were punished; Mistress Alice Perrers was banished from court and her property confiscated. Sir Richard Sturry went to visit the Prince as he lay on his death-bed. The Prince, almost in his agony, said, for the old Plantagenet temper was still alive: "Come closer, Richard, so that you may see what you have long wished to see." Sturry swore that he had never desired the Prince's death. "That is not so," the Prince answered, "you have been afraid for your skin; your conscience has suggested to you that I would some time punish your misdeeds and the evil counsel that you have not failed to offer to the King.  And so it would have been, if I lived, and you would have found the proverb true which says that, evil advice is worst for the giver.  But I go whither God calls, and I beg and beseech Him that if the hand of man fails, He will put an end to your wickedness."  Sturry wept and prayed for forgiveness.  "God will render you justice," the Prince added, "according to your deserts, I do not wish you to trouble me more.  Get hence out of my sight, you shall not see my face again."

The reforming Parliament, which has been named "the Good," sat until July sixth, but before its dismissal the great Prince had died.

# CHAPTER XXX

## THE END

IN THE beginning of June, 1376, the reformers were still continuing their zealous efforts to uproot corruption; but the Black Prince could do no more. Life was ebbing away. For five years he had been very ill, often in great pain. Scarce a month passed without some hemorrhage, and often his attendants had thought he was dying. "But he bore it all so patiently that he was never heard to breathe a word of complaint against God." On June seventh he made his will, in which he appointed his brother John, and also William of Wykeham, with some others, his executors. He made gifts to his household servants and retainers, whatever their rank or station, and begged the King to cherish and favor his friends and servants. He made provision for his funeral, and because the words are authentic, and are among the last that he uttered, I will quote a passage from them:

*"Et volons qe a quele heure qe notre corps soit amenez par my la ville de Canterbers tantqe a la priorie qe deux destrez covertez de nos armez et deux hommes armez en noz armez et en nos heaumes voisent devant dit notre corps / Cest assavoir lun pur la guerre de nos armez entiers quartellez / et lautre pur la paix de noz bages des plumes dostruce ove quatre baneres de mesme la sute / et qe chacum de ceux qe porteront les detz baneres ait sur sa teste un chapeau de nos armez. Et qe celi qe sera armez pur la guerre ait un homme armez portant a pres li un penon de noir ove plumes dostruce."*

284

THE END 285

[ And it is my will that at the time, when my body shall be conducted throught the City of Canterbury up to the priory, two war-horses covered with my arms, and two men armed in my arms and in my crests proceed before my body. That is to say, one for war with my arms in full quartered, and the other for peace with my badge of ostrich feathers, with four banners with the same, and that each of those that shall carry said banners shall have on his head a cap with my arms. And that he that shall be armed for war shall have a man armed carrying after him a black pennon with ostrich feathers. ]⁻

After he had made his will he had little Richard, now nine years old, brought in, and bade him never take away the gifts he had given. He expressed deep religious conviction, and said to his household: "Dear Gentlemen, consider, for God's sake, that we are not masters in this life. All must pass by this path; no man can turn aside from it. So, very humbly, I beg you please to pray for me." The next day, June eighth, was Trinity Sunday, and the Prince prayed: "Blessed Trinity, whose name I have always honored on earth, whose glory I have sought to magnify, in whose faith, although in other respects a miserable sinner, I have always lived, I beseech Thee, as I have always celebrated your festival on earth, and have called upon the people to be joyful and celebrate Thy feast with me, to free me from the body of this death, and deign to call me to that most sweet feast, which is celebrated in Heaven to-day." (From now on, I am quoting the Herald Chandos, who accompanied him on his last great campaign, in among that gallant company at Bordeaux, Sir John Chandos, Sir James Audeley, Sir Thomas Felton, and the rest.) "The Prince bade the doors of his room be opened wide, and had all the men in his service come in. 'Gentlemen, forgive me,' he said. 'By the faith that is due to you from me, you have served me faithfully, I can not of myself give to each his fitting reward, but God by His most holy name, will render it to you in the holy Heaven.' The room was full of the sound of sobbings and weepings. Then he said, loud and clear: 'I commend my son to you, he is very young and little; I pray you to serve him loyally, as you have served me.' Then he called the King, and his brother John, and commended to them his wife and also his son, whom he greatly loved, and he besought them both right then to help him. Both made oath on the Bible, and promised him without reservation to aid and comfort his son, and maintain him in his right. All the princes and barons, standing round, swore to this; and he gave them a hundred thousand thanks. Never, so God help me, was there such sore grief beheld as at his departing. The noble, beautiful Princess felt such grief at heart, that her heart was nigh to breaking. Of lamentation and sighing, of crying aloud and sorrowing, there was so great a noise, that not a man in all the world, if he had seen the grief, but would have had pity at heart."

According to the Monk of Saint Alban's, his last words were: "I thank thee, O Lord, for all Thy benefits. With all my power I ask for Thy mercy that Thou wilt forgive me for all the sins that I, in my wrongdoing, have committed against Thee. And I ask with my whole heart the grace of pardon from all men whom I have knowingly or unwittingly offended." So "ripe for heaven and full of honor," he breathed his last and his soul, as all good Christians believed, mounted to the banquet of the Holy Trinity, whose feast he so reverenced on earth. "With his death died the hope of Englishmen." In Paris, King Charles V held a memorial service in the Sainte-

Chapelle, and the Captal de Buch, then a prisoner, hearing of the Prince's death, began to neglect himself, abandoned all care of the world, abstained from sustenance, and gradually pined away from excess of grief at the loss of so brave a commander.

The coffin lay in state at Westminster for nearly three months, and then the funeral procession, attended by the Lords and Commons of Parliament, set out for London, and, across London Bridge, on by the Pilgrim's road to Canterbury. There the Prince's dying instructions were carried out. The coffin rested on a bier in front of the high altar, while the service was said. The Prince had directed his body to be laid in the crypt, in the Chapel of Our Lady, but his humility was not heeded; the body was laid in the world-famed Chapel of Saint Thomas, usually called Trinity Chapel, south of the saint's shrine, in the space within the central arch of the arcade. Here on a marble tomb, adorned with enameled shields, lies an effigy, in life size, of the Black Prince, clad in complete armor. On the tomb is engraved an epitaph in French verse:

> All ye that pass with mouth shut
> By where this body reposes,
> Hearken to what I shall tell you,
> According as I know how to tell it.
> Such as thou art, such was I,
> And thou shalt be such as I am.
> Of death I never thought
> So long as I had life.
> On earth I had great riches
> With which I lived royally,
> Lands, houses, great treasure,
> Clothes, horses, silver and gold;
> But now I am poor and wretched.
> Deep in the earth I lie.
> My great beauty is all gone,
> My flesh is all wasted away,

Very narrow is my house,
With me nothing but truth remains
And if ye now should see me,
I do not think that ye would say
That I had ever been a man,
So wholly changed am I.
For God's sake, pray the Heavenly King
That He have mercy on my soul.
And all that shall pray for me,
Or make my peace with God,
May God put in His paradise
Where no man can be wretched.

Above the tomb, a flat wooden tester with a representation of the Trinity, painted on the under surface, was extended from pillar to pillar, and his achievements were hung about, a helmet, a crest, a surcoat, a shield, a target, a sword, a scabbard, a dagger and gauntlets, such as he wore and used in life. The sword, the dagger and the target are gone; but the surcoat shows the quarterings of the golden lions *passant gardant* on a red ground and the golden fleur-de-lis on a blue; and on the crest, the lion *statant*, the "leopard" as heralds call it, pitifully reveals the perishability of the materials of which it was made.

His fame lived after him. "Wisdom did not in any way come short of his Courage: Both which were equall'd by his Exemplary Justice, Clemency, Liberality, Piety and Moderation, Virtues but seldom sincerely embraced by Persons of High Conditions. He was a Prince of whom we never heard any Ill, nor received any other Note than of Goodness, and the Noblest Performances, that Magnanimity, Generosity, Courage and Wisdom could ever show. Inasmuch as what Praise can be given unto Virtue is due unto him." (Joshua Barnes, 1688.)

APPENDIX

# BRIEF BIBLIOGRAPHY

## Sources

*Froissart's Chronicles,* Kervyn de Lettenhove's Edition.
Luce's Edition.
Translation by Lord Berners.
Translation by Johnes.
*Chronique de Jehan le Bel,* Viard et Déprez (1905).
*Chronicon Galfridi le Baker,* E. Maunde Thompson (1889).
*Eulogium Historiarum.*
*Robertus de Avesbury,* De gestis, etc., Edwardii Tertii.
*Historia Anglicana,* Thomas Walshingham.
*Chronicon Henrici Knighton.*
*Chronican Angliae,* a Monaco Sancti Albani.
*Adae Murimuth Continuatio Chronicarum.*
*Scalacronica,* Sir Thomas Gray.
*Anonimalle Chronicle.*
*Chronica Johannis de Reading.*
*Chronique Normande du XIV Siécle.*
*Chronique des Quatre premiers Valois.*
*Chroniques des regnes de Jean II et de Charles V.*
*Fœdera,* Rymer.
*Istorie Fiorentine,* Giovanni e Matteo Villani.
*Coronica del Rey Pedro,* Pero Lopez de Ayala.
*Roman de Bertrand du Guesclin,* Cuvelier.
*Chronique de Bertrand du Guesclin,* Gabriel Richou, editor.
*Life of the Black Prince* by, The Herald of Sir John Chandos, edited by Mildred K. Pope and Eleanor C. Lodge.
Laurence Minot's Poems.
*Political Poems and Songs,* Thomas Wright, editor.
*Wynnere and Wastour* (1352).
*Edward III* (1688), Joshua Barnes.
*Stow's Chronicle* (1580), John Stow.
*The Life and Times of Edward III,* William Longman.

*Edward III*, Mackinnon.
*The Black Prince's Register.*
*Life of the Black Prince*, G. P. R. James.
*The Black Prince* (1776), Alexander Bicknell.
*The Black Prince*, Louise Creighton.
*The Black Prince*, R. P. Dunn-Pattison.
*John of Gaunt*, Armitage-Smith.
*Froissart*, Marie Darmesteter.
*John Wyclif*, Herbert B. Workman.
*England in the Age of Wyclif*, G. M. Trevelyan.
*William of Wykeham*, Lowth.
*Memorials of the Order of the Garter*, Beltz.
*The Chronicles of London.*
*The Chronicler of European Chivalry*, G. G. Coulton.
*Crécy and Calais*, Hon. George Wrottesley.
*British Battles, Crécy*, Hilaire Belloc.
*A History of the Art of War*, C. Oman (1924).
*Histoire de France*, Lavisse.
*Histoire de Bertrand du Guesclin*, Luce.
*Don Pèdre I*, Prosper Mérimée.
*Las Mugeres del Rey Don Pedro*, J. B. Sitges.
*Histoire de Charles V*, R. Delachenal.
*Die Entwickelung des Kriegswesen*, G. Köhler.
*La Guerre de Cent Ans*, Denifle.
*Le Prince noir*, Moisant.
*Ich Dene*, Sir Israel Gollenz.
*Philippa of Hainault*, B. C. Hardy.
*Battles of English History*, H. B. George

# NOTES

THE three chief contemporary authorities are Geoffrey Baker, Froissart and Giovanni Villani. In 1346, Baker was apparently a grown man living in retirement in Oxfordshire, but he did not write his account of the battle, at least as it now stands, till after 1356. Froissart was probably about nine years old at the time of the battle, but he went to England in 1361, stayed five years and became acquainted with a great number of distinguished soldiers, and he seems to have been indefatigable in asking questions; no doubt he had a romantic fancy, and gave it rein. Baker in his narrative dashes off into rhetoric and quotations from Lucan. Giovanni Villani lived in Florence; but Florentine bankers and merchants had excellent correspondents, and some of the unfortunate Genoese crossbowmen may have lived to carry home tales of the battle. None of the three is very accurate, but Baker and Froissart give much information, and Villani some.

The controlling factors in understanding the course of the battle, are the topography, the numbers engaged and the tactics. Here only the topography is pretty certain. The English line is said to have extended from the slope above the River Maye to the village of Wadicourt. That statement must be wrong. Two battalions, of twelve hundred men-at-arms each, drawn up six deep, would not cover a front of more than eight hundred yards or so, and the archers could not have filled in the other twelve hundred yards. Villani is emphatic that the fight was on a narrow front, *essendo il luogo stretto da combattere,* and the narratives of Baker and Froissart confirm his statement. The English line therefore could not have extended all the way from the village of Crécy to the village of Wadicourt; and yet their left flank was not exposed, for if it had been, the French, owing to their numbers, if not to their tactics, would certainly have attacked it. I think that there must have been a forest this side of Wadicourt, and that it is likely (for a similar barricade was made at

293

Poitiers) that there was a barricade of carts on that flank, as
Villani says, from which the archers shot. That barricade was, of
course, in addition to the corral in the rear, where the horses and
baggage were placed. I assume, therefore, that the front was
narrow, and that on the edge of the Wadicourt forest a barricade
had been made to protect the left flank and was manned by archers.

The numbers of the English army are uncertain. Köhler reckons
3,900 men-at-arms, 10,000 archers, 5,000 Welshmen; Oman 2,000
men-at-arms, 5,000 English archers, 3,500 Welsh, half of them
archers, and 500 hobilars, a total of 11,000. Belloc puts the total
at 25,000; Wrottesley estimates it at about 19,000.

The traditional formation of three battalions was followed.
Froissart says they were in echelon; this was probably to prevent
an attack on the left flank. It is commonly said that the first and
second battalions were nearly on a line. I think that the echelon
was slight, and that the second battalion was pretty well behind the
first; my reason being that pits were dug only in front of the first
battalion. Baker says so explicitly, *effodierunt multa foramina in
terra coram acie prima.* This formation accords with the theory
of the narrow front. The King's battalion was stationed to the
rear as a reserve.

The position of the archers has called forth much discussion.
Froissart says: *missent les archiers tout devant en fourme de une
herce, et les gens d'armes ou fons.* Church and Oman assume
that *herce* is a triangular harrow, and exercise their ingenuity in
arranging the archers in that form, somewhat like the stars in
Cassiopeia's Chair. I find it difficult to accept such a formation.
Froissart makes the same statement as to the position of the English
archers at Poitiers; but nobody thinks that they were drawn up
there in the form of a triangle.

Foreign writers, I think, do not adopt the triangular theory;
they accept the other meaning of *herce* which is a portcullis.
Napoleon III holds that the English archers were placed in a long
line in front of the men-at-arms, in a disposition that enabled
them to use their bows to the best advantage; and says that
Froissart's simile refers to a portcullis. Lettenhove says that
Froissart's *herce* means a front five times longer than the depth;

which is a formation that came into use in the following century. General Köhler places the archers in a long line in front of the whole English position, and says that Froissart's *herce*, which he derives from *heriçon*, means an obstacle in front; he cites the *Chronique de Valenciennes* which states that the archers were drawn up *à la manière d'un escut*, in the manner of a shield. My own idea is that all the archers were drawn up in front and on the wing of the whole English front line, and that Froissart had in mind the teeth of a harrow, meaning that, with two or more ranks of archers, those behind could shoot between those in front.

Oman and George believe that the archers that belonged to each battalion stayed with their separate battalions during the battle. As the main reliance of the English army was upon its archers, I think King Edward's plan must have been to bring all the artillery into play as soon as the enemy came within range. There is an objection to this hypothesis as to the position of the archers; for Baker says: *Sagittariis eciam sua loca designarunt, ut, non coram armatis, set a lateribus regis exercitus quasi ale astarent et sic non impedirent armatos neque inimicis occurrerent in fronte, set in latera sagittas fulminarent.* The explanation of this contradiction is, according to my theory, that Baker here refers to the second stage of the battle, after the discomfiture of the Genoese crossbowmen when Alençon's battalion charged and the English archers withdrew to the sides as they were not armed to withstand the charge of men-at-arms. Incidentally, Baker's statement disposes of the theory that the archers of each battalion remained with that battalion; for he expressly says that they were placed "on the wings of the *exercitus*," the whole army, and not of the *acies*, a battalion.

As to the French numbers, it is impossible to say anything definite, except that they were very great. Their battalions evidently came on in a ragged continuous multitude, with virtually no regard to formation. The diagrams that represent them drawn up in orderly battalions are misleading.

Villani's statement that the English had cannon at Crécy, is confirmed by one of the Froissart manuscripts (see Lettenhove's edition, V, p. 46), and by *Grandes Chroniques de France*, V, p. 460.

### THE BURGHERS OF CALAIS

The story of Eustace de Saint-Pierre has been unnecessarily doubted. Jehan le Bel tells the story and names only Saint-Pierre; Froissart names the others, showing independent research. *La Chronique Normande* refers briefly to the episode of six burghers, giving no names; which makes it clear that the chronicler did not invent the episode in order to do honor to Saint-Pierre and his associates. Luce believes the story (*Froissart* IV, XXV, N. 1), Lavisse (IV, p. 68) also, as well as the editors of Jehan le Bel, (1905).

### THE BATTLE OF POITIERS

The figures of the English army seem here more trustworthy; Baker and Froissart agree on about 7,500 men, only Baker says 4,000 men-at-arms and 2,000 archers, while Froissart reverses those figures. The numbers of the French have been variously computed. Froissart shifts from 50,000 to 70,000, Lord Burghersh who was in the Prince's army said 8,000 men-at-arms and 3,000 foot. Delachenal suggests (II, p. 218) double the number of the English. Oman merely suggests that Burghersh may have underrated the French numbers, while Köhler says that his estimate is decidedly too small.

Delachenal's idea (II, p. 186) that King John had dismissed all the contingents from his *bonnes villes* is contradicted by Froissart, in that he makes the King address the men of Paris, Rouen, Orléans and Chartres just before the battle.

Neither Baker nor Froissart, nor the Herald Chandos, was present, nor, so far as it appears, even saw the battle-field. Baker's idea of the site is obviously wrong; and Froissart is obviously wrong in his assumption that the Prince's battalions at the time of the battle remained in the same places they had taken on Sunday.

There are, in my judgment, two controlling facts to be remembered in any attempt to reconstruct the position of the English army. One is, that the Prince knew that he was greatly outnumbered and wanted to avoid a battle; this of course was due to prudence, as for courage, he was bold as a lion. The second is that the hedge-and-ditch, behind which the English army was stationed, did not bisect the road, as in Oman's plan, but ran alongside the road; the earth from the ditch had been flung up and a hedge grown on top of it, in order to fence in the vineyards and other land beyond. The opening in the hedge, of which Froissart says so much, has been wrongly assumed to be made by this road passing through; on the contrary, it was an opening out from the road into the enclosed vineyards and fields, and was made by carters in the vintage season. Baker makes this plain; he does not say that the road passed through the hedge, but that there was a *"temesis quedam patula vel hyatus, quem bigarii fecerunt in autummo* [a broad cutting or opening which had been made by carters in the autumn]."

The truce, arranged by the Cardinal of Périgord, expired at dawn on Monday, September nineteenth. The *Anonimalle Chronicle* (which, I think, was not published till 1927 and therefore neglected by Oman and Köhler) says definitely that Warwick started at dawn and crossed a narrow causeway over a marsh, but the baggage train was so large that his division had not crossed by *prime,* which we may assume to be about six o'clock. In other words Warwick began to cross the Miosson. This movement is definitely confirmed by Herald Chandos, and must be accepted as a fact. Baker, in a confused narrative says: *Ad satis angustum vadum principis turma cum cariagiis torrentem preterivit.* I suggest that *principis* here does not mean *of the prince* but *of the first battalion,* and, if so, Baker confirms the other two but his ideas are (according to the topographical map) all upside down. Warwick had started at the first streak of light, while the Prince remained where he was in order to conceal Warwick's movements, and was still there till *mye prime,* meaning perhaps till half past seven or more (Delachenal II, p. 227, Note 2). As soon as the Cardinal had gone, Salisbury must have started at once, and the Prince followed at seven-thirty A.M. All three battalions kept well up near the wood of Nouaillé, on the farther side of the road from the

French, so that, in case of attack, the army should have the protection of the hedge-and-ditch that lined the road, and be in a position
very similar to that which, according to Froissart, they held on
Sunday. On learning that a battle could not be avoided, Warwick
returned and took his station on the east side of the road, between
the marshy land by the Miosson and the gap in the hedge, while
Salisbury moved up to stop the gap. Baker has got that right:
*campus in quo residebant nostre prima secundaque custodia, dis-
tinguebatur a planicie quam occupavit exercitus Francus sepe
longa subterfossata, cuius alterum extremum declinavit in mariscum
prefatum,* i.e. the field occupied by the English, separated from the
French by a long hedge and ditch, extended to the Miosson marsh.
The Prince's battalion was drawn up behind the others as a reserve.

I think that the battle with the cavalry, and afterward with the
Dauphin's battalion, was fought along this hedge, which would be
on a north and south line, near the edge of the Nouaillé wood. There
is some evidence to support this position, apart from inference:
*Commissum est praelium in extrema parte saltus Nobiliacensis*
(*Nouaillé,* Delachenal, II, p. 212, N.). I also think that the
English in the pursuit and afterward, crossed the road and advanced to meet King John's battalion on the land between it and
the little valley, somewhere near the spot known in the eighteenth
century as the Champ d'Alexandre.

THE FLANK ATTACK. Baker ascribes it to the Captal de Buch,
and says that he fell upon King John's battalion; Knighton says
that Warwick, coming back from pursuing fugitives, attacked the
King's flank; Froissart, does not name the leader, but refers to
an attack upon the Dauphin's flank. As the struggle with the
Dauphin's battalion was the real crisis of the battle, I think Froissart is right. The Prince knew that he must defeat the Dauphin
before King John came up, or all was lost. Very likely the Captal
commanded the flanking party.

Oxford's maneuver in changing the position of Warwick's
archers is to me unintelligible. Baker says that they had been
stationed *in marisco,* in a marsh, in order to be safe from the
French cavalry, but that they were useless there. *"Hoc perpendens,
comes Oxonie descendit a principe et sagittarios ductos in obliquum
jussit ad equorum posteriora sagittare,* which Oman paraphrases

"Oxford hastily led out part of the archers of the vaward into the marshy low ground by the Miosson at right angles to the English line, and bade them shoot up the valley at the flank of the French" (II, p. 171). Now Baker says these archers were in the marsh and that Oxford moved them to a place from which they could enfilade the French, and there is nothing but Oman's hypothesis of the topography to justify his saying that Oxford led them into the marsh. Besides, Oman's diagram of the battle-field shows the Prince's battalion was stationed between Warwick's and the marsh. Baker is confusing, because it is hard to see why Oxford, unless the order came from the Prince, should have been giving orders to Warwick's men, but Oman's explanation makes him more confusing still.

### THE SACK OF LIMOGES

The Prince was ill, probably in pain, harassed by care, perhaps young Edward, who died soon afterward, was already ailing. Delachnal, the most thorough of the historians of French history at this time (*Histoire de Charles V*, Tome IV, p. 293), criticizes Froissart's figures of 3,000 persons massacred on the ground that the total population hardly reached that figure. "*Qu'il y ait 300 morts,—le dixième du total indiqué par le chroniquer,—c'est déjà beaucoup;*" and he cites a monk of the abby of Saint-Martial de Limoges as authority for the figure 300. He believed the city "*decimée mais non exterminée.*" At all events, it was a bad business. It must be remembered that Limoges was composed of two distinct towns, *la cité*, clustered about the cathedral, and *la ville*, which encompassed the Abbey of Saint-Martial. It was the *cité* that the Prince destroyed. (Delachenal p. 283, citing Alfred Leroux.)

### THE BATTLE OF NAVARETTE

The two authorities are the prose chronicle of Ayala, who was a standard-bearer in the Castilian army, and the Herald Chandos, who was present in the Prince's army. It seems reasonable to regard Ayala as the better authority for facts concerning the Castilian army, and Chandos for those concerning the English army.

Delachenal believes that Ayala invented the contents of the letters exchanged between the Prince and Don Enrique just before the battle; he says that the real letters are preserved in the British Museum. But the B. M. letters possess no guarantee apart from their contents, while those which Ayala gives have the support of his authority.

INDEX

# INDEX